Paula Peck

Drawings by Grambs Miller

A FIRESIDE BOOK

NEW YORK LONDON TORONTO

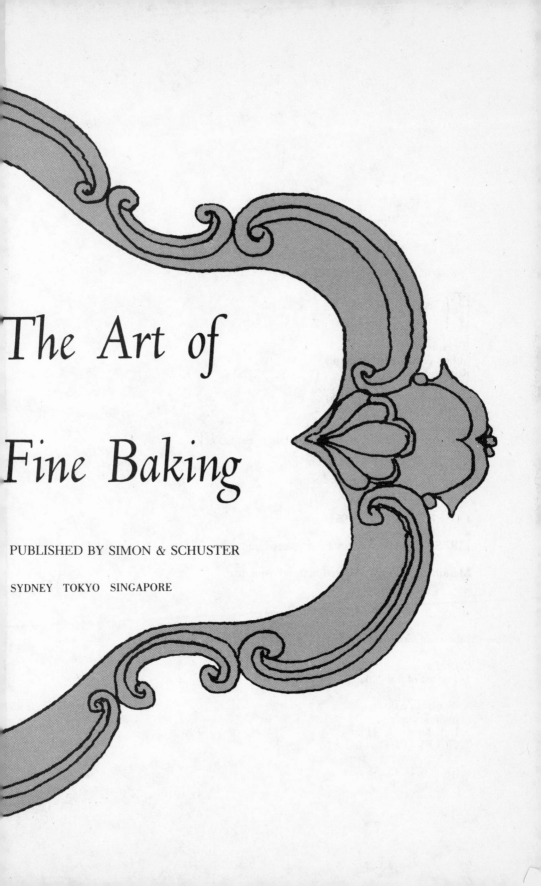

The Art of Fine Baking

PUBLISHED BY SIMON & SCHUSTER

SYDNEY TOKYO SINGAPORE

Fireside
Simon & Schuster Building
Rockefeller Center
1230 Avenue of the Americas
New York, New York 10020

First Fireside Edition, 1961

Manufactured in the United States of America

10 9 8 7 6 5 4 3 2 1 Pbk.

Library of Congress Cataloging in Publication Data

Peck, Paula.
The art of fine baking.

"A Fireside book."
Includes index.
1. Baking. I. Title.
TX763.P3 1984 641.8'65 84-20280

ISBN: 0-671-74627-8 Pbk.

For Jim
Sam
and Charles

I want to thank the many friends who have encouraged and helped me with this book, particularly Joseph Baum, Albert Stockli, and Albert Kumins of Restaurant Associates, who allowed me to observe in their pastry kitchen.

P.P.

Contents

Introduction

Paula Peck was born with a natural talent for creative cooking. She has an intense interest in all that is traditional in fine cuisine and a zestful curiosity that leads to experimenting.

It has been my privilege to work with Mrs. Peck as her instructor, later as a co-worker in my own cooking school and in demonstrations of cooking in various sections of the country. Her enthusiasm for the work table and range is refreshing. Her way to combat fatigue and worry is to get into the kitchen and turn out a hundred or so croissants or two or three batches of puff paste with all embellishments. She is an outstanding juggler with rolling pin and mixing bowl, and the magic results fill her larder and freezer to overflowing. Her home is an oasis for hungry travelers and guests, for there is always enough delectable food in her kitchen to serve a good-sized party.

In my opinion, this book is as complete a treatise on the art of baking as you will find in the English language. It contains some revolutionary ideas that Mrs. Peck developed through careful experimentation. These modern short cuts take fear and drudgery out of baking without sacrificing one jot of quality.

If you are one of those who enjoys browsing through cookbooks at bedtime, I warn you, the reading here is so mouth-watering that you may find yourself rushing from the bedroom to the kitchen to whip up a batch of gênoise and butter cream before going off to sleep!

It is with great pleasure that I participate in the launching of this confection among cookbooks. I feel confident that Paula Peck's book on baking will sail majestically on seas of whipped cream and egg whites.

James A. Beard

Foreword

Many people like to cook. But why bother to bake in this era of cake mixes and even of fairly good commercial bakeries?

The reason is that no commercial cake can ever taste like a home-baked one made with fresh butter and eggs. Furthermore, baking is fun. It fills the house with delicious smells—and memories. There is great nostalgia connected with baking at home. Most people have fond memories of someone back in their childhood who made delicious breads and cakes.

I never learned to cook or bake at home. But I remember my grandmother, before I was eight years old, kneading dough and rolling it out on a big, old-fashioned table in preparation for the Sabbath. It is one of my most pleasant memories.

As a bride, I had not even an elementary knowledge of how to cook. At home, my mother's cooking was simple and good, but limited to a few dishes which my father preferred. My husband, Jim, is a man with entirely different tastes. He likes foods of all nationalities and is always eager for new dishes. During the first year we were married, we ate in all the various foreign restaurants with which New York abounds.

However, when our first son was born, we had to eat at home. It was then that I decided to try to bring the foods of the different nationalities into our home, some first tasted in restaurants, others found in books.

I was fortunate in having seasoned advisers. Angele, the wife of a professional French chef, and an old family friend of Jim's, visited us once a week. She was invaluable in imparting to me her knowledge of French cooking.

My interest soon turned to baking. Jim's lack of appetite for desserts offered a challenge. The only cake he really liked was a spongecake version of the French baba au rhum. Angele described exactly how she made her spongecake—a truly simple recipe. But each time I tried to make it, something would go wrong. Once there was a rubbery layer on the bottom of the cake. Many times the cake was simply heavy. On some occasions I thought I had succeeded, but Jim would shake his head. So I tried again. By the time I learned to make that simple spongecake, I had grasped thoroughly the principles of air-raised cakes and had even managed to simplify the process of making them.

Another source of great help and comfort in those days was Mrs. Sokolowski, an elderly Polish lady who lived next door and did most of our baby-sitting. With her help I learned to work with yeast and to make the famous Polish babka. Once the principle of working with yeast is understood, making almost any bread or coffeecake becomes simple. Working with yeast is more fun than any other kind of baking because the dough has an alive quality, a wonderful texture, and smells better than anything else in the world after it is put in the oven.

One summer we went to France. In Paris we tasted the delicious, buttery, flaky rolls called croissants. Once a week for the following eight years, I tried making them. Sometimes they would turn out too yeasty, other times too bready, still other times wet in the center. The possible pitfalls seemed innumerable. Puff paste, which is famous —or perhaps infamous—for being difficult to make, was almost child's play compared to croissants. Finally, I achieved a perfect croissant and with a simplified recipe! Nine years after our first trip to France, we went there again. Again we tasted the croissants, and Jim decided that in most instances the ones I make at home are better.

Unfortunately, many people today feel that baking, particularly the kind described in this book, is too time-consuming and difficult for our fast-moving, complicated lives. Thanks to modern innovations such as the electric mixer, the blender, and the freezer, this is not true.

It might seem very silly to make a batch of 36 croissants for a family of three or four, since they would turn stale in two days. However, baked croissants can be kept, frozen, for months. And heating a frozen croissant—such a delicacy for breakfast—in a hot oven takes less than five minutes. Breads of all kinds can be frozen and then thawed at room temperature or even more quickly in the oven, whenever desired.

A cake or torte which requires an icing plus a different kind of filling plus a decoration of chocolate truffles or toasted chopped nuts may seem overwhelming in terms of labor. But, if the toasted nuts and truffles are on hand in the refrigerator; if at least one kind of butter cream is ready in the freezer; if a supply of cake layers has already been prepared in advance; if a jar of basic, simple syrup is handy—then making the most elaborate cake becomes just an assembly-line job requiring no more than twenty minutes.

Use the snowy and rainy days to prepare and lay in the composite parts of a cake. Discard the old way of making just one entire cake at a time. On a particular day, make many tart shells, several cake layers, etc.—and then freeze them. On another day, make butter cream, toasted nuts, etc., or prepare other miscellaneous items which are ingredients for so many desserts. In this manner, plan to spend a few hours each week making a supply of one composite part of one cake or another. Then, sit back, relax and prepare to enjoy watching others marvel at the results of your well-organized baking.

P. P.

Chapter 1

General Information

General Information

Please don't read this chapter straight through. You probably already know much of what it says, and it is too technical to be much fun. Go ahead and find a recipe you want to try in one of the next chapters. But when you have any sort of doubt—about beating or clarifying butter or buying a pastry bag—please come back here and see what it says. You'll be happier to know exactly what you're doing, and the results will amaze everyone including yourself.

A *Baking Terms and Techniques*

BEATING

There are 2 kinds of beating. The word is often used in this book to describe the process of filling eggs or cream with air. For such beating, a rotary beater, an electric mixer, or a wire whisk can be used.

In the second kind of beating, fairly stiff mixtures are stirred hard after the ingredients appear to be combined (as when making pâte à chou, the mixture used in baking such pastries as cream puffs and éclairs). This is done with a wooden spoon or a standard electric mixer.

CREAMING

Creaming is the combining of 2 or more ingredients by rubbing or beating them together with the back of a wooden spoon, an electric mixer, or with the bare hand.

This is usually done until the ingredients to be creamed together have acquired a light, fluffy appearance and seem to have lost their individual characteristics. For example, butter and sugar will acquire a lighter color and will not look sugary or greasy when they have been creamed together sufficiently; well-creamed butter and flour will also become lighter in color and fluffy.

FOLDING

Folding is the process of combining 2 or more ingredients in the gentlest possible manner to retain the air. It generally involves at least 1 light, delicate-textured ingredient, such as beaten eggs or whipped cream, which would be reduced to nothing if it were handled crudely. Folding is most efficiently done by hand or with an electric mixer, although most people fold with a spatula.

FOLDING BY HAND

If both ingredients to be combined are liquids, pour the less fluffy one on top of the other. If dry ingredients are to be folded in, sprinkle them on top of the fluffy mixture, folding in gradually.

To fold with an electric mixer: Put ingredients to be folded together in a bowl. Turn mixer to lowest speed and fold for no more than a minute or 2. If necessary, use a spatula to gently push the batter on sides of the bowl toward the center. Be careful not to overmix. It is often wise to stop the mixer just before the job is completed and finish folding with a rubber spatula or by hand.

To fold by hand: Your hands, properly used, are the most efficient, sensitive tools you will ever own. Hand folding has the special advantage of giving the actual feel of the lightness of a mixture.

To fold, keep the fingers of the right hand spread slightly apart. Cut through batter gently, being sure to go to the bottom of the bowl. Pull your hand across the bowl, scraping the bottom and sides. Then bring up your hand, bringing some of batter from bottom of bowl. Twist hand to empty it of batter. Cut down through batter again in a different place. Repeat the entire process, folding the batter over and over until the ingredients are combined but still light.

3

4

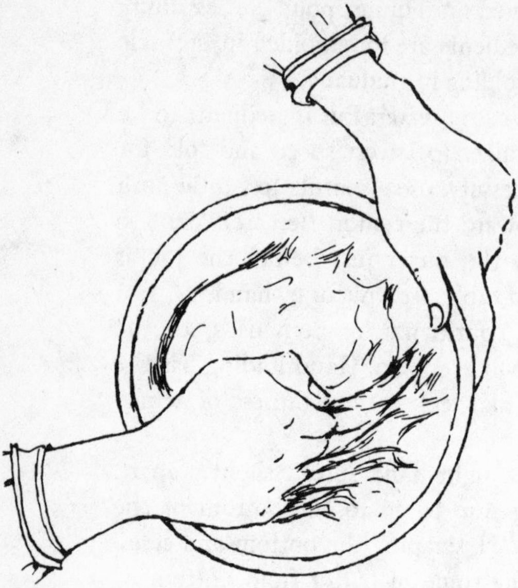

KNEADING SOFT DOUGH IN A BOWL

KNEADING

Kneading is the technique by which doughs are made smooth and elastic. It is used primarily in making dough for puff paste and yeast breads, or in working any mixture that is too heavy to be beaten with a spoon.

One type of kneading, used with soft, sticky doughs, is done right in the bowl. Such kneading is actually a pulling of the soft dough again and again from the walls of the bowl. A low, wide, dishpan type of container is best. It is held steady with the left hand while the right hand pulls the dough at different points. Doughs are sometimes worked in this manner until they come away completely from the sides of the bowl, or until they no longer stick to the hand when it is pulled abruptly out of the mixture. Another final test for very soft doughs (like savarin, used for making such pastries as manon and baba au rhum) is to watch for the appearance of air blisters on the surface of the batter after 8 or 10 minutes of kneading.

Kneading medium and heavy doughs is usually done on a flat surface (any type of table top or wooden board) which first has been lightly sprinkled with flour. The dough is folded in half, pressed down and pushed with the heel of one or both hands, rotated a little, folded over and pressed again. This is continued over and over, lightly sprinkling more flour on the working surface if necessary, until the dough has been made very smooth and elastic.

Some home mixers have a dough hook attachment which can be used for kneading.

KNEADING FIRMER DOUGH ON A FLAT SURFACE

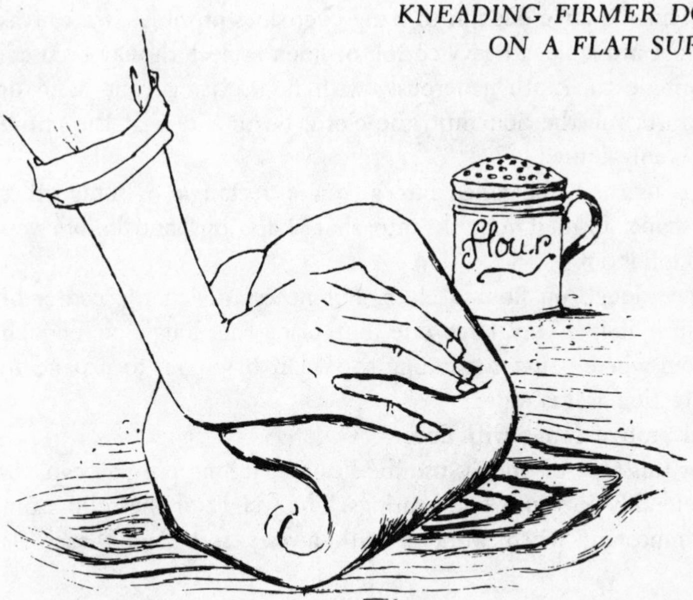

ROLLING OUT DOUGH

It is much easier to roll out dough on a table which is the right height. If a table is too high, it is impossible to bear down and thus give proper weight to the rolling pin, particularly when working with a rubbery type of dough. A table which is too low requires more bending over than should be necessary. My own preference is that a table top be 29 or 30 inches high, so that it reaches just to the top of my thigh. Taller people will want a higher table, and those less than 5 feet 2 inches tall will certainly find it easier to use a lower one.

When rolling out any chilled dough, such as for cookies, puff pastries or croissants, never roll all the dough at once unless a very small amount has been made. This is because the time interval between the rolling and the shaping of a large amount of dough will result in the dough's becoming soft, sticky and difficult to handle. Most recipes should be divided into two or three rollings.

Soft, Sticky, or Rubbery Doughs (such as strudel, puff paste, yeast dough)

1. Cover the table with a cloth, preferably one made of heavy canvas which is large enough to hang over sides of table. If a canvas cloth is not available, a heavy cotton or linen tablecloth may be used.

2. Sprinkle the cloth generously with flour. Using your hand or a soft brush, rub the flour into the cloth, being sure that the entire cloth is evenly floured.

3. If dough is to be rolled into a square, rectangle or some other special shape, form it roughly into that shape by hand before you begin to roll it out.

4. Place dough on floured cloth, not necessarily in the center of the table if it is a very large one; but place the dough far enough away from where you are standing so that it has room to expand in every direction as it is rolled.

5. Dust top of dough with flour.

6. For this type of dough, use the heaviest rolling pin you can obtain, preferably one with ball bearings. The weight of the rolling pin is less important when working with a *very* soft dough such as strudel.

7. Begin to roll back and forth. Bear down as hard as necessary to force the dough to take the shape you want. Only experience can teach you the correct amount of pressure necessary each time.

8. Bear in mind the particular shape you are making, and change the position of the dough on the cloth as often as necessary to end with that shape.

9. Dust dough with additional flour if it begins to stick to the rolling pin. If the cloth has been well floured, it is unlikely that the dough will stick to it. However, be sure to check underneath the dough occasionally to be certain.

10. Roll with even pressure. This will prevent unshapeliness, as well as spots which are too thick or thin in the rolled-out sheet of dough. Beginners tend to bear down too hard as they start to roll, thus destroying the rough shape of the dough and making it more difficult to end with the correct shape.

Rich, Short, Non-sticky Doughs (such as for cookies and tart shells)

1. Temperature of the dough is important. It should be neither ice cold nor warm and sticky. Very cold dough of this type, because it contains a large amount of fat, is too hard to be rolled out easily. While it is certainly possible to roll out warm, sticky dough by the method described below, it is almost impossible to shape or cut it as required. The dough should be firm, yet not hard. It should "give" if a finger is pressed into it but should not stick to the finger.

2. If dough is to be rolled into a square, rectangle or some other special shape, form it roughly into that shape by hand before you begin to roll it out.

3. Place dough on a sheet of wax paper. If a large amount of dough is being rolled, overlap two sheets of wax paper.

4. Cover dough with a sheet (or overlapping sheets) of wax paper.

5. Using a rolling pin which is not too heavy, begin to roll back and forth. Use only enough pressure to expand dough. Bearing down too hard on this type of dough will make it tear and crack. However, if dough should, unhappily, be very cold and hard, it will be necessary to exert much more pressure.

6. Bear in mind the particular shape you are making and change the position of the wax-paper-sandwiched dough as often as necessary to achieve that shape.

7. After a few minutes, you will find that the dough does not move as easily as it did. When this happens, carefully peel off the top sheet of paper. Then, with the help of the bottom paper, flip dough over on the peeled-off paper (which will now be underneath instead of on top). Peel off top sheet. Replace paper and proceed to roll as before. Repeat this as often as necessary to keep dough moving.

8. When rolling is complete, peel off top paper. Use bottom sheet to help flip dough over flan ring or tart shells (if that is what is being made); or, if cookies are to be cut out, simply be sure that the top sheet of paper is removed and the bottom one completely loose and unattached to the dough.

9. The advantage of this method for rolling is that less flour is absorbed in delicate cookies and pastries. Scraps left after cookies are cut out may be re-rolled with little if any impairment to the flavor or texture of the baked cookies.

STIRRING

Stirring is usually done with a wooden spoon, rotating it through a mixture as long as necessary, usually until the ingredients are combined. No particular care in stirring is necessary except to remember to stop stirring as soon as the ingredients are combined. Stirring beyond this point becomes *beating*. The texture of many kinds of delicate cakes and cookies can be spoiled by overstirring.

Often sauces and other things prepared on the stove are stirred slowly as they cook, until they thicken. This is a special kind of long stirring.

WHIPPING

Whipping is a synonym for the kind of beating done with eggs or cream to fill them with air and make them thick and fluffy.

SIFTING

Sifting is the putting of flour, sugar, cocoa, cornstarch, or any dry ingredient through a strainer or special sifter designed for this function. It has 2 main purposes:

1. To remove lumps.
2. To make a dry ingredient airier so that it can be more easily combined with a light batter.

Most recipes specify sifted measurements. (One cup of unsifted flour contains more flour than 1 cup of sifted flour.) It is often unnecessary to sift flour for any reason except for measurement purposes. An experienced cook frequently does not bother to sift flour for such mixtures as cooky doughs, yeast doughs, or pâte à chou. She can tell how much flour to add by the texture of these mixtures.

On the other hand, flour for any light cake, such as gênoise or spongecake, should be sifted not only to achieve correct measurement but also because the aeration which results from sifting allows the flour to be folded in more easily.

To sift flour: Place a measuring cup on a sheet of wax paper. Fill the flour sifter. Holding the sifter at least 1 inch above the cup, lightly sift the flour into the cup. Do not bang or jar the cup. This would cause the flour to pack down again. When the cup is filled to overflowing, level off the top, using the flat edge of a knife or a spatula.

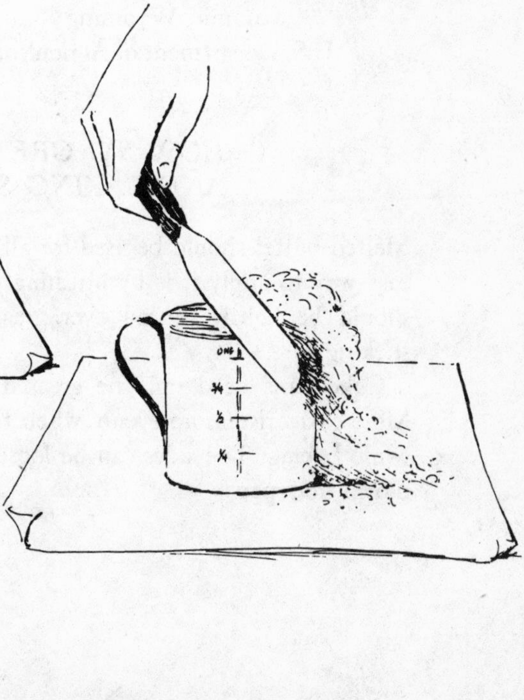

SIFTING

HIGH ALTITUDE BAKING

Baked products as well as sugar cookery are affected by elevations of 1,500 feet or more above sea level.

For example, yeast doughs rise more rapidly at high altitudes; therefore, less yeast may be used.

Flour dries quickly at high altitudes; it is often necessary to use more liquid or to decrease the amount of flour.

Baking temperatures at elevations over 3,500 feet must be increased slightly.

Sugar cookery at high altitudes will be more accurate when the thermometer is discarded (at least temporarily) and the manual tests of thread, ball, and crack stages (see p. 43) are used. A sugar thermometer may be used, however, in conjunction with manual tests and the temperatures noted for future use.

Write to the following sources for free or very inexpensive pamphlets on high-altitude baking:

General Foods Corporation, 250 North Street, White Plains, New York

Colorado Agricultural Experiment Station, Colorado A. and M. College, Fort Collins, Colorado

University of Wyoming Agricultural Experiment Station, Laramie, Wyoming

U.S. Department of Agriculture, Washington 25, D.C.

HOW TO GREASE PANS AND BAKING SHEETS

Melted butter should be used for all pans which require greasing. An easy way to apply it is by brushing it on with a pastry brush. Flour should be lightly dusted over greased surfaces to further prevent sticking.

Cake pans need only be greased at the bottoms, not the sides. Most cakes rise more evenly when they can cling to ungreased sides while baking. The sides can be loosened with a thin knife before removal from pans.

The greasing of pans and baking sheets can be entirely dispensed with if they are lined with Baking Pan Liner Paper, a silicone-treated parchment made by the KVP Paper Company in Kalamazoo, Michigan. It is available in the larger department stores. Even candy and nougat poured on Baking Pan Lining Paper will not stick. The paper can often be wiped off with a damp sponge and reused.

HOW TO USE AN OVEN

Even a perfect oven will not bake a perfect cake if it is not used correctly.

Unless a recipe instructs to the contrary, always preheat the oven for at least 15 minutes before putting anything into it to be baked. Most ovens need that amount of time to reach the temperature at which they are set.

Never overload an oven. It is poor economy. When 2 racks, one over the other, are filled with pans of cake or cookies, nothing bakes well. The cakes on the lower rack are usually too brown on the bottom and uneven on top; the cakes on the upper rack are too dark on top and often only half-baked on the bottom. Good baking requires even heat circulating all around the pans.

Most cakes, puff-paste pastries and cookies bake best on the second rack from the bottom. Filled tarts should be baked on the lowest rack because they need more intense heat from underneath to help them bake through properly .

Unfilled pastry shells and tartlets should be baked on the second rack from the bottom so that the heat is even all around.

Nohing should be baked on a rack near the top of the oven because this would result in a brown top and an uncooked bottom. The high rack is useful when only the tops of tarts or other pastry need last-minute browning.

HOW TO USE A PASTRY BAG

A number of excellent books have been written on the subject of cake decorating. These should be referred to by those who want to master such intricacies as flower and animal piping.

Here we are chiefly concerned with showing some of the practical ways in which a pastry bag and decorating tubes can be used at home with minimum effort and training.

Most home bakers who want to decorate cakes make the error of buying one of the cake-decorating sets consisting of a small plunger-type metal container and about 12 small tips. This equipment is practical mainly for intricate flower work but has little general value at home.

Pastry bags, preferably the type lined with plastic, offer a quick and easy way to accomplish any number of jobs, such as:

decorating cakes and petits fours
making drop cookies
shaping some types of molded cookies
shaping cream puffs and éclairs
filling hors d'oeuvre and sweet tartlet shells
filling cream puffs, éclairs and jelly doughnuts
decorating or piping jelly into centers of cookies
forcing mashed potatoes or purée of chestnuts around entrées to decorate

To take maximum advantage of this wonderful, time-saving technique, 2 bags should be purchased:

One 14-inch bag: a size small enough to use for small to moderate amounts of whipped cream or butter creams.

One 21-inch bag: big enough for large quantities of cooky mixtures, mashed potatoes, or fillings.

In addition to 2 pastry bags, paper cornucopias rolled from triangles of parchment paper or even heavy brown paper can be used with small amounts of icing or butter cream to decorate petits fours and to write with icing on birthday cakes. (See illustrations for rolling a paper cornucopia, p. 30.) After the cornucopia has been filled and the top folded down firmly against the icing, the sharp tip is cut off to make a small round hole; or it can even be cut to approximate the serrated edge of a star tube. A paper cup with a pointed bottom may be substituted for a paper cornucopia.

In addition to the equipment suggested above, a simple selection of metal pastry tubes (which are actually cone-shaped) should be purchased. If possible, buy large tubes rather than small ones useful only for decorating. The large tubes, about 2 inches long, are made with openings of various sizes and they can be used directly in a pastry bag without a coupling or any other hardware. They are available in department stores and in bakery- and restaurant-supply houses.

It's great fun to experiment with tube sizes and shapes, but here is a list of the most useful ones:

PLAIN ROUND TUBES

No. 0 has an opening of ⅛ inch. Used for filling such pastries as small cream puffs or jelly doughnuts.

No. 3 has an opening of ¼ inch. Same uses as No. 0.

No. 5 has an opening slightly larger than ¼ inch. Useful for shaping small cookies.

No. 7 has an opening of about ½ inch. Useful for making small cream puffs, cookies; filling large numbers of tartlets.

No. 9 has an opening of about ¾ inch. Useful for making large cream puffs, éclairs, large cookies, rings for Vacherin.

OPEN STAR TUBES

Nos. 1 and 2 are almost the same size. Both have openings of less than ¼ inch. For decorating small pastries.

No. 4 has an opening of about ⅓ inch. For making medium-size decorations or borders.

No. 6 has an opening of about ½ inch. For forming small molded cookies or whipped-cream decorations.

No. 9 has an opening of about ¾ inch. For making cookies containing pieces of nut meat, and for large decorations of whipped cream.

RIBBON TUBES

No. 47st, a flat tube with one serrated edge, has an opening about ¾ inch long. Primarily for making cookies. Press out dough in long ribbons on baking sheet, one right next to the other. Cut ribbons into 2-inch lengths before baking. They will come together again, but after they are baked, they will readily break apart. A very easy method of making a great many cookies.

MAKING AND USING A PAPER CORNUCOPIA

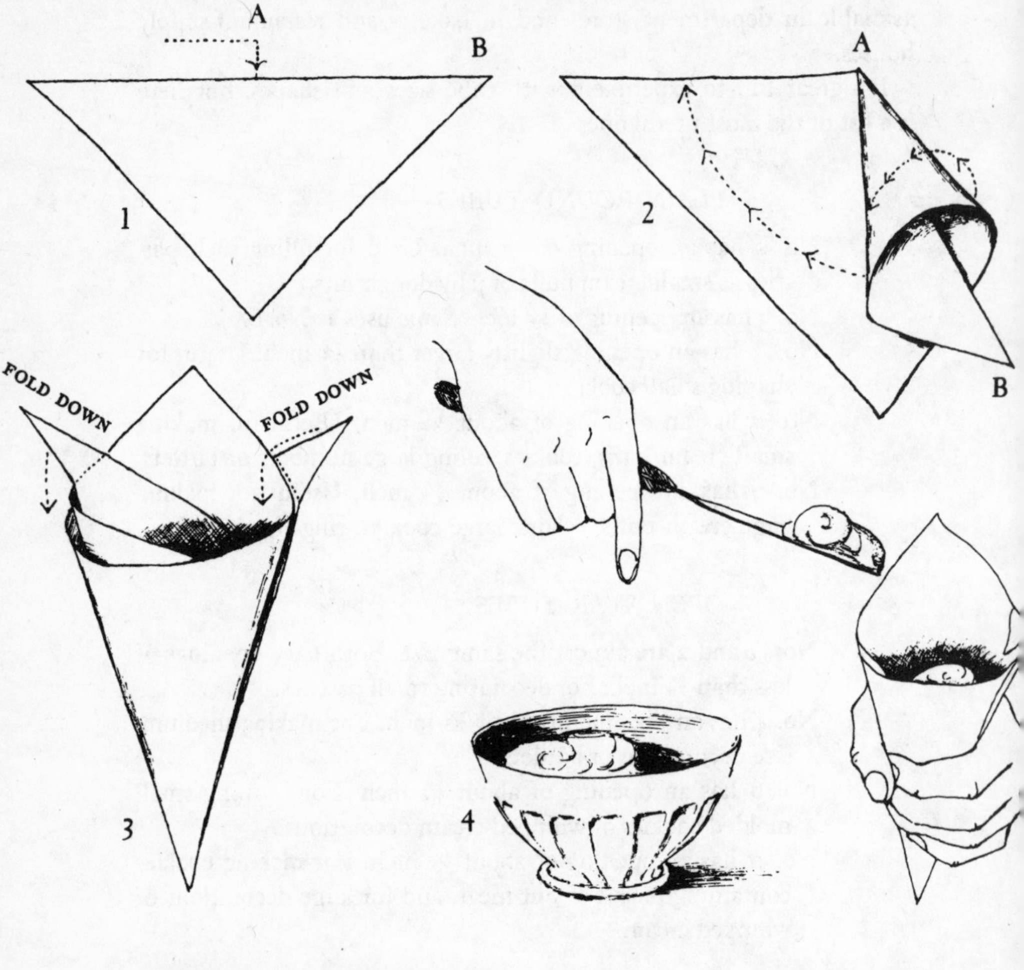

1. *On triangle of parchment paper find center* A. *This will be the pointed end of cornucopia.*

2. *Holding* A *between left thumb and forefinger, grasp* B *with right hand and make first roll, pulling* B *firmly to make* A *into a sharp point.*

3. *Continue to roll up cornucopia, keeping point sharp. Fold down two short ends to secure cornucopia.*

4. *Fill cornucopia no more than ⅔ full.*

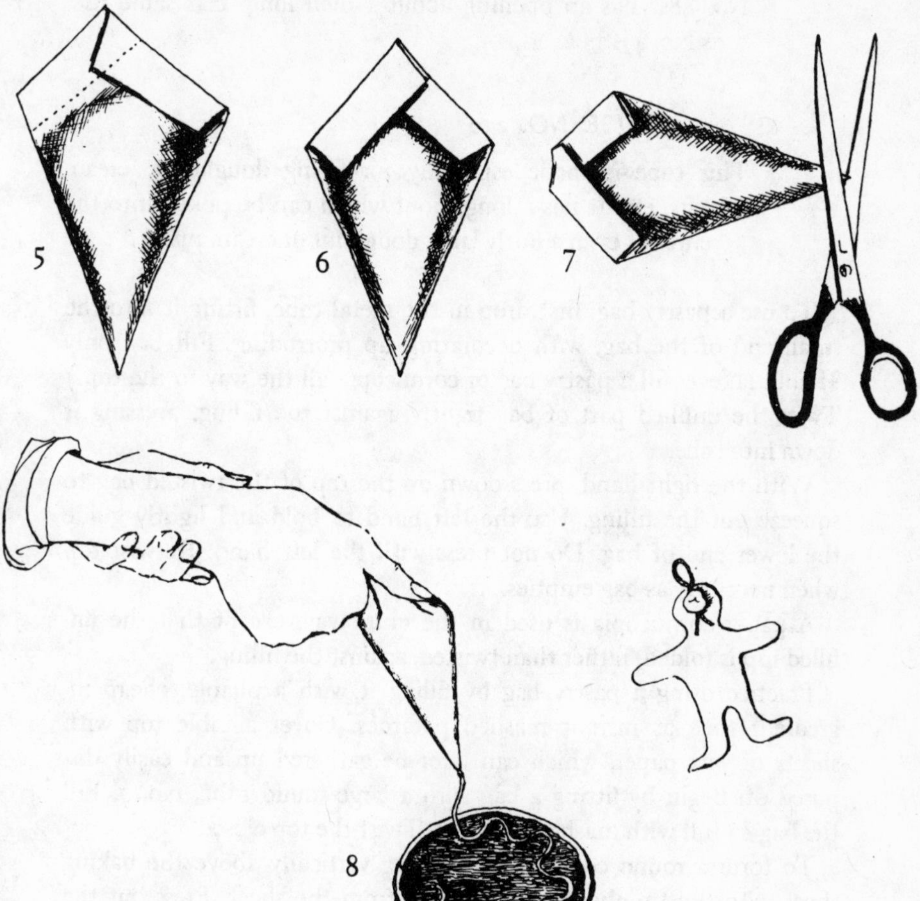

5. Fold down one side of top to enclose filling.

6. Fold down other side. Continue to fold top, first one side, then the other, till filling is pressed firmly into tip of cornucopia.

7. With scissors, cut off tip to make an opening through which filling can be forced.

8. Holding cornucopia at least 1 inch away from surface to be decorated, press filling out to decorate cookies or petits fours. Support the working hand at wrist by holding it with the other hand.

No. 48st has an opening about 1 inch long. Has same uses as No. 47st.

TUBE NO. 230

This tube is made especially for filling doughnuts, cream puffs, etc. It has a long snout which can be poked into the center of even a fairly large doughnut or cream puff.

To use a pastry bag, first drop in the metal tube, fitting it into the small end of the bag, with decorating tip protruding. Fill bag only ⅔ full. (Never fill a pastry bag or cornucopia all the way to the top.) Twist the unfilled part of bag tightly against the filling, pressing it down into tube.

With the right hand, press down on the top of the twisted bag to squeeze out the filling. Use the left hand to hold and lightly guide the lower end of bag. Do not press with the left hand. Retwist top when necessary as bag empties.

A paper cornucopia is used in the same way, except that the unfilled top is folded, rather than twisted, against the filling.

Practice using a pastry bag by filling it with a pliable, cheap ingredient such as instant mashed potatoes. Cover a table top with sheets of wax paper, which can later be gathered up and easily disposed of. Begin by fitting a bag with a large round tube, No. 7. Fill the bag ⅔ full with mashed potatoes. Twist the top closed.

To form a round cooky, hold the bag vertically above the baking sheet with the tip about ¼ inch away from the sheet. Press out the filling without moving the bag or tube, making a 1-inch round. Release pressure on the bag and pull away. Practice making other rounds of the same size. When you can make them with ease, try other sizes and shapes.

Pressure and release are the keys to making even-sized cookies.

To shape cream puffs, hold the bag about ¾ inch away from the baking sheet. Press out pâte à chou (see p. 79), raising bag slightly, to make a high mound about 1 ½ inches in diameter.

Tiny cream puffs are shaped by holding the bag closer to the baking sheet. Press out smaller mounds, making them high, no more than ½ or ¾ inch in diameter.

Rosette shapes are made in the same way. Use an open star tube.

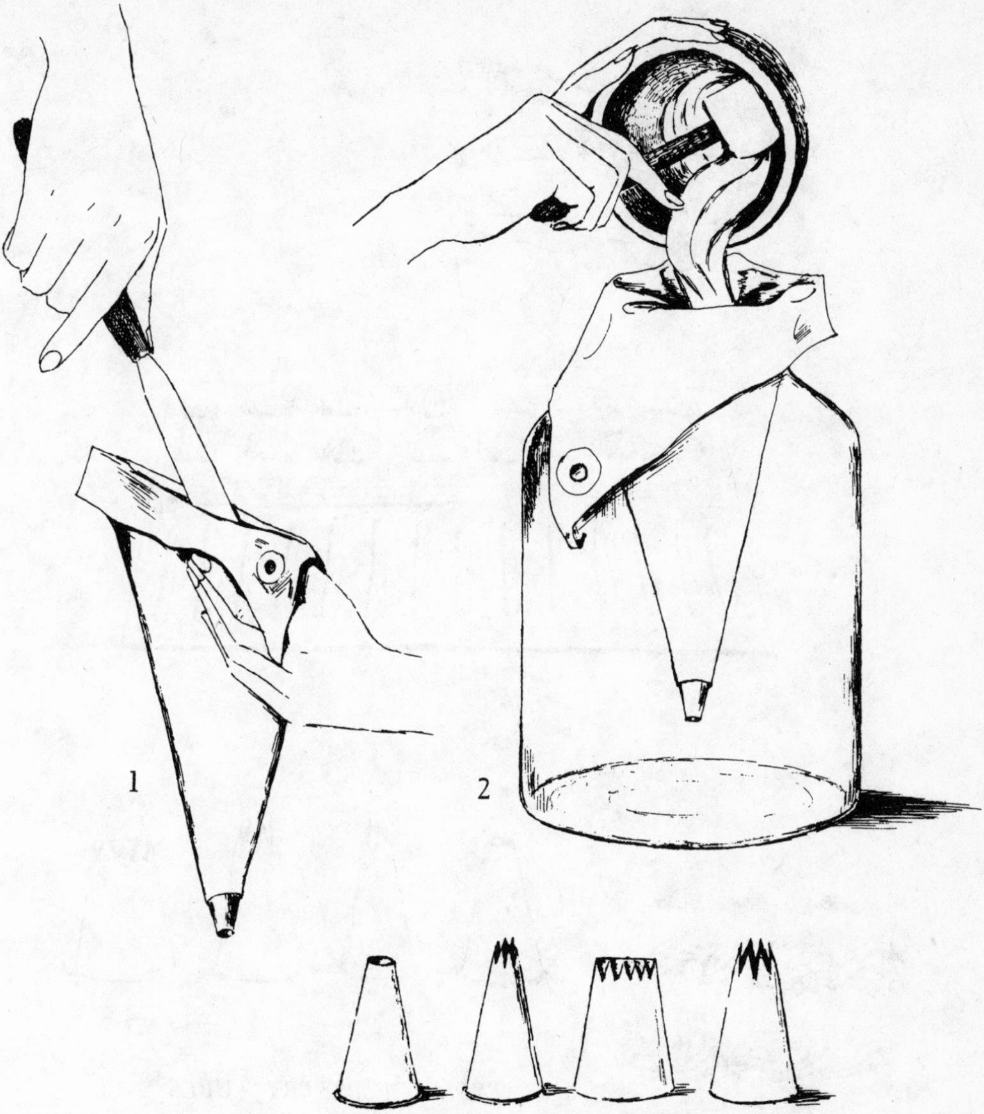

1. *To fill pastry bag by conventional method, hold it in the left hand. Keeping it open, fold top edge over the hand. Using a spatula, fill bag ⅔ full. Remove excess filling from spatula by pinching bag while spatula is being withdrawn.*

2. *Another method is to fit pastry bag into a large jar, draping upper edge over edge of jar. This frees both hands for transferring ingredients from bowl to bag.*

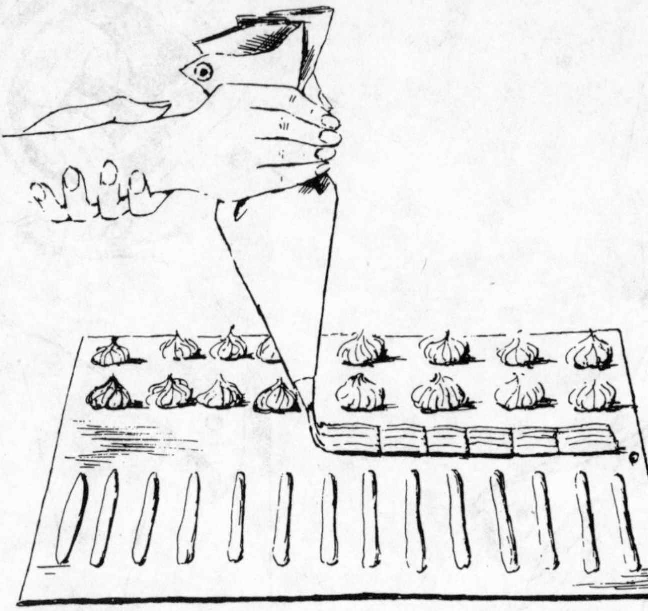

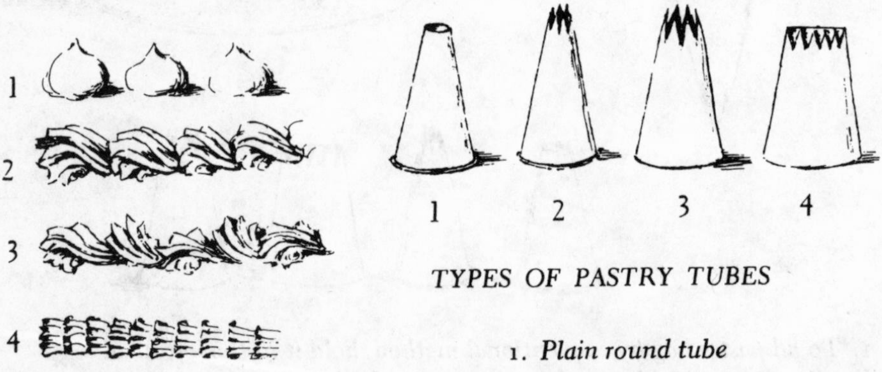

TYPES OF PASTRY TUBES

1. *Plain round tube*
2. *Open star tube*
3. *Larger open star tube*
4. *Ribbon tube*

Numbers of decorations correspond with numbers of tubes.

A simple border can be made by pressing out rosettes, one right next to the other. The shapes of rosettes can be varied by twisting the bag in different ways. (See illustrations for simple rosette borders, p. 34.)

B Basic Baking Ingredients

ALMOND PASTE

Almond paste is made primarily from blanched almonds. It is almost impossible to make a satisfactory almond paste at home. Commercially it is made with large, heavy rollers which produce a smooth, homogenized paste. It can be purchased in department stores and delicacy shops. Unfortunately, what is available is not always of best quality; and some hunting around might prove worth while.

Good almond paste should not be cloyingly sweet; nor should it be overpungent with bitter almond flavor. H. Roth and Son in New York City sells loose almond paste by the pound, of excellent quality.

If the only almond paste available is one of poor quality, increase the quantity of grated lemon rind in the recipe you are using; cut down the sugar; add an extra 2 or 3 spoonfuls of butter.

Fresh almond paste has a pliable consistency. If it is tightly covered, it can be kept in the refrigerator for months.

BUTTER

The best butter for baking is fresh sweet butter. Lightly salted butter may be substituted if sweet butter is unavailable. Vegetable shortenings and margarine have little place in fine baking.

Clarified butter is pure fat from which all the milk solids and water have been removed. If refrigerated, it can be kept for months without becoming rancid. It has many uses. It adds richness to certain delicate cakes, and fine restaurant chefs often use it for sautéeing chicken, veal, and fish, because it does not burn as easily as whole butter.

To make clarified butter, place any quantity of sweet butter in a deep saucepan. Melt it over low heat, and continue cooking the butter until the foam disappears from the top and there is a light brown sediment on the bottom of the pan. Salt butter may be used equally well, but it will yield slightly less clarified butter.

A small amount of butter, such as ¼ pound (½ cup) takes no more than 10 minutes to cook. A larger amount, such as 10 pounds, may take over 2 hours. The liquid butter must not brown, but should remain golden.

When the butter looks perfectly clear, remove it from the heat. Skim any brown crust from the top. If a large amount of clarified butter is being made, let it cool. Pour through a cheesecloth-lined strainer into containers, leaving the sediment in the bottom of the pot.

When only a small amount of clarified butter is being made, it is not necessary to strain it. Simply pour off the clear butter, leaving the sediment in the pot.

CHESTNUT PURÉE

Chestnut purée is often used in European pastries. It is easily made if canned whole chestnuts are available.

To make, heat chestnuts in their liquid until boiling hot. Drain off the liquid. Mash the hot chestnuts with a potato masher or in an electric mixer as you would mash potatoes.

Canned chestnut purée is also available but is not satisfactory for desserts because it is usually too soft and liquid.

Shelled, dry chestnuts can often be found in Italian neighborhoods. These are inexpensive and fairly good. Cover 1 pound of dry chestnuts with boiling water to which has been added ¼ teaspoon baking soda. Soak overnight. Boil the chestnuts in their soaking liquid until they are tender. They may then be mashed to a purée.

Fresh chestnuts in the shell are prepared as follows:

Cut a cross with a sharp knife on the flat side of each chestnut. Place in a saucepan. Cover with cold water. Bring to a boil. Remove from heat. Take out only a few chestnuts at a time and peel off outer and inner skins while still hot.

Cover shelled chestnuts with milk or fresh water. Simmer until chestnuts are tender. Drain off liquid. Mash while still hot with potato masher or electric mixer.

CHOCOLATE

There are 3 types of chocolate commonly used in home baking: unsweetened chocolate (primarily for baking), semisweet chocolate and unsweetened, dark, Dutch-type cocoa.

Unsweetened and semisweet chocolate should be melted in the top of a double boiler to avoid scorching. If you own a heavy saucepan, chocolate can also be melted by heating the saucepan, removing it from the heat, then adding the chocolate to melt from the heat of the pan. Another way of melting chocolate is in a saucepan placed in a low oven for 5 or 10 minutes. This can be done while other ingredients are being prepared. Be careful not to forget the chocolate if this method is used.

Sometimes you may have the unfortunate experience of stirring melted chocolate with a slightly wet spoon or spatula. Suddenly the chocolate will lose its smoothness and become rough and lumpy. This is the result of introducing a small quantity of liquid into the melted chocolate. It is not necessary to throw away the chocolate and begin all over. Simply stir in a tablespoon or 2 of a homogenized vegetable shortening for each 6 ounces of chocolate. This will not affect the flavor, and the chocolate will become smooth again.

Unsweetened, Dutch-type cocoa can be substituted in recipes using unsweetened chocolate. Substitute 2 level tablespoons of sifted cocoa for each ounce of chocolate. In recipes where flour is also used, the cocoa should be sifted with the flour after both ingredients have been measured separately. This type of cocoa has an attractive dark color. It is frequently called for in this book for finishing the outside of pastries.

EGGS

Eggs are one of the most important ingredients in baking. In this book they play a vital role as the sole leavening agent in many cakes.

Eggs also give color and richness to any food to which they are added. They should always be as fresh as possible.

For cakes using whole beaten eggs: The eggs and sugar should be lightly stirred together for only a minute, then heated over hot water

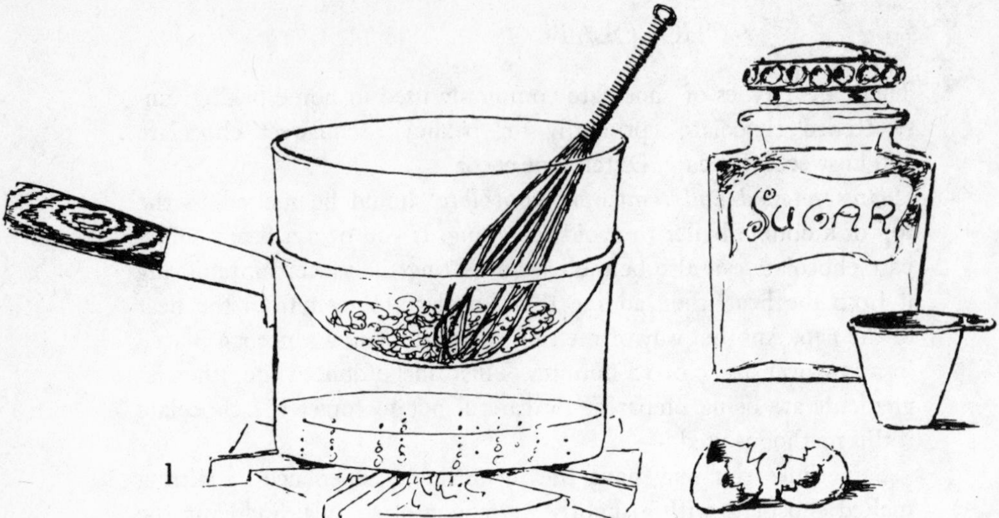

1

2

1. *Eggs and sugar being warmed*

2. *Eggs and sugar after having been warmed and beaten*

until they are slightly warmer than lukewarm. The eggs do not have to be stirred continually while heating; but they must be watched to prevent overheating and curdling.

Heating the eggs before beating helps them to become fluffier and lighter, producing more volume than by ordinary methods.

After being heated, the eggs must be beaten with an electric mixer or with a rotary beater until they are very thick, fluffy, and entirely cool. This beating will fill them with air, which in turn leavens the cake.

It is especially important to fold in the remaining ingredients very carefully so that the air is not forced out of the light batter. Rough handling or overmixing after the eggs have been beaten results in a heavy cake.

In making cakes which use separated eggs: The whites are placed in 1 bowl, the yolks in another.

To separate an egg: Crack it, part the shell gently, letting the white fall into a bowl underneath. Carefully transfer the yolk from one half of shell to the other, letting any additional white fall into the bowl also. Place the yolk in a separate bowl.

Egg whites to be beaten should be at room temperature if possible. A clean, dry bowl with no trace of greasiness must be used.

More volume will be obtained from egg whites if there are absolutely no specks of yolk in them. However, contrary to general belief, a bit of egg yolk will not make beating impossible. Sometimes tiny bits of egg yolk can be removed with a piece of eggshell.

We have made what we consider an important discovery concerning separated-egg cakes. You may throw to the winds all the theories about dry, overbeaten egg whites or thick, lemony egg yolks. It has been found, after repeated tests, that it is almost impossible to overbeat egg whites, particularly after sugar is gradually beaten into them. Furthermore, nothing need be done to egg yolks except break them up with a fork. The egg yolks and any other ingredients are folded into the stiffly beaten egg whites together, at the very last.

This method makes the lightest, most even-grained cakes imaginable. There are also fewer utensils to clean.

Egg yolks are given special emphasis in this book because they have a wonderful effect on the texture of yeast doughs, in particular, and certain butter cakes. Poultry-parts stores often sell raw yolks (incompleted eggs) at very low prices. Such egg yolks can be utilized in baking when available. Remove the outer membrane simply by squeezing the liquid yolk inside the membrane into a measuring cup, remembering that 1 cup equals approximately 12 yolks.

In making yeast doughs, egg yolks are preferable to whole eggs. They give incomparable texture and richness. In any yeast recipe 2 yolks can be substituted for each whole egg.

Egg yolks are often used to thicken sauces and sweet custards. Since eggs curdle easily from overheating, they should be added to any hot mixture with care, preferably near the end of cooking.

The technique is a simple one: Before adding egg yolks (or whole beaten eggs) to anything hot, first add 2 or 3 spoonfuls of the hot mixture to the eggs, stirring briskly. Then pour the warmed eggs into the hot sauce, continuing to stir. Cook the sauce over low heat, or in a double boiler, stirring constantly, until the eggs have thickened the sauce.

FLOUR

Grocery shelves offer a confusion of flours: self-rising cake flour, plain cake flour, self-rising all-purpose flour, plain all-purpose flour, not to mention cake mixes, which are usually placed all around and in between the flours.

Plain, all-purpose flour is the only flour which is absolutely essential to the recipes in this book. It can be used for making cakes, breads, cookies, and almost anything else you might decide to try.

Self-rising flours contain salt and baking-powder leavenings.

Cake flours are made from flour-starch blends in varying proportions. They are generally more expensive than all-purpose flours, and they produce lighter cakes in recipes using baking powder. In cakes leavened with beaten eggs they make little, if any, difference.

Bread flour, which contains a higher percentage of gluten than cake or all-purpose flours, is obtainable only from those little bakeries which will agree to sell it. Bread flour is especially good for making breads, coffeecakes, and puff paste. However, all-purpose flour can always be substituted.

More information on flour is contained in the chapters on yeast doughs and puff paste.

LIQUEUR FLAVORINGS

The alcoholic flavorings in any of the recipes in this book can be omitted. However, these flavors help to achieve the famed delicacy of European pastries.

In most recipes, one liqueur can often substitute for another. For example, cognac may always be used instead of rum; fruit liqueurs can substitute for each other. Innovations are always in order.

A bottle each of cognac, an orange-flavored liqueur such as Cointreau or Grand Marnier, and kirsch will provide enough variety to flavor the recipes in this book.

NUTS

Nuts are a widely used baking ingredient. They give flavor, texture and, often, beauty to cakes. Most nuts with the exception of peanuts and cashews are suitable for fine home baking.

Nuts can be purchased in the shell or shelled. Shelled nuts freeze well for many months; or they can be kept fresh in a closed container in the refrigerator.

Shelled almonds have a brown inner skin which often must be removed. This is called blanching. To blanch almonds, cover them with boiling water. Let them stand for 5 minutes. The brown skins can then be slipped off easily.

Filberts, too, have a brown inner skin. To blanch, place shelled filberts in a 350 degree oven for 10 or 15 minutes, or until the brown skin is dark in color. Cool slightly. Rub nuts in a towel or between the hands to remove the flaky brown skin.

Nuts are prepared and used in the following ways:

Whole nuts: Blanched almonds, walnut halves, pecan halves, and filberts (also called hazelnuts) are generally used as decorations.

Large pieces of nuts can often be substituted for whole nuts.

Thinly sliced (or flaked) almonds or filberts are often used as a final decorative touch on pastries. They also add taste and texture. Blanched, sliced almonds or filberts can be prepared at home, but it is a time-consuming chore unless you have a nut-slicing attachment for your mixer or grinder. Fortunately they can be purchased ready to use in some large department stores and in some small first-class bakeries. When using sliced blanched almonds or filberts on small pastries and dessert cakes, they should be broken or crushed (after toasting) to a size in keeping with the size of the pastry. Toasting sliced almonds or filberts adds to their flavor and appearance. Place them on a flat baking sheet in a 325 degree oven for 10 or 15 minutes, stirring once or twice, until they are a light golden brown. Toasted nuts can be refrigerated or frozen.

Crushed nuts: Lightly toasted pecans, walnuts, or filberts make an excellent substitute for sliced blanched nuts. They are delicious, and look as appetizing as sliced nuts. To prepare crushed nuts, place nuts (after toasting) on a table top or working surface. Using no more than ½ cup at a time, crush the nuts with a rolling pin, being careful not to make them too fine. Crushing nuts releases their oils, giving more flavor.

Finely ground or grated nuts can be prepared in an electric blender or in any of the little nut graters made especially for this purpose.

POTATO WATER

The water in which potatoes have been boiled is often preferred as the liquid in bread dough. It adds a unique flavor and is also said to give bread a longer-keeping quality.

SUGAR

Sugar has been the subject of inexhaustible studies. For home use, only a few basic principles need be understood.

Sugar in baking provides not only sweetness but also brownness and texture. Granulated sugar, brown sugar, light-brown sugar, and confectioners' sugar are those most often used at home.

Granulated sugar is used most frequently and can be measured just as it pours from the package, unless it is lumpy and needs straining.

Brown sugar and light-brown sugar are darker-colored and more strongly flavored. When fresh, they are moist and contain many soft lumps. These are easily eliminated by placing the sugar in a plastic bag and rolling the lumps out with a rolling pin. Stale brown sugars are very hard and almost not worth the trouble of getting them back into usable form. To prevent brown sugars from hardening, the opened packages should be emptied into jars which can be tightly closed. The jars should be kept in a cool place.

Confectioners' sugar is used mainly in icings and for dusting cakes before they are served. When fresh, it is soft and may contain some lumps, which can be removed by pressing sugar through a strainer or sifter. Stale confectioners' sugar may develop very hard, difficult-to-remove lumps.

COOKED SUGARS

Sugar syrups, made with granulated sugar mixed with water and corn syrup or cream of tartar, have many uses in baking. It is most important to remember, when cooking any syrup, to dissolve the sugar slowly, stirring constantly in the beginning. Rushing this process will result in incompletely dissolved sugar. A *single grain of undissolved sugar can cause an entire batch of syrup to crystallize after it has cooled.* After the sugar has been completely dissolved, the syrup is generally boiled. The longer it boils, the more water evaporates, and the thicker the syrup becomes.

Except at high altitudes, where adjustments are necessary (see p. 26), a candy thermometer is the most accurate way of determining the condition of a boiling syrup. Here is a brief outline of syrup temperatures and what they mean:

230 to 234 degrees (heavy syrup), THREAD STAGE: Slightly cooled syrup spins a 2-inch thread when rubbed between thumb and forefinger.

234 to 240 degrees, SOFT BALL: A bit of slightly cooled syrup, dropped into a cup of very cold water, can be picked up in a soft ball.

244 to 248 degrees, FIRM BALL: Syrup, when dropped into very cold water, forms a ball which does not flatten upon removal from water.

250 to 266 degrees, HARD BALL: Syrup, when dropped into very cold water, forms a ball hard enough to hold its shape, yet soft enough to be flattened between thumb and forefinger if pressed.

270 to 290 degrees, SOFT CRACK: Syrup, when dropped into very cold water, separates into bits which are hard but not brittle.

300 to 310 degrees, HARD CRACK: Syrup, when dropped into very cold water, separates into bits or threads which are hard and brittle.

320 degrees, CARAMELIZED: Syrup turns brown.

Caramelized sugar is generally made by melting granulated sugar in a heavy pan, over very low heat. A little lemon juice or corn syrup added to the sugar helps it to dissolve more evenly, with less possibility of hard lumps. *The sugar must be stirred constantly while it is melting*. It can be cooked until it is a light golden brown or until it is somewhat darker in color. It needs careful watching, however, because the changes in color occur very rapidly.

Be especially careful when it is necessary to add liquid to hot caramelized sugar. Serious burns can result from the sudden boiling and spattering.

BASIC SIMPLE SYRUP

This is for making mock fondant, butter creams, sauce for baba au rhum, and many other delicious things. Keep in a covered jar at room temperature.

2 ½ *cups sugar*
¾ *cup white corn syrup*
1 ¼ *cups water*

Combine sugar, corn syrup, and water in a large saucepan. Stir over low heat until sugar is completely dissolved. When it looks clear, wash down sides of saucepan with a brush dipped in cold water. Place lid on saucepan for 5 minutes so that steam will further dissolve any sugar crystals.

Remove lid. Raise heat. Boil for 5 minutes without stirring. Cool syrup, pour into jars, and cover tightly. Store for future use.

Note: If sugar has not been thoroughly dissolved, the syrup, after a week or even less, may form large crystals in the bottom of the jar (one way to make rock candy). The presence of crystals will not hurt the syrup, but it is wasteful, because the more crystals the less syrup you will have.

FLAVORED SUGARS

CINNAMON SUGAR

2 *cups granulated sugar*
2 *tablespoons cinnamon*

Mix together. Store in a covered jar.

LEMON SUGAR

Grating lemon rind is a chore and a bore. People often use dry substitutes which, however good, never taste quite like fresh lemon. Here is a simple way always to have the flavor of freshly grated lemon rind on hand. Lemon sugar will keep in the refrigerator for months.

6 lemons
1 cup sugar (approximately)
lemon juice, if needed

Grate the outer rind of 6 whole lemons or, using a potato peeler, peel rind very thin. The white substance just beneath the yellow is bitter and should be left on the lemon.

If a potato peeler has been used, grind the lemon peel twice in meat grinder, using finest blade. Measure ground or grated lemon peel. Add twice as much sugar (approximately 1 cup). Stir and mash very well. Sugar should look slightly dampened. If it looks very dry, add just a drop or 2 of lemon juice.

Keep refrigerated in a covered jar. One tablespoon of lemon sugar substitutes for 1 teaspoon of grated lemon rind.

ORANGE SUGAR

Follow recipe for lemon sugar (see above), substituting 4 oranges for lemons.

TANGERINE SUGAR

Follow recipe for lemon sugar (see above), substituting tangerines for lemons.

VANILLA SUGAR

Vanilla sugar is used more for the aroma than for the taste. It should not be substituted for regular vanilla flavor in a recipe. It is best used for dusting cakes just before serving. To make it, bury 3 or 4 vanilla beans in a canister containing a pound of confectioners' sugar. After a few days the sugar will have absorbed some of the fragrance. It can be kept almost indefinitely.

VANILLA FLAVORINGS

VANILLA COGNAC

Vanilla cognac can be used to flavor any pastry or cake filling in which cognac is used. It should not be used to take the place of vanilla extract.

To make vanilla cognac, place 3 or 4 vanilla beans in a bottle of cognac. Let stand at least a week.

VANILLA POWDER

Vanilla beans kept in confectioners' sugar eventually dry up. These should be replaced. Save the dry vanilla beans. Put them all into a jar. When there are several, and they are as dry as firewood, break them up slightly. Put them into the blender and turn it on. A fine vanilla powder will result, delicious for flavoring custards, ice cream, whipped cream, anything in which you won't mind the tiny vanilla specks. Vanilla powder keeps indefinitely in a tightly closed jar.

VANILLA EXTRACT

Pure vanilla extract should be used in all recipes requiring liquid vanilla flavoring. Artificial vanilla should never be substituted. It is preferable to use grated orange or lemon peel in a recipe if pure vanilla is unavailable.

YEAST

Yeast is discussed in the chapter entitled "A Few Breads, Many Coffeecakes."

C *Equipment for Baking*

Electric Blender: An electric blender is certainly a great help, although if a choice is to be made, a mixer is far more important in baking. A blender will grind nuts and make any number of delectable butter creams and desserts very quickly.

Electric Mixer: If you really love to bake, don't run out and buy a little portable job, or even the first standard-model home mixer which comes your way. Some electric mixers have very special, worthwhile features such as a paddle for creaming, a wire whisk for beating, and a dough hook for kneading.

Rotary Egg Beater: A good, modern rotary egg beater should be purchased if an electric mixer is out of the question. Some modern hand beaters are very efficient. Don't by any means try to get by with an old, grandma-vintage egg beater.

Measuring Cups: Use standard measuring cups to measure any ingredient. If possible, do not use a 1-cup size to measure ½ or ¼ cup. Metal and plastic measuring cups can be purchased in sets consisting of sizes from ¼ cup to 1 cup. These should be used to measure exact quantities of dry ingredients.

Oven: A dependable oven is a valuable piece of equipment. An oven should have a thermostat for even heat control. If this is not available, place an oven thermometer on a baking rack. When glass containers are used for baking, oven temperatures should always be reduced by 25 degrees to avoid a tough crust.

Unfortunately an oven thermometer cannot be depended on to remain reliable indefinitely. Check it every month by placing in a saucepan of boiling water. If the thermometer registers about 212 degrees, it is still accurate.

Fortunately for all of us, variations of 25 to 50 degrees in oven temperature will not mean utter baking failure. Most cakes, even delicate ones, survive slightly warmer or cooler ovens than directions call for with little impairment.

Pastry Cloth: A pastry cloth is not, by definition here, a small 18-inch square of canvas. To be of practical value a pastry cloth should be as large as the table on which you work.

A heavy pastry cloth should be used to roll anything which is apt to give trouble by sticking, such as puff paste and cooky doughs. Well floured, it will make rolling any dough almost foolproof.

Heavy canvas for this purpose can be purchased inexpensively in shops selling boat supplies. Most department stores sell canvas in their upholstery departments. The edges of the canvas can be hemmed if desired (not necessary however); and they can be elasticized to make the cloth fit snugly (also not necessary, if the canvas is heavy enough and hangs over the sides of the table).

After each use, flour and all other substances should be carefully scraped off the pastry cloth with a metal scraper or spatula. This will eliminate the need for laundering every time the cloth is used. It should be stored in a dry, airy place.

DESIRABLE MISCELLANEOUS EQUIPMENT

FOR MIXING

flour sifter
measuring cups, 2 or more sets
measuring spoons, 2 or more sets
wire whisks, 2 if possible
rotary egg beater
rubber spatulas, 2 or more
mixing bowls, assorted sizes
heavy saucepans, 1 or more
wooden spoons

FOR SHAPING

assorted cooky cutters
rolling pin, as heavy and large as you can find, preferably with ball bearings
sharp knives, 2 or more
baker's scraper—looks like an old-time meat chopper with a straight edge. Excellent for cleaning pastry cloth as well as cutting off pieces of dough
round pastry knife wheel—a pastry wheel with a knife instead of a fluted edge (sometimes used for cutting pizzas)
pastry bag and assorted tubes

FOR BAKING

jelly-roll pan, 11 x 16 inches
tube pans, 1 9-inch and 1 10-inch
loaf pans, 9 x 5 x 3 inches, 3 or more
baking sheets, as large as your oven will accommodate, 2 or more
flan rings, 1 or more
layer-cake pans, 9 inches in diameter, 1 inch deep, 2 or more
spring-form pan, 9 inches in diameter

tartlet tins, 12 or more
square 9-inch pans, 2
assorted tins and molds for making babas, madeleines, savarins
muffin tins
fluted ring mold (kugelhopf pan), 10 inches in diameter

FOR DECORATING

cake racks, 1 large and 2 smaller ones
metal spatulas, 2 or more
pastry brushes, 2 or more
parchment paper for cornucopias
paper cups with pointed bottoms
pastry bag and assorted tubes

Note: When choosing pans for baking, try to select solid, well-made ones which feel slightly heavy when picked up. Pans made of tinned steel or *heavy* aluminum are preferable to lightweight cheap ones, which often warp in baking and fail to bake through properly. Suitable pans can best be purchased at restaurant- and baking-equipment-supply firms, which are located in all sizable cities. A few stores which fill mail orders are listed below.

If possible, select baking sheets which are only slightly smaller (1 inch all around) than your oven. Sheet-metal shops usually will cut pieces of aluminum to size. This is an inexpensive way to acquire large, heavy aluminum baking sheets tailored to fit your own oven.

A FEW SHOPPING SOURCES FOR SUPPLIES AND EQUIPMENT

(All the shops listed below will fill mail orders)

August Thomsen & Co., Inc., 37-28 56th Street, Woodside 77, N. Y. Manufacturer of Ateco pastry tubes and bags. Will fill retail mail orders or advise as to local sources. No catalogue. Some printed literature available.

BAZAR FRANÇAIS, 666 *Avenue of the Americas, New York City.* French baking tins, madeleine molds, baba molds, tartlets, flan rings, kugelhopf pans; also wire whisks. Catalogue available.

BAEHM PAPER COMPANY, 53 *Murray Street, New York City.* Paper supplies of all kinds: paper cases for small pastries, parchment paper, freezing papers, and other supplies. No Catalogue.

THE BRIDGE COMPANY, 498 *Third Avenue, New York City.* French baking tins: madeleine molds, baba molds, tartlets, flan rings; wire whisks, kugelhopf pans, pastry bags and tubes. Fair prices. No catalogue.

H. ROTH AND SON, 1577 *First Avenue, New York City.* Hungarian and German type baking supplies: spring-form pans, kugelhopf pans, wooden spoons, cooky cutters, nut grinders, poppy-seed grinders. An excellent source of almond paste, vanilla beans, spices, shelled and unshelled nuts, candied and dried fruits. Catalogue available.

LA CUISINIERE, 903 Madison Avenue, New York City. Continental baking and cooking equipment. Descriptive price list available.

MAID OF SCANDINAVIA, 3245 *Raleigh Avenue, Minneapolis, Minn.* Many baking specialties: pans, cake-decorating tubes, pastry bags, books. Catalogue available.

TRINACRIA IMPORTING COMPANY, 415 *Third Avenue, New York City.* Nuts, spices, different kinds of flour, special dipping chocolate for candymaking, a few types of pans. No catalogue.

WILLIAMS-SONOMA, 576 Sutter Street, San Francisco, California. Imported aids to the baker and cook. Descriptive price list available.

D *To Make and Keep*

Unexpected company, a joyous celebration, a long-awaited anniversary or a bit of good luck call for festive desserts. A beautiful, luscious homemade cake can turn a simple meal into a party.

Delectable pastries need never—should never—become an all-day production. Many seemingly complicated desserts can be quickly put together with supplies from a well-stocked pantry, refrigerator, or freezer.

Some days—the rainy and snowy ones—seem made for working at home. Take advantage of them to prepare shelled nuts, fruit-rind sugars, layers and crumbs of broyage, nougat powder, and chocolate shapes.

If you own a freezer, you already know some of the advantages of keeping it well-stocked. Homemade bread freezes perfectly, as does almost every conceivable type of baked product.

Freezing-time-limit estimates given in this section are admittedly conservative. Bread can be frozen for 1 year, cake layers for 6 months, say the frozen-food manuals. This is true only if these products are especially well wrapped, and conditions within the freezer absolutely perfect. Some freezer owners maintain such conditions. Too often, however, air finds its way into freezer packages. The result is bread, cake, or butter cream with a distinct "freezer" taste. For that reason, freezing-time limits given here have been reduced.

Although a freezer is definitely an asset in planning ahead, a great number of cake decorations, fillings, and even cake layers can be kept for some time in the refrigerator or pantry.

Items recommended for refrigeration or pantry storage should be well wrapped or covered. Put fillings and butter creams into jars with tight covers; wrap cake layers with Saran or aluminum foil, or cover with a bowl; keep nuts in jars with tight covers, cookies in clean, dry, tightly covered tins. Proper wrapping of foods to be made and kept cannot be overemphasized.

Plastic containers, jars, and canisters with tight covers generally provide the best storage.

TO MAKE AND KEEP

(If no storage time is indicated under a heading of the following chart, it is best not to store the food in that location. Pastries, for example, that show no storage time under *Pantry* should either be served shortly after baking or stored in the *Refrigerator* or *Freezer* as designated.)

	Pantry	*Refrigerator*	*Freezer*
BASIC SUPPLIES			
Chestnut purée		2-3 days	6-8 weeks
Clarified butter		3 months	indefinitely
Egg whites		1-2 weeks	3-4 months
Egg yolks		1-2 days	3-4 months (to freeze, add ½ teaspoon salt or 2 teaspoons sugar for each 6 yolks)
Liquored cherries and brandied fruits	indefinitely		
Mincemeat	indefinitely		
Nougat powder	4-6 weeks	indefinitely	
Nuts, shelled		indefinitely	3-4 months
Preserves, fruit	indefinitely		
Sugar			
Cinnamon	indefinitely		
Lemon		indefinitely	
Orange		indefinitely	
Tangerine		indefinitely	
Vanilla	indefinitely		
Syrup, basic simple	indefinitely		
Vanilla powder	indefinitely		
Yeast			
dry granulated	3 months		
fresh compressed		2-6 weeks	

MAINLY FOR DECORATING

	Pantry	Refrigerator	Freezer
Chocolate			
rounds, shapes, animals		2-3 months	4-6 months
truffles		1 month	
Crumbs (broyage, cooky)	1-2 weeks	3-4 weeks	3-4 months
Crystallized flowers	indefinitely		
Fruits, preserved, liquored, brandied, or candied	indefinitely		
Nougat powder, shapes, cutouts	4-6 weeks		
Nuts, shelled, sliced: toasted or untoasted		indefinitely	3-4 months
Vanilla sugar	indefinitely		

FILLINGS AND FROSTINGS

	Pantry	Refrigerator	Freezer
Butter creams, general		1-2 weeks	3-4 months
Meringue		1-2 weeks	only in filled pastry; 4-6 weeks
Chocolate glazes, cooked		3-4 weeks	
Coffeecake fillings			
Frangipane, Ground Nut, Poppy Seed, Potato Cream, Prune		2-3 days	2-3 months
Others		2-3 days	
Fondant	2-3 weeks	1-2 months	
Lemon cream		3-4 months	
Pastry creams		3-4 days	
Sour cream (homemade)		4-5 weeks	
Whipped cream			
plain, or with sugar and flavoring		2-3 hours	

	Pantry	*Refrigerator*	*Freezer*
Whipped cream (con't) gelatin added, with or without sugar and flavoring		1-2 days	
BASIC CAKES			
Broyage, Swiss, Chocolate, baked	1-2 weeks		3-4 months
Cream Puffs, Éclairs, baked, unfilled			2-3 months
Fruit Cake (dark)	indefinitely		
Gênoise, Sponge, Almond Butter, Basic Sponge Sheet, Chocolate Pastry, etc., baked	2 days	3-4 days	3-4 months
Meringue, Swiss, baked loosely wrapped, in dry place	1-2 weeks		
Pastry			
unshaped, unbaked		5-7 days	
shaped, unbaked (flan rings, tartlets)		4-5 days	2-3 months
baked, unfilled	4-5 days	4-5 days	4-6 weeks
baked, filled		4-5 days	2-3 weeks
Custard filled		2-3 days	
Pâte à Chou, unbaked, unshaped		1-2 days	
Pound cakes	1-2 weeks	2-3 weeks	3-4 months
Puff Paste			
unshaped, unbaked		2-3 days	
shaped, unbaked		1-2 days	2-3 months
baked	3-7 days		3-4 weeks
Savarin dough, baked		1-2 days	2-3 months
Strudel,			
filled, unbaked		1-2 days	
filled, baked (unless filling needs re-			

	Pantry	*Refrigerator*	*Freezer*
Strudel (con't) frigeration, strudel keeps better at room temperature)	2-3 days	2-3 days	3-4 weeks

COOKIES

	Pantry	*Refrigerator*	*Freezer*
Cooky bars and slices, baked	3-5 days		4-6 weeks
Drop cookies,			
unbaked, shaped or unshaped		3-4 days	
baked	1-2 weeks		6-8 weeks
Florentines (do not freeze)	3-5 days	7-10 days	
Molded cookies,			
unbaked, unshaped		4-5 days	
shaped but unbaked		1-2 weeks	2-3 months
baked	1-2 weeks		4-6 weeks
Rolled cookies,			
unbaked, unshaped		4-5 days	
shaped but unbaked		4-5 days	2-3 months
baked	at least 2 weeks		6-8 weeks

YEAST BREAD, ROLLS, AND COFFEECAKES

	Pantry	*Refrigerator*	*Freezer*
Bread,			
unbaked, unshaped dough		1-2 days	
shaped, baked			3-4 months
Brioche,			
unshaped, unbaked		3-4 days	
shaped, baked			3-4 months
Croissants,			
unshaped, unbaked		2 days	
shaped, unbaked		6-8 hours	1-2 days
shaped, baked			3-4 months

	Pantry	*Refrigerator*	*Freezer*
Basic, Rich and Sour Cream Coffeecake Doughs			
unshaped, unbaked		3-4 days	
baked without icing			2-3 months
Danish and Butter Roll Pastries			
unshaped, unbaked		2-3 days	
shaped, unbaked		6-8 hours	1-2 days
baked, without icing			3-4 months
Yeast			
dry granulated	3 months		
fresh compressed		2-6 weeks	

PASTRY HORS D'OEUVRES

Cheese Bites,			
unbaked		5-7 days	3-4 months
baked	5-7 days		4-6 weeks
Pâte à Chou Hors d'Oeuvres:			
Gougère, Cocktail Puffs, baked, unfilled			2-3 months
Spiced Pufflets, baked	2-3 weeks		3-4 months
Potato Puff Sticks,			
shaped, unbaked		2-3 days	2-3 months
baked			4-6 weeks
Russian Rolls, baked			4-6 weeks
Short Hors d'Oeuvres Pastry and Cream Cheese Pastry Hors d'Oeuvres: barquettes, turnovers, salt sticks			
unbaked		3-7 days	2-3 months
baked	2-3 days		4-6 weeks

Note: Baked turnovers with meat and fish fillings must be refrigerated.

	Pantry	Refrigerator	Freezer
Sponge Pinwheel Slices,			
before slicing		2-3 days	4-6 weeks
sliced, untoasted		2-3 days	4-6 weeks

HORS D'OEUVRE FILLINGS

	Pantry	Refrigerator	Freezer
Cabbage		3-4 days	4-6 weeks
Ham		2-3 days	
Liver		3-4 days	4-6 weeks
Meat, Basic		3-4 days	4-6 weeks
Onion		3-4 days	4-6 weeks
Sea Food, Basic		2-3 days	3-4 weeks
Spinach		3-4 days	4-6 weeks

TABLE OF EQUIVALENTS

Almond paste	2⅛ cups	=	1 pound
Baking soda	2½ tablespoons	=	1 ounce
Butter	2 cups	=	1 pound
	1 cup	=	16 tablespoons
	½ cup	=	⅜ cup clarified butter
Cornstarch	3½ cups (stirred)	=	1 pound
Eggs (large)	2 cups	=	1 pound
whole	5	=	1 cup
whites	8-9	=	1 cup
yolks	12	=	1 cup
Flour			
all-purpose and bread	4 cups (sifted or stirred)	=	1 pound
cake	4½ cups (sifted or stirred)	=	1 pound
whole wheat	3¾ cups (stirred)	=	1 pound
Fruits			
apples	1 pound	=	3 cups peeled, cored, sliced
apricots (dry)	3 cups	=	1 pound (5 cups after cooking)
currants	3¼ cups	=	1 pound
figs (cut fine)	2⅔ cups	=	1 pound

TABLE OF EQUIVALENTS (*continued*)

ginger, crystallized			
(diced)	2⅔ cups	=	1 pound
prunes, dry pitted	2¼ cups	=	1 pound
raisins, whole			
seeded	2½ cups	=	1 pound
seedless	3 cups	=	1 pound
Gelatin	3 tablespoons	=	1 ounce
Honey	1⅓ cups	=	1 pound
Milk, whole			
or skimmed	2 cups	=	1 pound
Nuts			
almonds	1 pound in shells	yields	⅔ cup
	3 cups shelled	=	1 pound
filberts	1 pound in shells	yields	1⅔ cups
	3⅓ cups shelled	=	1 pound
pecans	1 pound in shells	yields	1¼ cups
(halves)	4¼ cups	=	1 pound
walnuts	1 pound in shells	yields	1¾ cups
(halves)	4½ cups	=	1 pound
Oils (liquid fats)	2 cups	=	1 pound
Sugar, granulated	2¼ cups	=	1 pound
superfine	2⅓ cups	=	1 pound
brown (well			
packed)	2¼ cups	=	1 pound
confectioners'	3½–4 cups	=	1 pound
Water	2 cups	=	1 pound

TABLE OF WEIGHTS

3 teaspoons	=	1 tablespoon (½ ounce)
16 tablespoons	=	1 cup
4 tablespoons	=	¼ cup
5 tablespoons plus 1 teaspoon	=	⅓ cup
¼ cup plus 1 tablespoon	=	⅜ cup
½ cup plus 2 tablespoons	=	⅝ cup

TABLE OF WEIGHTS (*continued*)

¾ cup plus 2 tablespoons	=	⅞ cup
1 cup	=	½ pint (8 fluid ounces)
2 pints	=	1 quart
4 quarts	=	1 gallon

FOREIGN WEIGHTS

454 grams	=	1 pound
227 grams	=	½ pound
30 grams	=	2 tablespoons
5 grams	=	1 teaspoon
1 kilogram	=	2⅕ pounds
1 gill	=	½ cup (¼ pint)
1 liter	=	slightly over a quart of liquid

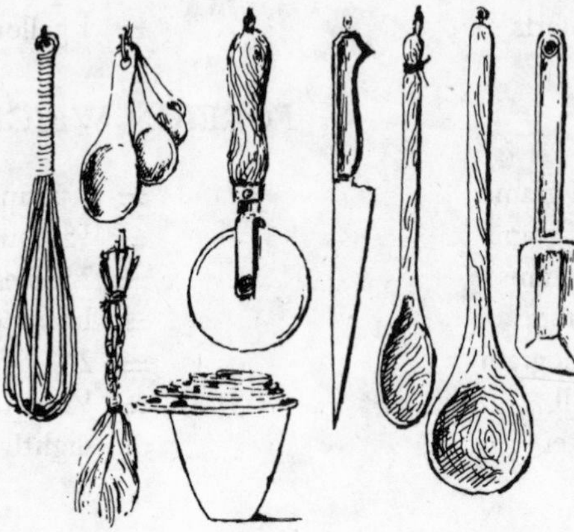

Chapter 2

Basic Cakes and Mixtures

2 *Basic Cakes and Mixtures*

Here you will find all the cakes and mixtures with which old-world cooks create their magic of dainty petits fours, extra-rich torten and delicate gâteaux. Learn to make these basic cakes and your baking scope will become unlimited. Give extra heed to this chapter. Understanding it is essential to much that follows.

Put away the baking powder, a necessity in 1-, 2-, or 3-egg cakes. Beaten eggs will be our leavening.

GETTING ORGANIZED FOR BAKING

Making any cake can be simplified by planning a workable routine. For example, making a gênoise with an electric mixer might go like this:

1. Set oven temperature at 350 degrees.
2. Gather all ingredients and utensils.
3. Begin to clarify butter so it will be ready when you need it.
4. Combine eggs and sugar in a bowl. Place bowl over a saucepan of hot water. Place saucepan over low heat to warm eggs.
5. While eggs are warming, prepare sifted flour and grease pans. Do not forget to check on eggs to prevent over-heating.
6. Remove warmed eggs from stove. Beat with mixer.

7. While eggs are beating, check on butter. When it is ready, pour into a clean cup, leaving sediment in pan.
8. Check eggs in beater to prevent overflowing. Scrape sides of bowl with rubber spatula occasionally, if necessary.
9. When eggs have been beaten until light, fluffy, and tripled in bulk, stop mixer. Sprinkle flour lightly on top of eggs. Turn mixer on to lowest speed. Add vanilla and melted butter in a thin stream, folding in with the flour. Or, follow directions given for folding in flour and butter by hand (p. 19).
10. Pour into prepared pans. Bake until cake is golden brown and top is springy when touched lightly with index finger. Do not open oven door until at least ⅔ of baking time has elapsed.
11. Remove cakes from pans immediately by inverting onto rack, unless other directions are given in a particular recipe. Cool cakes on a rack which permits air circulation all round.

When a cake is made with a hand beater, the routine must be changed, but only slightly. All ingredients should be prepared, pans greased, and everything made ready before actual mixing is begun. Beaten eggs cannot wait while flour is sifted, butter clarified, pans greased. The longer the beaten eggs are left to stand, the more air is lost.

GÊNOISE

Gênoise, the French butter spongecake, is the most versatile cake you can make. It is rich, yet light and delicate. Any dessert cake made with layers of gênoise is unforgettably delicious. It is a 1-bowl cake and not at all difficult to make when directions are followed.

Note that an alternate method is given for mixing gênoise batter. For those who do not own an electric beater, the second method is much easier, cutting down the beating time by at least half. Cakes made by the alternate method have a slightly less fluffy texture, which is actually preferred by some people.

6 large eggs
1 cup sugar
1 cup sifted flour
½ cup sweet butter, melted and clarified (p. 35)
1 teaspoon vanilla

Set oven at 350 degrees. Grease and lightly flour 1 of the following:

two 9-inch layer-cake tins
three 7-inch layer-cake tins
one 11 x 16 jelly-roll pan
two shallow 10-inch layer-cake tins

In a large bowl combine eggs and sugar. Stir for a minute, or until they are just combined. Set bowl over a saucepan containing 1 or 2 inches of hot water. Water in pan should not touch bowl; nor should it ever be allowed to boil. Place saucepan containing bowl over low heat for 5 to 10 minutes, or until eggs are lukewarm. Heating the eggs helps them whip to greater volume.

It is not necessary to beat them continuously as they are warming. *They should, however, be lightly stirred 3 or 4 times to prevent them from cooking at bottom of bowl.*

When eggs feel lukewarm to your finger and look like a bright yellow syrup, remove bowl from heat. Begin to beat, preferably with an electric mixer. Beat at high speed for 10 to 15 minutes, scraping sides of bowl with a rubber spatula when necessary, until syrup becomes light, fluffy, and cool. It will almost triple in bulk and look much like whipped cream. It is the air beaten into the eggs that gives gênoise its lightness.

Beating by hand with a good rotary beater will take about 25 minutes.

Sprinkle flour, a little at a time, on top of the whipped eggs. Fold in gently, adding slightly cooled, clarified butter and vanilla. Folding can be done with electric mixer turned to lowest speed, or by hand. Be especially careful not to overmix. (See illustration p. 66.)

Pour batter into prepared pans. Bake in preheated oven 25 to 30 minutes, or until cakes pull away from sides of pans and are golden brown and springy when touched lightly on top.

Remove from pans immediately and cool on cake rack.

Folding flour, clarified butter and vanilla into eggs

ALTERNATE METHOD FOR MIXING GÊNOISE

Separate eggs. Add vanilla to egg yolks.

Beat egg whites until they hold soft peaks. Beat in sugar, a tablespoon at a time, beating well after each addition. Continue to beat until egg whites are very stiff, about 5 minutes in all.

Fold about ¼ of egg whites into yolks. Pour over remaining stiffly beaten whites. Sprinkle flour lightly on top. Fold eggs and flour gently but thoroughly together, adding cooled clarified butter at the same time. Fold only until flour and butter disappear into batter.

LEMON OR ORANGE GÊNOISE

gênoise recipe (*p.* 64)
1 *teaspoon grated orange or lemon rind*
2 *tablespoons orange or lemon juice*

Follow recipe for gênoise, adding 1 teaspoon grated orange or lemon rind and 2 tablespoons orange or lemon juice to clarified butter before folding it into cake batter.

GÊNOISE FOR PETITS FOURS

Gênoise for petits fours should be a little firmer than regular gênoise. Follow the basic recipe (p. 64), substituting 1½ cups flour for the regular flour measurement. Bake in an 11 x 16 jelly-roll pan.

NUTTED GÊNOISE

gênoise recipe (p. 64)
½ cup almonds, walnuts, filberts, or pecans

Follow the recipe for gênoise. Grate or grind nuts fine. Toasting the nuts slightly before grinding improves their flavor. When folding in flour, sprinkle in nuts.

NOUGAT GÊNOISE

gênoise recipe (p. 64)
⅔ cup nougat powder, p. 111 (measured after grinding)

Follow the recipe for gênoise. When folding in flour, sprinkle in ⅔ cup nougat powder.

CHOCOLATE GÊNOISE

Follow the recipe for gênoise (p. 64). Substitute ½ cup dark unsweetened Dutch cocoa for ½ cup of flour. Sift cocoa and flour together once before folding into batter.

GOLDEN VELVET CAKE

Here is an especially rich yellow cake with a most unusual texture. It is an expensive cake that uses 12 yolks to make only two 9-inch layers. But it is a very special treat. Layers of golden-velvet cake can substitute for layers of gênoise; or, if preferred, this batter can be baked in a deep, 9-inch tube pan. Serve plain or decorated.

12 *large egg yolks* (1 *cup*)
1 *cup sugar*
1 *teaspoon grated lemon rind*
1 *teaspoon vanilla*
3 *tablespoons water*
½ *cup sifted flour*
½ *cup sifted cornstarch*
½ *cup butter, melted and cooled* (*not clarified*)

Set oven at 350 degrees. Grease and flour the bottoms of two 9-inch layer-cake pans, or one 9-inch tube pan.

Combine egg yolks and sugar in a large bowl, stirring for a minute to mix them. Place the bowl over a saucepan of hot water. Heat as for gênoise (p. 64), until the yolks are slightly warmer than lukewarm, stirring occasionally.

When mixture is warm, beat with an electric mixer (hand beating would take about 25 minutes) until it is completely cool, light, and very thick and fluffy. Beat in grated lemon rind and vanilla, then water.

Sprinkle flour and cornstarch lightly on top. Begin to fold, preferably by hand, adding melted butter. Fold only until dry ingredients and butter have disappeared. Be careful not to overmix.

Pour into prepared pan(s). Bake in preheated oven about 30 minutes for layer cakes, 50 to 60 minutes for a tube-pan cake, or until top of cake is a deep golden brown and springy to a light touch. Cool cake in pan for 10 minutes before loosening sides and turning out on a cake rack to finish cooling.

ALMOND BUTTER CAKE

This is a very fine cake for cutting into petits fours, or just for eating as is. Much of its delicacy depends on the quality of the almond paste.

¾ *cup sifted flour*
¼ *cup butter, melted and clarified* (*p.* 35)

3 whole eggs
2 egg yolks
½ teaspoon vanilla
½ cup sugar
1 teaspoon grated lemon rind
¼ cup almond paste

Set oven at 350 degrees. Grease the bottom of an 11 x 16 jelly-roll pan or one 9-inch square or round layer-cake pan. Fit a sheet of wax paper into bottom. Grease wax paper.

In a bowl combine whole eggs, 1 egg yolk, vanilla, sugar and grated lemon rind. Follow directions in gênoise recipe (p. 64) for heating eggs and sugar over hot water.

While eggs are warming, cream almond paste with remaining yolk until it is soft, smooth, and fluffy.

When eggs feel warm and look like a bright-yellow syrup, begin to beat them, preferably with an electric mixer. Beat as for gênoise until eggs are almost triple in bulk and like whipped cream.

Pour softened almond paste over fluffy egg mixture. Sprinkle flour on top. Fold gently together, adding slightly cooled clarified butter. Folding can be done with electric mixer turned to lowest speed, or by hand. *Be careful not to overmix.*

Pour batter into prepared pan. Spread it evenly. Bake about 15 minutes or until cake is golden brown and springy to the touch.

Remove from pan and cool on cake rack.

OLD-FASHIONED SPONGECAKE

This spongecake makes a fine substitute for gênoise.

6 eggs
pinch of salt
1 cup granulated sugar
1 tablespoon lemon juice
1 teaspoon grated lemon rind
1 teaspoon vanilla
1 cup sifted flour

Set oven at 350 degrees. Grease and dust with flour the bottom of a high, 9-inch tube pan or two 9-inch layer-cake tins. Do not grease sides of pan. Cake will cling to sides as it rises.

Separate eggs. Beat egg whites with salt until they form soft peaks. Beat in sugar gradually, a tablespoon at a time. Continue beating until egg whites are very stiff, about 5 minutes in all.

Stir egg yolks with a fork to break them up. Add lemon rind, juice, and vanilla. Fold ¼ of the stiffly beaten egg whites thoroughly into egg yolks. Pour egg-yolk mixture over remaining stiffly beaten whites. Sprinkle flour on top. Fold all gently together, using hand or mixer turned to lowest speed. Fold only until no separate pieces of egg white show, with batter still very fluffy and light. *Do not overmix.*

Pour batter into prepared pan, spreading it with a spatula. Hit pan sharply on table twice to remove air pockets.

Bake cake 35 to 40 minutes in preheated oven.

Cake is done when top is golden brown and springy to the touch. Remove cake from oven and cool in pan. It is not necessary to turn it upside down while cooling. When completely cool, loosen sides of cake with a knife and remove it from pan.

MAKING A CAKE BY THE SEPARATED-EGG METHOD

1

2

1. *When egg whites have been combined with sugar and beaten very stiff, add ¼ of mixture to egg yolks stirred with fork to break up, but* not beaten. *Fold together.*

2. *Pour folded mixture over remaining egg whites.*

3. *Sprinkle flour or cornstarch lightly on top. Fold all* gently *together.*

3

WHOLE EGG SPONGECAKE

gênoise recipe, omitting butter (p. 64)
⅓ cup additional flour
1 teaspoon grated lemon rind
1 tablespoon lemon juice

Set oven at 350 degrees. Grease and lightly flour bottom, not sides, of a 9-inch tube pan.

Follow the recipe for gênoise, omitting butter. Use 1 ⅓ cups flour and add lemon rind and juice with vanilla.

Bake in prepared pan for 35 to 40 minutes or until top of cake is golden brown and springy to the touch. Cool cake in pan.

BASIC SPONGE SHEET

For making jelly roll, petits fours and a great variety of other cakes.

4 eggs
pinch of salt
¼ cup sugar
½ teaspoon vanilla
¼ cup sifted cornstarch
¼ cup sifted flour

Set oven at 400 degrees. Grease an 11 x 16 jelly-roll pan and line with wax paper. Grease and lightly flour paper.

Separate eggs. Beat egg whites with salt until they hold soft peaks. Gradually beat in sugar, sprinkling it in a tablespoon at a time. Continue beating until whites are very firm, about 5 minutes in all.

Stir yolks with a fork to break them up. Add vanilla. Fold ¼ of the stiffly beaten egg whites thoroughly into egg yolks. Pour egg-yolk mixture on top of remaining stiffly beaten whites. Sprinkle cornstarch and flour over mixture. Fold all very gently together, by hand or with mixer turned to lowest speed. Fold until no pieces of egg white show. *Be careful not to overmix.*

Pour into prepared pan. Spread batter evenly. Bake 10 to 12 minutes or until cake is very lightly browned. Be careful not to overbake. Loosen sides and remove cake from pan at once. Cool on rack before peeling off paper. Cake should be flexible from end to end.

CHOCOLATE BASIC SPONGE SHEET

4 eggs
pinch of salt
¼ cup sugar
½ teaspoon vanilla
⅛ cup sifted flour
⅛ cup sifted cornstarch
¼ cup sifted dark, unsweetened cocoa

Follow the recipe for making basic sponge sheet (p. 72), using above ingredients. Sift cocoa with flour and cornstarch before folding into batter.

SPICED BASIC SPONGE SHEET

basic sponge sheet recipe (p. 72)
1 teaspoon cinnamon
1 teaspoon nutmeg
½ teaspoon ground cloves

Follow the recipe for making basic sponge sheet, adding spices with other dry ingredients.

SWISS MERINGUE

For making such delightful pastries as vacherin, meringue layers and shells.

5 egg whites, at room temperature
¼ teaspoon cream of tartar
¼ teaspoon salt
1 teaspoon vanilla
1 ¼ cups sugar

Grease and flour 2 baking sheets. Combine egg whites, cream of tartar, salt and vanilla in a large bowl. Beat (at medium speed if a mixer is used) until egg whites hold soft peaks. Gradually add ¾ cup sugar, a tablespoon at a time, beating continuously. Continue beating until meringue is very stiff and dull. It has been beaten enough when a bit, rubbed between thumb and finger, is no longer grainy. The meringue should be stiff enough to hold its shape when formed with a pastry tube. Gently fold in remaining sugar.

Meringues should actually be dried rather than baked. Herein lies the secret of making meringues which are tender, delicate, and light-colored, rather than overly crisp, tough, and too dark to be either attractive or delicious. The best meringues are baked by the following method:

Set oven temperature at 200 degrees before beginning to beat the egg whites. After shaping the meringue mixture on baking sheets, place in the preheated oven for 15 minutes. Then turn off the oven heat. Allow the meringues to remain in the oven with the heat turned off for at least 4 to 5 hours—the longer the better. If your oven has a pilot light, the meringues will be ready a little sooner. The meringues should be totally dry before removing them from the oven. If you can, leave them in the oven overnight.

For many of us, however, time is a factor. If you can't take the time to bake meringues this slow, slow way, accept second best and simply bake them slowly, setting the oven temperature for 200 degrees or less if possible. At 200 degrees, meringue layers will need to bake for about 40 minutes; small meringues may take a little less time.

Whatever method you use, it is important to prevent the meringues from coloring, since even a light tan color changes their texture and taste as well as their appearance.

When thoroughly dry, meringues can be kept covered in a dry airy place (*not* in a tightly covered box) for several weeks.

ALTERNATE MIXING METHOD BY ELECTRIC BEATER FOR SWISS MERINGUE, SWISS BROYAGE, CHOCOLATE BROYAGE

Combine egg whites, cream of tartar, salt, ½ cup sugar and vanilla in large bowl. Beat at high speed until egg whites hold peaks. Add ½ cup sugar, all at once. Beat at high speed until mixture is very stiff and there are no grains of undissolved sugar. Fold in remaining sugar.

To shape Swiss meringue into layers and rounds follow directions given below.

SWISS BROYAGE

Swiss broyage has the texture of a meringue, although it is not as sweet, and it has the added flavor of ground nuts. Completely delicious by itself, Swiss broyage is most often used in combination with other cakes and icings to make party desserts.

It is crisp when it comes from the oven, but broyage will mellow to semisoftness if it is spread with butter cream and stored in the refrigerator for a day or two. For this reason it is an especially good dessert to prepare ahead of time.

3 egg whites
1/8 teaspoon cream of tartar
pinch of salt
1 teaspoon vanilla
3/4 cup sugar
1/4 cup blanched almonds, finely grated
1/3 cup sifted cornstarch

Combine egg whites, cream of tartar, salt, and vanilla in a large bowl. Beat (using medium speed if a mixer is used) until egg whites hold soft peaks. Add 1/2 cup sugar, a tablespoon at a time, beating constantly. Continue beating until meringue is very stiff and dull.

Combine ground almonds, cornstarch, and remaining sugar. Fold into meringue.

This will make 2 thin 9-inch layers or 24 thin 2-inch cookies.

TO SHAPE SWISS MERINGUE AND BROYAGE

Grease and flour a large baking sheet. Press the rim of a 9-inch layer-cake pan or a 2-inch cooky cutter lightly into the flour on baking sheet to make guides. If Baking Pan Liner Paper is used, the guiding circles will have to be traced with a pencil. Spread mixture within circles.

Or: Fill a pastry bag fitted with a No. 3 or 5 tube with prepared

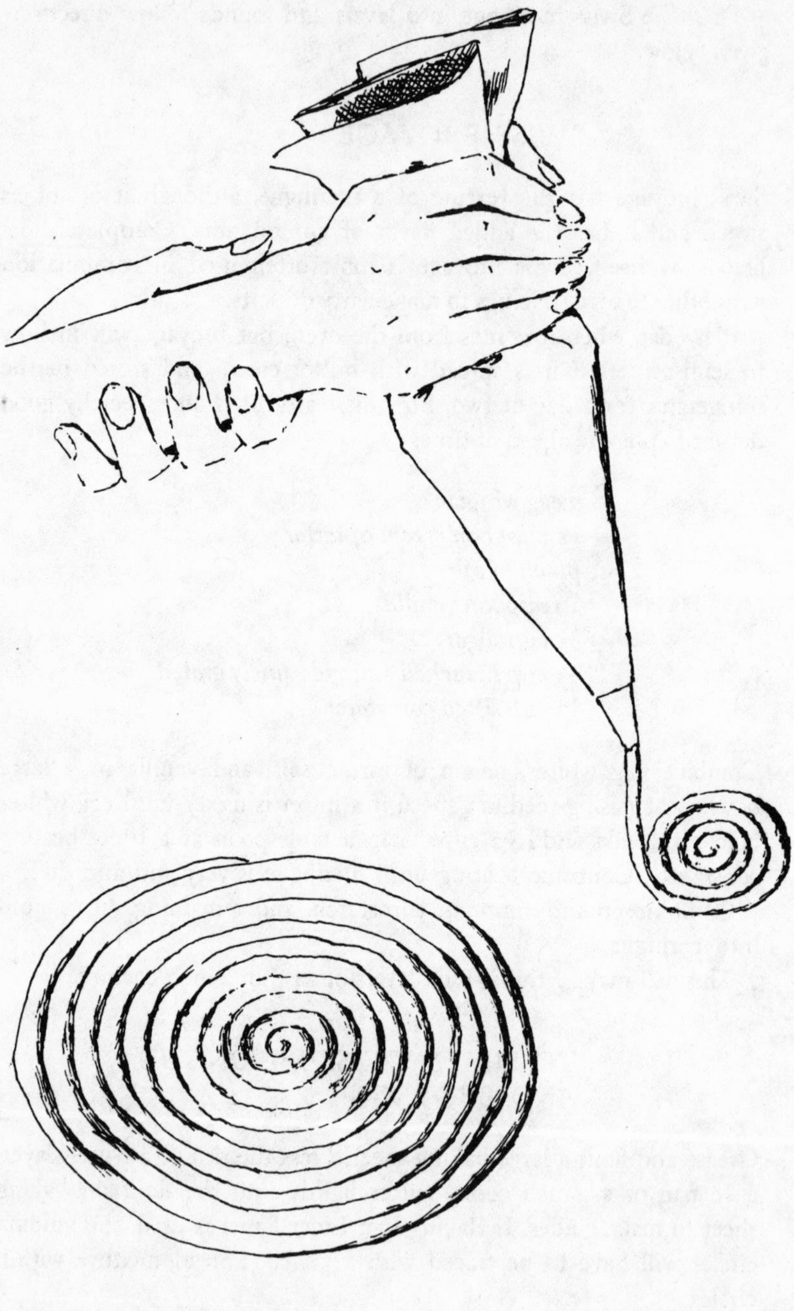

SHAPING LAYERS OF SWISS BROYAGE OR MERINGUE

mixture. Starting in center of each circle, press out batter in a long, continuous, pencil-thick strip, curling it round and round until traced circle is completely filled in. For best control, press out batter slowly, holding bag at least 1 inch away from sheet.

Bake in a 325 degree oven, 25 minutes for small rounds, 35 to 40 minues for 9-inch layers.

CHOCOLATE BROYAGE

Chocolate broyage is used like Swiss broyage.

Follow recipe for Swiss broyage (p. 75), using only 1 tablespoon cornstarch and adding 2 tablespoons sifted unsweetened, dark cocoa. Combine cocoa with sugar, ground nuts and cornstarch before folding into meringue.

CHOCOLATE PASTRY

Neither a pastry in the real sense nor a cake, chocolate pastry is actually a soufflé mixture baked in a large flat pan and then cooled. It provides a delicate contrast in texture as well as flavor when used in combination with cakes and butter creams.

6 eggs
pinch of salt
¾ cup sugar
6 ounces semisweet chocolate, melted
2 tablespoons strong coffee
1 teaspoon vanilla
½ cup dark, unsweetened cocoa

Set oven at 375 degrees. Grease 11 x 16 jelly-roll pan. Line it with wax paper. Grease wax paper and dust with flour.

Separate eggs. Beat egg whites with salt until they hold soft peaks. Add sugar, a tablespoon at a time, beating after each addition. Continue beating until mixture is very firm, about 5 minutes in all.

Stir egg yolks with a fork to break them up. Stir in melted chocolate, coffee, and vanilla. Fold ¼ of the stiffly beaten egg whites into chocolate mixture. Pour back over remaining egg whites. Fold all gently together.

Pour into prepared pan. Spread evenly. Bake in preheated oven for 10 minutes. Reduce heat to 350 degrees and continue to bake about 5 minutes longer, or until top of pastry is firm. Cool in pan.

Sift cocoa evenly over a sheet of wax paper. Turn out pastry on cocoa-covered paper. Carefully peel off paper lining. Use to make such pastries as chocolate roll and monettes.

CHOCOLATE PASTRY WITH EGG WHITES

Here is an alternative recipe for making chocolate pastry. It is as delicious as the first. It is a good thing to make when egg whites have accumulated in the refrigerator.

5 *to 6 egg whites* (⅔ *cup*)
pinch of salt
½ *cup sugar*
6 *ounces semisweet chocolate, melted*
2 *tablespoons strong coffee*
1 *teaspoon vanilla*
½ *cup dark, unsweetened cocoa*

Set oven at 375 degrees. Grease an 11 x 16 jelly-roll pan. Line it with wax paper. Grease wax paper and dust with flour.

Add salt to egg whites. Beat them with a rotary beater or with electric mixer until they hold soft peaks. Add sugar, a tablespoon at a time, beating after each addition. Continue beating until mixture is very firm, about 5 minutes in all.

Fold about ¼ of stiffly beaten egg whites thoroughly into melted chocolate, adding coffee and vanilla at the same time. Pour back over remaining egg whites. Fold all gently together.

Pour into prepared pan. Spread evenly. Bake in preheated oven for 10 minutes; reduce heat to 350 degrees and continue to bake about 5 minutes longer, or until top of pastry is firm. Cool cake in pan.

Sift cocoa evenly over a sheet of wax paper. Turn out pastry on cocoa-covered paper. Carefully peel off paper lining.

CREAM PUFF PASTRY
(*Pâte à Chou*)

For making cream puffs, éclairs, and a variety of pastries, sweet and savory.

½ cup butter
1 cup water
1 cup sifted flour
¼ teaspoon salt
4 eggs

Combine butter and water in a saucepan. Cook over medium heat until butter is melted and mixture is boiling. Turn heat to very low. Add flour mixed with salt, all at once. Stir vigorously until a ball forms in center of the pan. This takes from 3 to 5 minutes.

Remove from heat. Add 3 eggs, 1 at a time, beating hard after each addition. This beating can be done in an electric mixer.

The final egg should be lightly beaten with a fork and added gradually. The paste must be just stiff enough to stand in a peak when a spoon is withdrawn. Therefore it is sometimes necessary to add slightly less—or even more—egg than the 4 specified in the recipe. This depends on the dryness of the flour and the size of eggs.

Shape pâte à chou according to instructions below and bake immediately, or refrigerate in a covered bowl up to 2 days.

Pâte à chou is baked in a 375 degree oven. Bake until pastries are golden brown and no beads of moisture show. Then stick the point of a small knife into the sides of pastries. Turn heat off. Leave small pastries in oven 10 minutes longer, large cakes 15 to 20 minutes more. This will allow steam inside to evaporate and help prevent sogginess.

Makes approximately 90 small puffs or 25 medium-size puffs.

TO MAKE CREAM PUFFS

Fit pastry bag with a large, round No. 9 tube. On a lightly greased baking sheet, press out high mounds of pâte à chou about 1 ¼ inches in diameter. These will swell and puff in oven.

Bake 40 to 50 minutes, or until no moisture is evident on the golden-brown puffs. Stick the point of a small knife into the sides of each puff 2 or 3 times. Turn off oven heat. Leave puffs in oven for 15 minutes more before removing.

TO MAKE TINY PUFFS

Use a plain, round No. 7 tube. Press out small rounds of pâte à chou, equal to a scant teaspoon. Keep the little rounds as high as possible. Bake 25 to 30 minutes. Stick point of a small knife into sides of each little puff once or twice. Turn off oven heat. Leave puffs in oven for 10 minutes more before removing.

Puffs can also be shaped with 2 spoons as is done with drop cookies. Take care to keep mounds high.

SAVARIN DOUGH

For making such pastries as baba au rhum and manon.

½ ounce fresh yeast or 1 package dry yeast
3 tablespoons sugar
½ teaspoon salt
½ cup lukewarm milk
4 eggs, slightly beaten
2 cups flour, approximately
⅔ cup soft butter

Cream fresh yeast with sugar and salt. (See directions for using dry yeast on p. 252.) Stir in milk, then beaten eggs. Add enough flour to make a soft batter. Beat vigorously for 8 minutes with a wooden spoon.

Cover bowl. Let batter rise about 40 minutes, or until it has doubled in bulk. Stir it down. Beat in softened butter.

Set oven at 400 degrees. Grease a 9-inch savarin ring or approximately 2 dozen small individual baba tins. Fill tins halfway. Let dough almost double in bulk. Place in preheated oven. Bake for 10 minutes. Reduce heat to 350 degrees and continue baking until cake or cakes are golden brown—10 to 12 minutes for small babas, up to 35 minutes for a large cake.

Chapter 3

Frostings, Fillings, and Decorations

CURRANT
JELLY
APRICOT
JAM

3 *Frostings, Fillings, and Decorations*

Look in other books for gooey marshmallow and confectioners'-sugar toppings. We will concentrate on satin-smooth butter creams, extra-shiny icings, and cake decorations of chocolate, nougat, and fruit, which are delicious as well as beautiful.

At the end of this chapter are the coffeecake fillings and toppings, which will turn the simplest yeast dough into party fare.

HOW TO DECORATE A CAKE

The first and most important step in frosting and decorating a cake is to have one that is even and symmetrical in shape. This does not mean that cakes which seem light but lopsided must be discarded.

Many delicious cakes are so delicate that in cooling or being removed from pans they are apt to shrink slightly or fall a bit in one spot. If this should happen, a bit of surgery is in order.

First, the cake should be completely cool. Using a long, thin, serrated knife, cut off crisp edges extending from sides. Examine layers and use most symmetrical for top. If necessary, cut some cake away so the top is certain to be level. In sandwiching a layer cake, turn alternate layers upside down so that bottoms are joined to bottoms and tops to tops. This generally helps to keep surgery to a minimum.

After cake has been trimmed, brush away all loose crumbs. If possible, decorate cake on a Lazy Susan type of turntable. (Cakes which are to be masked completely with a poured icing must be placed on a rack so that excess can drip underneath.) Some people prefer to frost a cake right on a serving plate in order to avoid having to transfer it

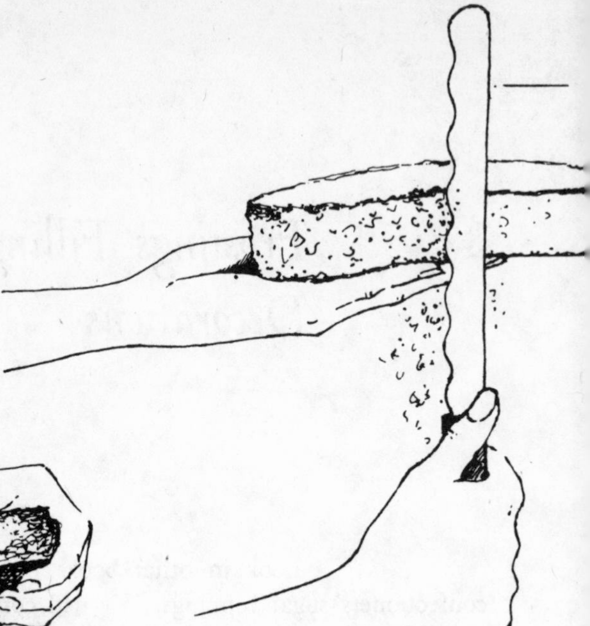

1

2

1. *Before beginning decoration, trim cake to be sure it is symmetrical.*

2. *After spreading bottom layer with filling, set top layer in place. Trim again if necessary. Brush away crumbs.*

3. *Brush top with hot apricot glaze. When cooled (about 5 minutes) pour fondant or other icing glaze on top, smoothing with a spatula when necessary. Let icing dry for a few minutes, then scrape off any excess which may have dripped on sides.*

4. *Spread sides with butter cream or apricot glaze. Coat sides with sliced toasted blanched almonds or filberts, or crushed cooky crumbs..*

5. *Make butter cream border around top of cake.*

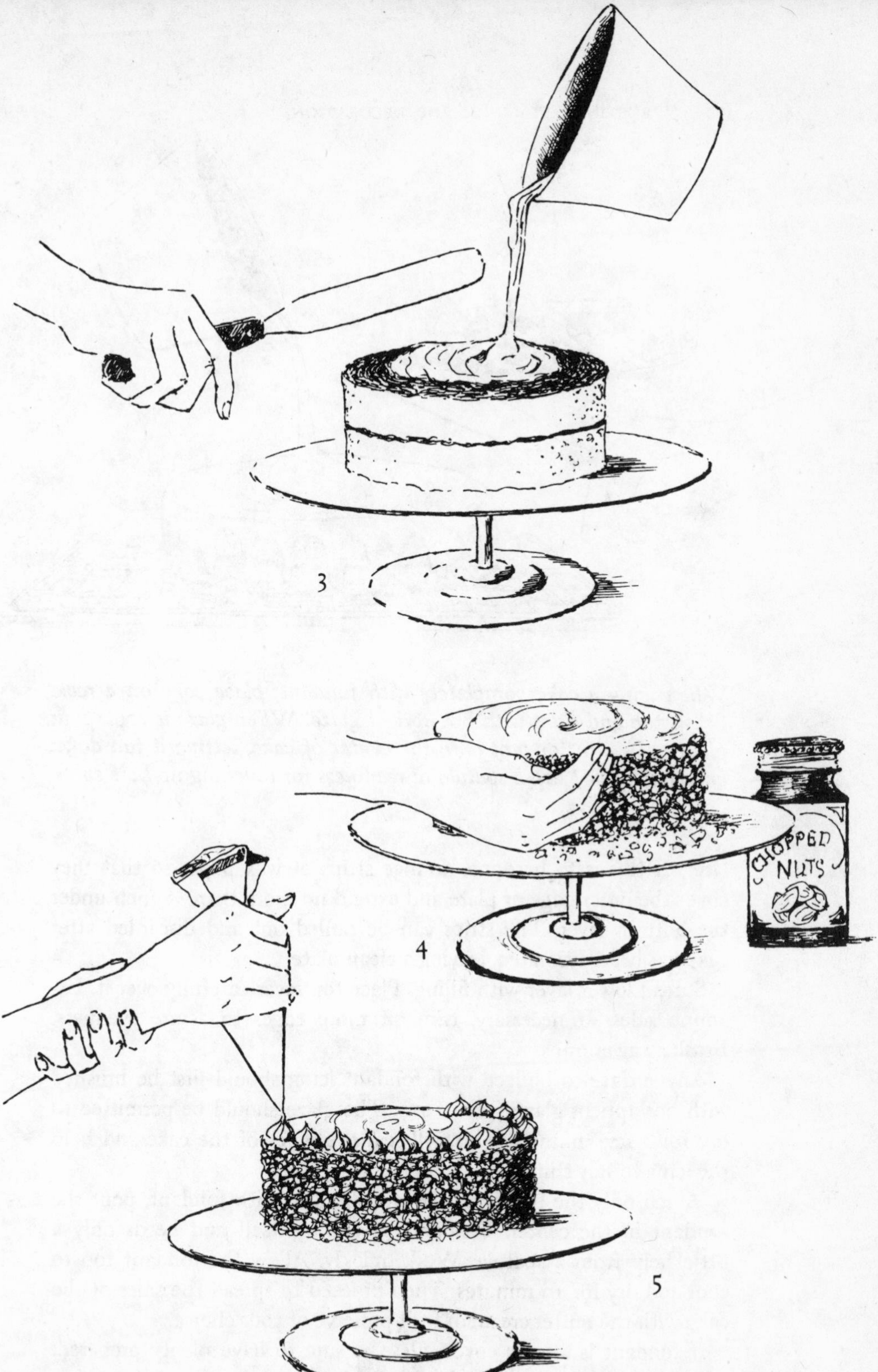
3
4
CHOPPED NUTS
5

When icing a cake completely with fondant, place cake on a rack. Brush top and sides with hot apricot glaze. When glaze is cool, pour plenty of warm fondant onto the center of cake, letting it run down and coat sides. Keep a spatula in readiness for touching up bare spots.

later. If this is to be done, arrange strips of wax paper so that they cover the outer edge of plate and extend no more than ½ inch under the bottom layer. The strips can be pulled out and discarded after cake has been decorated, leaving a clean plate.

Spread lower layer with filling. Place top layer carefully over it. Examine sides. If necessary, trim off more edges to assure evenness. Brush away crumbs.

Any surface to be iced with fondant icing should first be brushed with hot apricot glaze (see p. 92). The glaze should be permitted to dry for a few minutes. This will seal the pores of the cake and help the icing to stay shiny.

When only the top of a cake is to be iced with fondant, pour the fondant in the center. Fondant spreads by itself and needs only a little help from a spatula. Work quickly. Allow the fondant top to cool and dry for 10 minutes. Then proceed to spread the sides of the cake with the butter cream or fruit preserve of your choice.

If fondant is also to cover sides, be sure to have plenty prepared. Pour it onto center of top of cake, letting it run down and coat sides.

Use a spatula to touch up bare spots. Let fondant icing dry about 10 minutes before attempting to transfer cake.

Sliced toasted almonds or filberts, crushed pecans, or crisp cooky or cake crumbs may be pressed into butter-cream sides, if desired. One of these should always be used if sides are spread with apricot jam, to give it a finished look. To coat sides, fill palm of hand with nuts or crumbs. Press lightly into cake, moving hand up and down and around the cake until sides are completely covered.

Make a butter-cream border around top of cake. Fit a pastry bag or cornucopia with open-star tube No. 4. Fill ⅔ full with butter cream. Press out a circle of even rosettes, one touching the other, all around top of cake.

ICINGS AND GLAZES

FONDANT

Real fondant is not easy to make or to use. Yet it is the perfect icing for petits fours and cakes. When properly used, it stays shiny for many days. For home baking there are a number of icing alternatives; but, just in case you want to try, here is the recipe for real fondant:

6 *cups granulated sugar*
3 *tablespoons white corn syrup*
2 *cups cold water*

Combine sugar, corn syrup, and water in a large, heavy saucepan. Heat slowly, stirring constantly, until sugar is completely dissolved. Dissolving the sugar properly is probably the most important step in making fondant. If, in this initial stage, a grain or two of sugar is left undissolved, it will later cause crystallization of the entire batch of syrup.

When the syrup looks clear, wash down sides of pan with a brush dipped in cold water. Put a lid on the pan for 5 minutes. This will create steam, which will further wash away clinging sugar crystals. Remove the lid. Without stirring, boil syrup over high heat until it reaches 238 degrees on a candy thermometer. If you lack a thermometer, drop a little syrup into cold water. If you can roll the cooled bit into a soft ball between thumb and forefinger, the syrup is cooked enough.

Remove from heat and allow it to stop bubbling. Pour out on a large platter or tray to a depth of not more than 1 inch.

When temperature has dropped to lukewarm, begin to stir briskly with a wooden spoon. Work the mixture, missing none of it, until it becomes white and begins to stiffen. Scrape it together and cover with a slightly dampened towel.

Taking a little at a time, knead well until the entire batch has been made soft and pliable and has been worked into a smooth white ball.

Wrap fondant in a towel that has been wrung out in cold water. After 1 hour, remove the towel. Knead fondant once more to make it creamy.

Place in an airtight container. Tightly covered, it can be kept in an average room for several weeks. It should not be frozen.

USING FONDANT

For best results, first brush cake to be iced with thick, hot apricot glaze (see p. 92). Allow glaze to dry. For the top of a 9-inch cake, put 1 cup of fondant into a heavy saucepan. Add a tablespoon or two of liquid. Water, vanilla, any liqueur, or simple syrup (see p. 44), can be used. Warm over very low heat, working and stirring fondant constantly until it is barely lukewarm and creamy. Be careful not to overheat as this will make it lose its shine. Use only enough liquid to thin the fondant to pouring consistency. It should be thick enough to mask the cake, yet soft enough to pour and spread by itself. To further enhance the shine, stir in briskly a teaspoon of egg white for each cup of fondant, just before pouring.

Fondant can be colored or flavored in any way desired.

Chocolate fondant is made by adding 1 ounce melted unsweetened chocolate to 1 cup fondant as it is being warmed.

Punch, coffee, orange juice and rind, lemon juice and rind, cognac or any liqueur can be used to flavor and thin fondant to the right consistency.

MOCK FONDANT

Much easier to make than real fondant, and more quickly prepared, this recipe provides an excellent substitute if you have on hand a jar of the basic simple syrup, which keeps almost indefinitely. For best results, pour mock fondant over cake which has first been lightly brushed with hot apricot glaze.

½ cup cooled basic simple syrup (p. 44)
1 ½ cups sifted confectioners' sugar (approximately)
1 teaspoon egg white
1 teaspoon melted butter

Place syrup in a saucepan. Add enough sifted confectioners' sugar to make a fairly stiff paste. It should be a bit too thick to pour or spread by itself. Place saucepan over low heat and warm, stirring constantly till fondant is lukewarm. Be careful not to overheat, or the icing will not be shiny.

Beat in a teaspoon each of egg white and melted butter. If icing is still too thick, add additional syrup or flavoring liquid to thin it. If it becomes too thin, add more confectioners' sugar. This is enough mock fondant for the top of a 9-inch layer cake.

Flavor with any one of the following, or any flavor of your choice:

1 ounce melted unsweetened chocolate
1 tablespoon extra-strong coffee
2 tablespoons rum
2 tablespoons any liqueur
1 teaspoon vanilla

ROYAL ICING

(For decorating holiday cookies.)

1 ½ cups sifted confectioners' sugar
1 egg white
pinch of salt
1 teaspoon lemon juice
food coloring

Combine first 4 ingredients in a bowl. Beat, preferably in a mixer, until light and fluffy and mixture stands in peaks when beater is withdrawn. If necessary, add a little more sugar or egg white to obtain the right consistency. The more this is beaten, the better it is. Keep covered with a damp cloth when not used. In this manner, icing may be kept (at room temperature) for several days.

To use, spoon some of icing into another bowl. Add a few drops of food coloring. Mix and add more color if necessary.

Use paper cornucopias (see pp. 30-31 for how to make and use) for decorating cookies. Fill cornucopia no more than ⅔ full. After folding the top down, cutting off tip, etc., push the icing out by pressing against the folded top with the right-hand thumb. Guide the right hand by holding it at the wrist with the left hand. Hold cornucopia about 2 inches away from cookies. Use icing to outline cookies, to make a center design, or to make eyes on animal cookies. Icing will dry in a few minutes and become hard. Cookies may then be transferred to storage boxes.

APRICOT GLAZE

1 *cup sieved apricot jam*
2 *to* 4 *tablespoons cognac, kirsch, applejack, or any liqueur (optional)*

Heat apricot jam in a saucepan until it is boiling. Stir in preferred flavoring. Use glaze while it is hot.

CURRANT GLAZE

1 *cup currant jelly*
2 *to* 4 *tablespoons cognac, kirsch, applejack, or any liqueur (optional)*

Follow directions for making apricot glaze.

CREAMY CHOCOLATE GLAZE

This is also a delicious cake filling.

3 *ounces unsweetened chocolate*
¾ *cup heavy cream*
1 *cup sugar*
¼ *cup water*
1 *tablespoon corn syrup*
1 *egg slightly beaten*
1 *tablespoon vanilla*

Combine chocolate, cream, sugar, water, and corn syrup. Stir over low heat until chocolate is melted and sugar is dissolved. Raise heat a little and cook without stirring for about 5 minutes, or until mixture is thick enough so that a bit, dropped into a glass of cold water, forms a soft ball.

Stir 2 or 3 tablespoons hot chocolate into beaten egg. Pour egg mixture back into remaining chocolate, stirring briskly. Replace over low heat and cook a few more minutes or until chocolate is a little thicker. Stir constantly.

Remove from heat. Add vanilla. Cool slightly before pouring over cake. This frosting stays shiny and cuts easily even after many days. It will make enough chocolate glaze for the top and sides of one 9-inch cake.

To use as a cake filling, cool completely.

BITTER CHOCOLATE GLAZE

This rich chocolate glaze can be kept covered in the refrigerator for several weeks. It should be reheated to boiling before it is used.

1 cup dark, unsweetened cocoa, sifted
pinch of salt
⅔ cup heavy cream
⅓ cup sweet butter
1 ⅓ cups granulated sugar
1 teaspoon vanilla

Combine all ingredients except vanilla in a heavy saucepan. Cook over low heat, stirring constantly, until smooth and thick, about 5 minutes. Let mixture stop bubbling. Stir in vanilla. This provides enough chocolate glaze for top and sides of one 9-inch layer cake.

Use while hot. (See directions for pouring fondant, pp. 88, 90.)

If cake to be glazed has a butter-cream filling, the entire cake should be well chilled, even frozen, for an hour or so, before the hot glaze is poured over it.

CREAMS, BUTTER CREAMS, AND FILLINGS

WHIPPED CREAM

Cream for whipping should be at least 1 day old. It can be kept in the refrigerator in a sealed container for more than a week. Before being whipped, it should be very cold. In hot weather the bowl and beater should also be chilled.

1 cup heavy cream
1 to 2 tablespoons fine granulated sugar (optional)
1 teaspoon vanilla

Using a well chilled bowl, or setting the bowl over ice, beat cream with an electric mixer or rotary egg beater. As cream begins to thicken, beat in sugar and vanilla. Continue beating until stiff. If not to be served at once, place in refrigerator, where it may be kept 2 to 3 hours.

The yield from a cup of cream can be increased (with very slight difference in texture) by adding 1 egg white to each cup of whipped and flavored cream. Beat the egg white until it holds soft peaks. Sprinkle in 1 ½ tablespoons granulated sugar. Continue beating till very stiff. Fold into whipped cream.

To prepare whipped cream a day or two ahead of time: Soften ½ teaspoon of granulated gelatin (for each cup of cream to be whipped) in a small metal cup containing a tablespoon of cold water. Set cup in a pan of boiling water or over low heat, until the gelatin dissolves and looks clear. Stirring is unnecessary. Beat dissolved gelatin into the cream just as cream begins to thicken.

Gelatin will also give whipped cream extra firmness so it can be used for decorating with a pastry bag.

FLAVORING WHIPPED CREAM

To each cup of whipped cream, 1 of the following flavorings can be added:

2 tablespoons sifted dark, unsweetened cocoa
2 to 4 tablespoons rum, cognac, or any liqueur
½ cup nougat powder
1 teaspoon instant coffee powder

Fold flavorings into cream *after* it has been whipped.

SOUR CREAM

Homemade sour cream is a true delicacy rarely encountered in the United States. What a shame, considering how easy it is to make!

Unlike commercial sour cream, the homemade kind—provided you've made it with heavy cream—can be whipped. When whipping it, be careful not to overwhip, because suddenly, in a flash, it can turn to butter.

Homemade sour cream, whipped or plain, makes a delicious topping for fruit tarts and for many chocolate desserts. It can be kept in the refrigerator a whole month, and it will get thicker and thicker and better and better.

2 cups heavy cream
5 teaspoons buttermilk

Combine cream and buttermilk in a screwtop jar. Shake the jar for a minute.

Let stand at room temperature for 24 hours. If room is especially cool (on a cold winter day) let stand an extra 12 to 24 hours. Cream will thicken.

Refrigerate at least 24 hours, preferably longer, before using.

PASTRY CREAM

2 tablespoons flour
1 cup light cream or milk
⅛ teaspoon salt
⅜ cup sugar
4 egg yolks
1 teaspoon vanilla

Combine flour with ¼ cup cream. Stir until smooth. Gradually add the remaining ¾ cup cream. Place in a heavy saucepan. Stir in salt and sugar. Cook over medium heat, stirring until mixture becomes as thick as a medium white sauce.

Stir a little of the hot sauce into egg yolks. Then pour egg yolks into saucepan, stirring briskly. Return pan to low heat for a few minutes to thicken a little more, continuing to stir. Be careful not to let the sauce boil. Remove from heat. Add vanilla. Cool as quickly as possible.

In order to prevent a skin from forming on top of the thick pastry cream while it is cooling, melted butter may be brushed over it. Stir pastry cream before using.

CHOCOLATE PASTRY CREAM

Add 2 ounces melted, unsweetened chocolate or 6 tablespoons dark, unsweetened cocoa to pastry cream (p. 95) after it is cooked.

COFFEE PASTRY CREAM

Add 1 tablespoon extra-strong coffee to pastry cream (p. 95) after it is cooked.

HALF-AND-HALF CREAM FILLING

1 envelope gelatin
¼ cup cold water
pastry cream, cooled (p. 95)
1 cup heavy cream, whipped, unsweetened, flavored with cognac

Soften gelatin in cold water in a small metal cup. Place cup into boiling water until mixture is clear. Stir dissolved gelatin into pastry cream.

Fold pastry cream and whipped cream gently together. Chill before using. Can be used to fill cream puffs, gâteaux, and millefeuilles.

PUNCH FILLING

1 ¾ cups sugar
1 orange, juice and grated rind
2 lemons, juice and grated rind
¼ cup water
¼ cup rum
a few drops red food coloring
2 teaspoons grated semisweet chocolate
2 to 3 cups cubed spongecake

Combine sugar, orange juice and rind, lemon juice and rind, and water in a saucepan. Place over low heat, stirring until sugar dissolves. Raise heat and boil, without stirring, about 5 minutes, or until syrup spins a thread (230 degrees). Remove from heat and let stand until cool. Flavor half of cooled punch with rum and add coloring; flavor remaining half with grated chocolate.

Apportion cake cubes in 3 containers. To first container add rum punch, being careful to use only enough to moisten cubes; to second container add chocolate punch, following same precaution. Leave remaining cubes unflavored.

To use, toss all cake cubes *lightly* together, without mashing.

BUTTER CREAMS

Traditionally, butter cream is an egg-syrup-butter mixture requiring cooking and much beating. It is used for both fillings and frostings. The classic recipe is given on p. 99. Also included are a brand-new recipe for making an uncooked, rich, smooth butter cream in the electric blender and an easy, delicious recipe that can be beaten by hand.

QUICK BLENDER BUTTER CREAM

Especially quick and simple to make, and as smooth and delicious as any of the cooked butter creams.

3 egg yolks
3 tablespoons granulated sugar
1 teaspoon vanilla
⅔ to 1 cup butter

Half of butter should be soft; the rest of it cold and firm, but not hard. Place eggs, sugar, and vanilla in blender. Turn on blender. Keep blender going 3 minutes, adding soft butter gradually until it is absorbed into yolks. Then, add enough firm butter, in small pieces, to make cream fairly thick. Add flavoring. (Makes approximately 1 ¼ cups butter cream.)

To flavor quick blender butter cream, stir in 1 of the following:

1 ounce melted unsweetened chocolate (cooled), or
2 tablespoons sifted dark, unsweetened cocoa
1 tablespoon extra-strong coffee
1 tablespoon liqueur (rum, cognac, Grand Marnier, etc.)
2 tablespoons nougat powder (p. 111)
⅓ cup chestnut purée (p. 36)

1 teaspoon grated lemon rind and 1 teaspoon lemon juice
1 tablespoon grated orange rind and 1 tablespoon frozen concentrated orange juice (undiluted)

Note: If butter cream should become thin after flavoring is added, place in refrigerator until it chills and thickens again

SIMPLEST BUTTER CREAM

1 cup very soft sweet butter
⅔ cup cool basic simple syrup (p. 44)
flavoring

Cream very soft butter till fluffy. Gradually beat in syrup, a little at a time.

Flavor with any of the following:

2 ounces melted, cooled unsweetened chocolate
1 to 2 tablespoons extra-strong coffee
3 tablespoons liqueur

(Makes approximately 1 ¾ cups butter cream.)

SPEEDY CHOCOLATE OR MOCHA BUTTER CREAM

½ cup soft butter
6 ounces semisweet chocolate, melted and cooled
1 egg yolk
½ teaspoon vanilla
2 teaspoons cognac
1 teaspoon instant coffee powder (optional)

Cream butter briefly until it is fluffy. Beat in cooled melted chocolate, egg yolk, vanilla and cognac. If mocha flavor is desired, add coffee powder. This can be used immediately or refrigerated until needed. It will harden in refrigerator and should be brought to room temperature before being used.

CLASSIC EGG YOLK BUTTER CREAM

2⁄3 cup sugar
1⁄8 teaspoon cream of tartar
1⁄3 cup water
5 egg yolks
1 cup soft butter

Combine sugar, cream of tartar, and water in a saucepan. Stir over low heat until sugar is completely dissolved. Raise heat and boil syrup without stirring until candy thermometer reads 238 degrees, or a few drops form a soft ball in cold water.

While syrup is cooking, beat egg yolks until they are fluffy. Pour hot syrup in a thin stream into yolks, beating constantly.

As the mixture cools, it will become thick and light. Continue to beat for a few minutes and then set aside until entirely cooled. If the syrup has not been cooked sufficiently, no amount of beating will make the mixture thick enough. If the syrup has been cooked too long, it will not beat smoothly into the egg yolks but will form little lumps of sugar.

Beat in softened butter. Flavor as desired. (Makes approximately 2 cups butter cream.)

MERINGUE BUTTER CREAM

Here is an especially fluffy light butter cream, good to make when you have extra egg whites.

This butter cream will not spread smoothly after it has been frozen. It may, however, be used to fill pastries which can be frozen.

1 cup sugar
1⁄2 cup water
1 tablespoon corn syrup
3 egg whites
1 cup sweet butter

Combine 2⁄3 cup of sugar with water and corn syrup in a saucepan. Stir over low heat until sugar is completely dissolved. Raise heat and boil syrup without stirring until a candy thermometer reads 238 degrees, or a few drops of syrup form a soft ball in cold water.

While syrup is cooking, beat egg whites until they form soft peaks. Gradually beat in remaining sugar, a little at a time, until whites are firm. Pour boiling syrup in a fine stream over whites, beating constantly. If beating by hand, use a wire whisk while adding syrup. Continue beating until completely smooth and stiff. Cool.

Cream butter until soft and fluffy. Beat meringue mixture into butter. Flavor as desired. (Makes approximately 2 cups butter cream.)

CHOCOLATE BUTTER CREAM

2 cups butter cream
2 to 3 ounces unsweetened chocolate, melted (or 4 tablespoons dark, unsweetened cocoa)
3 tablespoons cognac

Beat melted chocolate or cocoa into butter cream, adding cognac at the same time.

NOUGAT BUTTER CREAM

2 cups butter cream
1 cup nougat powder (p. 111)
3 tablespoons bourbon

Beat 1 cup nougat powder into butter cream, adding bourbon at the same time.

WALNUT RUM BUTTER CREAM

2 cups butter cream
1 1/4 cups finely ground walnuts
3 tablespoons rum

Moisten finely ground walnuts with rum. Beat into butter cream.

MOCHA BUTTER CREAM

2 cups butter cream
5 ounces semisweet chocolate, melted

4 tablespoons extra-strong coffee
3 tablespoons cognac

Beat melted chocolate and strong coffee into butter cream, adding cognac at the same time.

COFFEE BUTTER CREAM

2 cups butter cream
1 tablespoon instant coffee dissolved in a little water (or 3 tablespoons extra-strong coffee)
2 tablespoons cognac

Beat coffee into butter cream, adding cognac at the same time.

MARRON BUTTER CREAM

2 cups butter cream
⅔ cup stiff purée of chestnuts (p. 36)
3 tablespoons cognac

Beat chestnut purée into butter cream, adding cognac at the same time.

LEMON CREAM

This keeps for months in the refrigerator. In England, where it is called Lemon Curd, it is used as a spread for hot breads. It can be a quick tart or cake filling or the base of a lemon-cream dessert.

5 egg yolks
½ cup sugar
2 large lemons, juice and grated rind
¼ cup sweet butter

In a heavy saucepan or the top of a double boiler, combine egg yolks and sugar over low heat. Add lemon juice and rind. Stir, adding butter little by little. Cook until thick, stirring constantly.

Pour into clean jar. Cover top of cooled lemon cream with cognac paper (see p. 107). Keep in the refrigerator.

COFFEECAKE FILLINGS AND TOPPINGS

POPPY SEED FILLING

½ pound poppy seeds
½ cup butter
½ cup honey
2 tablespoons heavy cream
1 cup coarsely crushed walnuts
½ cup raisins
1 teaspoon grated orange peel

Pour enough boiling water over poppy seeds to cover. Let stand overnight. The following morning drain well. Grind poppy seeds 3 times, using the finest blade of the meat grinder. (There is also a grinder made especially for poppy seeds.) It is possible to have the seeds ground in the store where you buy them, but they will be cleaner and taste better if you soak and grind them yourself.

Cream butter and honey together. Add cream. Stir in ground poppy seeds, nuts, raisins, and grated orange peel.

GROUND NUT FILLING

1 ½ cups almonds or any other nuts except peanuts or cashews
3 eggs
½ cup sugar
½ cup melted butter
1 teaspoon grated orange rind
½ cup white sultana raisins
1 teaspoon vanilla

Grate nuts finely. Beat eggs and sugar for 5 minutes. Stir in grated nuts, melted butter, orange rind, raisins, and vanilla.

Note: Cake or cooky crumbs can be substituted for part of grated nuts.

ORANGE FILLING

⅔ cup soft butter
⅔ cup orange marmalade
⅔ cup coarsely crushed walnuts or pecans

Cream butter, marmalade, and nuts together.

CHEESE FILLING

2 tablespoons yellow raisins
1 tablespoon cognac
1 cup cream cheese or cottage cheese or ½ cup of each
¼ cup sugar
1 tablespoon flour
1 egg yolk
1 teaspoon melted butter
1 tablespoon sour cream
½ teaspoon grated lemon rind
½ teaspoon vanilla

Mix raisins with cognac. Cream together cheese, sugar, and flour. Stir in egg yolk, then melted butter, sour cream, lemon rind, and vanilla. Add cognac-soaked raisins.

PRUNE FILLING

1 cup cooked prunes, pitted
½ tablespoon lemon rind
⅛ teaspoon nutmeg
3 tablespoons melted butter
1 teaspoon grated orange rind
½ cup coarsely crushed walnuts
2 tablespoons sugar

Grind prunes or chop them fine. Stir in all remaining ingredients.

RAW APPLE FILLING

3 tart apples
½ teaspoon grated lemon rind
½ teaspoon vanilla
3 tablespoons cinnamon sugar
¼ cup currants
1 teaspoon lemon juice

Peel apples. Grate them on a coarse grater so that apple pulp is in shreds. Discard cores.

Add all remaining ingredients. Use as soon as possible to prevent apples from darkening.

FRANGIPANE FILLING

½ cup soft butter
1 cup almond paste
2 beaten eggs
1 teaspoon grated lemon rind
2 teaspoons flour

Cream butter. Stir in almond paste, a little at a time, adding beaten eggs alternately. Beat until smooth. Stir in remaining ingredients.

ORANGE HONEY FILLING

½ cup butter
1 grated orange rind
⅔ cup honey

Cream all ingredients together.

ALMOND CREAM FILLING

Almond cream has the consistency of pastry cream and can be used as a substitute.

¼ cup butter
1 cup almond paste
1 cup rich milk or light cream
½ cup sugar

½ cup toasted almonds, ground
6 egg yolks
1 teaspoon vanilla

Cream butter until it is soft. Add almond paste a little at a time, alternating with milk. Stir in sugar and ground nuts. Cook over medium heat, stirring constantly until cream thickens.

Stir a few tablespoons of hot, thickened cream into egg yolks. Then pour egg-yolk mixture into remaining cream, stirring briskly.

Return to low heat. Continue to cook and stir until cream thickens a little more, being careful not to let it boil. When mixture is cool, add vanilla.

APRICOT CREAM FILLING

⅓ cup sherry
2 tablespoons flour
⅔ cup strained apricot jam
½ teaspoon grated lemon rind
3 tablespoons lemon juice
3 tablespoons orange juice
3 egg yolks

Add sherry to flour. Mix until smooth. Add apricot jam, lemon rind and juice, and orange juice. Stir until smooth. Place in a heavy saucepan. Cook over low heat, stirring constantly until thick.

Stir a few tablespoons of hot sauce into egg yolks. Then pour egg yolks into remaining hot mixture, continuing to stir. Cook and stir a few more minutes, being careful not to boil, until cream is smooth and thick.

APPLE CUSTARD FILLING

3 large apples, peeled
1 lemon, juice and rind
¾ cup sugar
1 tablespoon flour
3 tablespoons water
2 egg yolks
2 tablespoons butter
½ teaspoon vanilla

Shred peeled apples on coarse grater. Discard cores.

Combine grated apple, lemon juice, lemon rind and sugar in a saucepan. Cook over medium-high heat, uncovered, until almost boiling. Stir in flour which has been mixed with water. Stir until apple mixture is thickened.

Stir 2 or 3 tablespoons of hot filling into egg yolks. Pour egg-yolk mixture into pan containing filling, continuing to stir briskly. Return to low heat 3 or 4 minutes longer, stirring until filling is a little thicker. Remove from heat. Stir in butter and vanilla.

POTATO CREAM FILLING

½ cup butter
1 cup mashed potatoes
¼ cup cream cheese
⅓ cup sugar
¼ cup sour cream
1 teaspoon grated orange rind
3 egg yolks
1 teaspoon grated lemon rind
1 teaspoon vanilla

Cream butter until soft. Beat in mashed potatoes and cream cheese. Stir in remaining ingredients.

BUTTER CRUNCH TOPPING

1 cup granulated sugar
1 teaspoon lemon juice
¼ cup heavy cream
½ cup butter
1 ½ cups blanched, sliced, toasted almonds or filberts
1 teaspoon vanilla

Combine sugar and lemon juice in heavy saucepan or skillet. Stir over low heat until sugar is completely dissolved and golden brown. Add cream and butter. Let mixture boil. At first the sugar will harden, but it will soon melt and blend with the liquid. Stir until smooth. Add nuts. Set aside to cool. Stir in vanilla before using. Enough topping for two 9-inch round coffeecakes.

STREUSEL TOPPING

⅓ cup butter
½ cup cinnamon sugar
1 teaspoon vanilla
1 cup coarsely chopped walnuts
1 to 1 ½ cups flour

Cream butter and cinnamon sugar. Add vanilla and nuts. Add flour gradually, stirring constantly. Use enough flour to make a crumbly mixture. The more flour added, the smaller the crumbs. Sprinkle on coffeecake before baking. Enough topping for two 9-inch round coffeecakes.

BRANDIED MINCE FRUIT

To use for flavoring butter creams and similar fillings. A tablespoon or two of this fruit, well drained, is enough to add spice and zest to any sweet.

Chop or grind coarsely an assortment of dried fruit, such as currants, raisins, apricots, figs. Place in a jar. Add cognac to cover. Let stand at least a week before using—the longer the better. Add more cognac when mixture seems dry.

SOME PRESERVES AND CAKE DECORATIONS

COGNAC PAPER

Paraffin is a comparatively modern product for sealing jars of sweet preserves.

Old-fashioned cognac paper is less messy than paraffin and also adds flavor.

To make cognac paper, cut out rounds of parchment or heavy brown paper the same size as the tops of the preserving jars. Soak paper rounds in any strong spirits for a minute or two. Cognac gives the best flavor, although rum or even vodka may be used.

Placed soaked paper rounds on top of cooled fruit preserves, jams, or lemon cream. Cover with jar lids.

APRICOT JAM

2 pounds dried apricots
9 cups water
2 pounds sugar
cognac paper

Wash apricots. Soak in water overnight. The following morning, simmer undrained fruit until it is tender.

Strain, undrained, through food mill or purée in a blender. Return fruit and juice to pan. Add sugar. Cook slowly, stirring frequently to prevent scorching, until jam is thick and clear.

Pour into sterilized hot jars. When jam has cooled, cover it with rounds of cognac paper. Top with jar lids.

LIQUORED CHERRIES

2 pounds sour cherries (preferably dark sour cherries called morellos)
3 cups sugar
1 fifth 100-proof vodka

Pit cherries. Crush ¼ cup of pits with nutcracker or mallet. Place cherries and crushed pits into a jar. The pits will add flavor. Add 1 cup sugar. Let stand at room temperature 4 days, shaking or stirring jar once a day. Add vodka. Cover jar. Put away for 2 months.

Drain liquid from cherries. Liquid can be used as a liqueur or to flavor desserts. Add 2 cups sugar to drained cherries. Let stand at least 1 more month before using them to decorate pastries, in fruit desserts, in butter-cream fillings, or as an after-dinner sweet.

PINEAPPLE PRESERVES

8 cups peeled, cored pineapple cut into 1-inch cubes (2 medium-size fresh pineapples)
4 cups sugar
¾ cup water (to be used only if pineapple is not juicy)

Be sure to keep as much juice as possible when peeling and coring the pineapples.

Put pineapple in a large saucepan. Add sugar. Stir. If sugar is well dampened by juice, water will not be needed. Otherwise add water.

Cover saucepan. Place over low heat for 10 minutes. Stir occasionally. Remove lid from saucepan. Sugar should be completely dissolved. If it isn't, continue to cook over low heat, stirring until sugar is dissolved.

Raise heat. Boil rapidly, about 15 minutes, or until syrup is thick and pineapple looks clear. It is not necessary to stir constantly, but be sure to watch preserves toward end of cooking to prevent pineapple from scorching.

Remove from heat. Let preserves stop bubbling. Pour into a sterilized 1-quart jar. When preserves are completely cool, place a piece of cognac paper on top and cover jar tightly.

WONDERFUL MINCEMEAT

2 *pounds lean uncooked beef*
2 *pounds uncooked tongue*
1 *pound beef suet*
4 *cups seedless raisins*
4 *cups seeded raisins*
2 *cups currants*
1 *cup diced citron*
1 *cup diced orange peel*
½ *cup diced lemon peel*
1 *cup chopped figs*
2 ½ *cups sugar*
2 *teaspoons salt*
2 *teaspoons nutmeg*
2 *teaspoons cinnamon*
2 *teaspoons allspice*
1 *teaspoon cloves*
5 *cups cognac (approximately)*
4 *cups sherry (approximately)*

Cook beef and tongue in water to cover until tender. Grind through the coarse blade of meat grinder, adding uncooked suet.

Add all remaining ingredients except cognac and sherry. Add enough cognac to make a thick, soupy mixture. Place in a clean crock. Cover and let stand at least 1 month. Refrigeration is unnecessary. Check after 1 week. If mixture has absorbed most of liquid and seems dry, add enough sherry to moisten it again. Continue to check every 2 or 3 weeks, adding cognac and sherry alternately as mincemeat absorbs moisture. It will keep indefinitely.

Add 1 cup chopped tart apples to each 1 ¼ cups mincemeat before using. Drain mincemeat before mixing with apples.

CHOCOLATE ROUNDS, TRIANGLES, ANIMALS

6 *ounces semisweet chocolate*
1 *teaspoon vegetable shortening*

Melt chocolate over hot water. Stir in shortening. Spread chocolate thinly on cooky sheet lined with wax paper or Baking Pan Liner Paper. Chill in refrigerator or freezer for a few minutes, or until chocolate just begins to set.

Cut out desired shapes, using cooky cutters or a knife. Any shape can be made—a turkey for a Thanksgiving cake, animals for a child's birthday cake, simple rounds for the sides of a gâteau.

Replace in refrigerator until chocolate is completely firm. Peel paper off chocolate and separate shapes. Keep in a covered tin box in the refrigerator or freezer.

CHOCOLATE TRUFFLES

bitter chocolate glaze (*p.* 93)
2 *tablespoons rum*
½ *cup sifted dark, unsweetened cocoa*

Cook bitter chocolate glaze until very thick. Cool. Add rum. Refrigerate until very cold and firm. Roll into ¾-inch balls. Roll balls in cocoa. Refrigerate or freeze.

CAKE CRUMBS FOR DECORATING

Bake 2 or 3 layers Swiss broyage (p. 75) or chocolate broyage (p. 77). When they are cool and dry, crush with a rolling pin or make crumbs in the blender. Store in a covered jar. Use for decorating and coating tops and sides of cakes.

COOKY WAFER DECORATIONS

Make cats' tongues (p. 202), shaping them a little wider than usual.

Or form round cookies instead. Arrange baked cookies, one right next to the other, to cover sides of a cake, first spreading cake sides with butter cream or apricot jam.

CRYSTALLIZED FLOWERS

Crystallized violets, roses, and leaves can be purchased in small packages from delicacy shops and department stores. These are used solely as decorations; they have practically no flavor, only sweetness.

To use, crush crystallized flowers or leaves slightly. Whole, they are too large and too much of a mouthful, particularly on small pastries.

NOUGAT

2 *cups granulated sugar*
2 *tablespoons lemon juice*
¾ *cup blanched almonds, toasted and chopped medium fine*
¾ *cup filberts, toasted and chopped medium fine*

Combine sugar and lemon juice in a heavy skillet. Melt over low heat, stirring constantly with a wooden spoon. When mixture is a deep golden color and sugar is completely dissolved, stir in nuts. Pour out on a very well oiled pan.

NOUGAT POWDER

Break cooled nougat into pieces. Grate into a powder with a nut grater or reduce to powder in the blender. Store nougat powder in a covered jar.

NOUGAT TRIANGLES AND ROUNDS

After nougat has been poured out on an oiled pan, spread it as thin as possible with an oiled spatula. Before it hardens, cut it into rounds or triangles, using a knife or cooky cutter dipped in oil. As nougat hardens very quickly, it is necessary to work with some speed. If the nougat should harden before all the shapes are cut, place uncut part in a 350 degree oven for a few minutes until it again becomes soft.

Chapter 4

Pound Cakes, Loaf Cakes

Raisins
Nuts
Spices
Flour

4 *Pound Cakes, Loaf Cakes*

Pound cakes, usually unadorned, are basic cakes and are delicious, adorned or plain. Long-keeping, they are convenient to have on hand as a "specialty of the house."

These cakes should be left in their pans for 15 or 20 minutes after baking, then turned out on a cake rack to finish cooling. Don't slice for at least 24 hours.

Pound cakes will last for several weeks if they are thoroughly cooled wrapped in aluminum foil and stored in a covered container. In a freezer they can be kept for months.

Rich fruit cakes wrapped in cognac-soaked cloths will keep almost indefinitely if the cloths are moistened once a month and completely replaced every 3 or 4 months.

Do note that eggs are the sole leavening in these cakes. They must be very well beaten: whole eggs should be as thick as whipped cream, egg whites as firm as possible.

When flour is added to a creamed mixture at the same time as beaten eggs, it should be lightly sprinkled on while the batter is being folded together. Fold thoroughly, but only enough to combine all the ingredients. Overmixing will result in heavy cake.

BASIC POUND CAKE

A delicious, old-fashioned cake, especially good toasted.

6 *eggs*
1 *cup sugar*
1 *cup butter*
2 *cups sifted flour*
1 *teaspoon vanilla*

Set oven at 350 degrees. Grease a deep, 9-inch tube pan and dust with flour.

In a large bowl, combine eggs and sugar. Beat for a minute. Set bowl over a saucepan of hot water. Place saucepan over low heat for about 10 minutes, or until eggs are slightly warmer than lukewarm. Do not let water boil. Stir eggs occasionally while they are being heated to prevent them from cooking on bottom of bowl.

While eggs are warming, cream butter and flour till light and fluffy. Add vanilla.

When eggs are lukewarm, beat them until cool, thick, and tripled in bulk. Quickly stir ¼ of beaten eggs into creamed mixture. Pour mixture over remaining beaten eggs. Fold in gently. Be careful not to overmix.

Pour batter into prepared pan. Bake about 50 minutes, or until cake is golden brown and pulls away from sides of pan.

ALTERNATE METHOD FOR MIXING BASIC POUND CAKE

Cream soft butter with ¼ cup sugar until light and fluffy. Add egg yolks, 1 at a time, beating well after each addition. Add vanilla.

Add pinch of salt to egg whites and beat until egg whites hold soft peaks. Add remaining sugar, a tablespoon at a time, beating well after each addition for at least 5 minutes, or until egg whites are very firm.

Fold ¼ of the stiffly beaten egg whites thoroughly into creamed butter-sugar-egg mixture. Pour mixture back on top of remaining egg whites. Fold gently together, while sprinkling in flour. Be careful not to overmix.

SEED CAKE

basic pound cake recipe (p. 116)
2 teaspoons caraway seeds

Follow recipe for basic pound cake, but add 2 teaspoons caraway seeds to creamed flour-butter mixture.

RAISIN CAKE

basic pound cake recipe (p. 116)
1 ½ cups mixed golden and dark sultana raisins
¼ cup cognac

Soak raisins in cognac at least ½ hour. Drain excess liquid from raisins. Toss raisins lightly in 1 cup flour.

Follow recipe for basic pound cake, creaming butter with only 1 cup flour. Fold floured raisins into batter with beaten eggs.

NUT CAKE

basic pound cake recipe (p. 116)
1 ½ cups crushed walnuts or pecans

Follow recipe for basic pound cake. Add 1 ½ cups crushed walnuts or pecans to creamed flour-butter mixture.

GINGER CAKE

basic pound cake recipe (p. 116)
¼ cup chopped preserved ginger or candied ginger
½ cup mixed, diced and candied fruit
¼ cup cognac
1 teaspoon ground ginger

Combine preserved ginger and fruit in a bowl. Add cognac. Let stand 20 minutes. Drain excess liquid. Toss fruit in 1 cup flour.

Follow recipe for basic pound cake, creaming butter with only 1 cup flour. Fold ground ginger and floured fruits into batter with beaten eggs.

SIMNEL CAKE

This is a long-keeping cake of English origin. It looks delicious and tastes even better than it looks.

½ cup mixed, diced candied fruit
½ cup currants
1 teaspoon grated lemon rind
1 teaspoon vanilla
2 tablespoons cognac
3 eggs
½ cup sugar
¼ cup butter
1 cup sifted flour
frangipane filling (p. 104)

Set oven at 325 degrees. Grease and dust with flour 1 round, 8-inch spring-form pan.

Combine all fruit and grated lemon rind in a bowl. Add vanilla and cognac. Let stand at least 20 minutes, then drain excess liquid from fruit.

In a large bowl, combine eggs and sugar, beating them together for a minute. Set bowl over a saucepan of hot water. Place saucepan over low heat for about 10 minutes, or until eggs are slightly warmer than lukewarm. Do not let water boil. Stir eggs occasionally while they are being heated to prevent them from cooking on bottom of bowl.

While eggs are warming, cream butter and flour together until light and fluffy. Stir fruit into the butter-flour mixture.

When eggs are warm, beat them until cool, thick, and triple in bulk. Immediately stir ¼ of the beaten eggs into creamed mixture. Pour mixture over remaining beaten eggs. Fold gently together. Be careful not to overmix.

Pour half of batter into prepared pan. Spread half the frangipane filling on top. Cover with remaining batter. Bake about 50 minutes, or until cake is golden brown and pulls away from sides of pan.

Fit a pastry bag with open star tube No. 4. Fill bag with remaining frangipane filling. Decorate top of cake with rosettes or scrolls. Return cake to the oven, placing it on a high rack for about 10 minutes, to set the frangipane decoration. Cool cake before removing sides of pan.

PLUM CAKE

This is a French cake with an English name, and a very special fruitcake in anybody's country.

¾ cup mixed, diced candied fruit
½ cup diced candied orange peel
½ cup dark sultana raisins
1 teaspoon grated lemon rind
½ cup sliced, blanched almonds
¼ cup cognac
1 teaspoon vanilla
5 eggs
¼ cup sugar
¾ cup butter
½ cup almond paste
1 cup sifted flour
½ cup sifted cornstarch

Set oven at 350 degrees. Grease and dust with flour a deep 9-inch tube pan.

Combine all fruit, grated lemon rind and nuts in a bowl. Add cognac and vanilla. Let stand at least 20 minutes, then drain excess liquid from fruit.

In a large bowl, combine 4 of the eggs with the sugar. Beat for a minute, then set bowl over a saucepan of hot water. Place saucepan over low heat for about 10 minutes, or until eggs are slightly warmer than lukewarm. Do not let water boil. Stir eggs occasionally while they are being heated to prevent them from cooking on bottom of bowl.

While eggs are warming, cream butter and almond paste together. Add remaining egg to this mixture, beating it in well.

When eggs are warm, beat until they are cool, thick and triple in bulk. Fold ¼ of beaten eggs into creamed butter-almond paste mixture. Pour mixture and drained fruit on top of remaining lightly beaten eggs. Fold all together, sprinkling in flour and cornstarch at the same time. Fold only till ingredients are combined. Be careful not to overmix.

Pour into prepared pan. Bake about 55 minutes, or until cake is golden brown and pulls away from sides of pan.

GERMAN SAND TORTE

1 *teaspoon grated lemon rind*
1 ½ *tablespoons rum*
1 *teaspoon vanilla*
½ *cup butter, melted*
8 *eggs*
4 *egg yolks*
1 ¼ *cups sugar*
⅓ *cup blanched almonds*
2 *cups sifted flour*
2 *tablespoons melted butter*
vanilla sugar (p. 45)

Set oven at 350 degrees. Butter and dust with flour a deep 10-inch tube or kugelhopf pan. Grind or grate almonds fine.

Add lemon rind, rum, and vanilla to ½ cup butter, melted and cooled to lukewarm but *not* clarified. Set aside.

In a large bowl, combine eggs, egg yolks, and sugar. Beat for a minute. Set bowl over a saucepan of hot water. Place saucepan over low heat for about 10 minutes, or until eggs are slightly warmer than lukewarm. Stir eggs occasionally while they are being heated to prevent them from cooking on bottom of bowl.

When eggs are warm, beat until they are cool, light and triple in bulk. Sprinkle grated almonds and flour over top. Fold in carefully, adding ½ cup melted butter at the same time. Continue to fold until there is no trace of butter. Be careful not to overmix.

Pour batter into prepared pan. Bake in preheated oven about 50 minutes, or until cake comes away from sides of pan. Cool cake for 10 minutes before removing from pan.

Brush with melted butter, then dust with vanilla sugar. Dust again with sugar just before serving. Slice thin.

MELTING TEA CAKE

Half sponge, half pound cake, light but buttery, this cake literally melts in your mouth.

½ cup whole, blanched almonds
1 *teaspoon vanilla*
1 *teaspoon grated lemon rind*
1 *cup butter, melted*
4 *eggs*
4 *egg yolks*
1 *cup sugar*
1 ½ *cups sifted flour*
2 *tablespoons sifted cornstarch*
⅛ *teaspoon mace*

Set oven at 350 degrees. Grease and dust with flour a 9-inch kugelhopf pan or a deep 9-inch tube pan. Arrange blanched almonds around bottom of pan.

Add vanilla and grated lemon rind to butter, melted over low heat and cooled to lukewarm but *not* clarified.

In a large bowl combine eggs, egg yolks, and sugar. Beat for a minute. Set bowl over a saucepan of hot water, and place saucepan over low heat for about 10 minutes, or until eggs are slightly warmer than lukewarm. Do not let water boil. Stir eggs occasionally while they are being heated to prevent them from cooking on bottom of bowl.

When eggs are warm, beat until they are cool, thick, and tripled in bulk. Sprinkle flour, cornstarch, and mace on top. Fold in gently, adding butter at the same time. Continue to fold until there is no trace of butter. Be careful not to overmix.

Pour batter into prepared pan. Bake about 45 minutes, or until cake is golden brown and comes away from sides of pan.

MARBLED TEA CAKE

melting tea cake recipe (p. 121)
2 ounces semisweet chocolate, grated
¼ teaspoon cinnamon

Follow recipe for melting tea cake.

Combine grated chocolate with cinnamon. Pour half of cake batter into prepared pan. Sprinkle half of grated chocolate on top. Cover with remaining batter. Sprinkle with remaining grated chocolate.

Cut through batter once or twice with a rubber spatula to streak chocolate throughout.

MARBLED ALMOND CAKE

¾ cup butter
1 ⅔ cups sugar
½ cup almond paste
5 egg yolks
1 teaspoon vanilla
12 egg whites
½ teaspoon salt
3 cups sifted flour
3 ounces semisweet chocolate, melted

Set oven at 350 degrees. Grease and dust with flour two 9 x 5 x 3 loaf pans.

Cream butter and ¼ cup sugar. Add almond paste, a little at a time, creaming it in well, until mixture looks light and fluffy. Add egg yolks, 1 at a time, beating well each time. Add vanilla.

Add salt to egg whites and beat until egg whites hold soft peaks.

Then add sugar, a tablespoon at a time, beating constantly, for at least 5 minutes, or until egg whites are very firm.

Stir ¼ of the stiffly beaten egg whites into creamed almond-paste mixture. Pour mixture back over remaining egg whites. Fold together, sprinkling in flour as you fold.

Add melted chocolate. Marble chocolate roughly in batter by drawing through it with a rubber spatula.

Pour into prepared pans. Bake 1 hour and 15 minutes, or until cakes are golden brown and pull away from sides of pans.

PRINCESS CAKE

This is a delicious pound cake made with egg whites.

1 cup butter
2 ⅔ cups sifted flour
1 teaspoon vanilla
8 egg whites
pinch of salt
¼ teaspoon cream of tartar
1 ⅔ cups sugar

Set oven at 350 degrees. Grease and dust with flour a deep 10-inch tube pan.

Cream butter and half of flour until light and fluffy. Add vanilla.

Beat egg whites with salt and cream of tartar until they hold soft peaks. Add sugar, a tablespoon at a time, beating well after each addition. Beat whites at least 5 minutes, or until they are very firm.

Quickly stir ¼ of the beaten egg whites thoroughly into creamed butter-flour mixture. Pour mixture back over remaining egg whites. Fold gently together while sprinkling in remaining flour. Be careful not to overmix.

Pour into prepared pan. Bake about 1 hour, or until the cake is golden brown and pulls away from sides of pan.

This cake can be substituted for basic pound cake in recipes for seed, raisin, nut and ginger cakes.

WHITE FRUIT CAKE

2 cups mixed, diced candied fruit
1 cup light sultana raisins
1 cup pecans, coarsely chopped
1 teaspoon cream of tartar
4 cups sifted flour
2 cups butter
2 cups sugar
12 eggs, separated
2 teaspoons vanilla
½ teaspoon mace
2 teaspoons grated lemon rind
pinch of salt

Set oven at 350 degrees. Grease and dust with flour two 9-inch tube pans.

Combine candied fruit, raisins and nuts in a bowl. Add cream of tartar and 4 tablespoons flour. Toss lightly.

Cream butter and ½ cup sugar until light and fluffy. Add egg yolks, 1 at a time, beating well each time. Stir in vanilla, mace, and grated lemon rind.

Add salt to egg whites and beat until they hold soft peaks. Then add remaining sugar, a tablespoon at a time, beating well after each addition for a total of 5 minutes, or until egg whites are very firm.

Fold ¼ of the stiffly beaten egg whites thoroughly into creamed butter-sugar-egg mixture. Pour mixture back over remaining egg whites. Sprinkle floured fruit on top. Fold all gently together, sprinkling in remaining flour at the same time.

Pour into prepared pans. Bake about 1 hour and 10 minutes, or until cakes are golden brown and pull away from sides of pans.

ENGLISH FRUIT CAKE

A rich, dark fruit cake which will keep indefinitely (if you have a good hiding place). By covering the batter with aluminum foil, the cakes are steamed before browning.

2 ½ cups mixed, diced candied fruits
1 ½ cups thinly sliced candied pineapple
1 cup light sultana raisins
1 cup thick fruit preserves
1 teaspoon vanilla
1 ½ cups currants
1 ½ cups black sultana raisins
½ cup cognac
1 cup filberts, coarsely chopped
1 cup pecans, coarsely chopped
6 eggs
1 cup dark-brown sugar
1 cup butter
2 cups flour
½ teaspoon nutmeg
½ teaspoon cloves
1 teaspoon cinnamon

The night before you bake English fruit cake, combine all the fruit, fruit preserves, vanilla, and cognac in a large bowl.

The following morning, grease and lightly flour three 9 x 5 x 3 loaf pans. Set oven at 300 degrees. Add nuts to bowl containing fruit.

Cream butter, flour, and spices together until light.

Beat eggs and sugar together until thick and fluffy. Stir beaten eggs thoroughly into creamed butter-flour mixture.

Pour batter over fruits and nuts. With hands, mix together gently but quickly.

Fill prepared pans ⅔ full. Pat batter down firmly. Cover each pan with a sheet of aluminum foil, sealing the batter in.

Bake cakes in preheated oven for 2 hours. Remove aluminum-foil covers. Bake about 40 minutes longer, or until tops of cakes are browned.

When cakes are completely cooled, turn them out of pans. Wrap each in a cognac-soaked cloth, then in aluminum foil. Store in an airtight box for at least 2 weeks before serving.

HUNTER CAKE

1 ¾ *cups unblanched almonds*
1 *teaspoon grated lemon rind*
1 *teaspoon vanilla*
6 *egg yolks*
3 *egg whites*
⅔ *cup sugar*
½ *cup raspberry jam*
vanilla sugar (*p.* 45)
topping (*p.* 127)

Set oven at 350 degrees. Grease bottom, but not the sides, of a 9-inch spring-form pan. Grate almonds fine.

Add lemon rind and vanilla to egg yolks. Stir lightly with a fork to break them up.

Beat egg whites until they form soft peaks. Add sugar, a little at a time, beating well after each addition, until whites are very stiff, about 5 minutes in all.

Pour egg yolks on top of whites. Sprinkle grated almonds over them. Fold all gently together, preferably by hand.

Pour into prepared pan. Bake about 40 minutes, or until cake is lightly browned and springy when gently touched.

Remove from oven. Quickly spread top with thin layer of raspberry jam. Over jam, spread half of topping (below). Press remaining topping through a pastry bag fitted with a large star tube. Replace cake in oven on a high rack. Bake 30 to 40 minutes longer, or until top is golden brown and set. Cool cake in pan. Dust with vanilla sugar before serving.

Begin to prepare the following topping when cake has baked about 20 minutes.

TOPPING

3 *egg whites*
2 *teaspoons lemon juice*
1 *teaspoon vanilla*
½ *cup sugar*
1 ¼ *cups unblanched almonds*

Grate almonds fine. Combine egg whites, lemon juice, and vanilla. Beat until egg whites hold soft peaks. Add sugar, a tablespoon at a time, beating well after each addition, until whites are very stiff, about 5 minutes in all. Fold in grated almonds. Use as soon as possible.

Chapter 5

Puff Paste and Strudel

5 *Puff Paste and Strudel*

MAKING PUFF PASTE

Puff paste is a crisp, light pastry consisting of hundreds of paper-thin layers of dough. These layers are prevented from sticking together by thin layers of fat—any fat, but usually butter. While the pastry is baking, steam caught between the layers of dough forces them to rise. As the baking continues, the steam evaporates and the fat is absorbed, leaving a high, crisp, flaky pastry.

Making puff paste is a simple mechanical process that is not at all difficult to learn if directions are followed carefully. Using puff paste is fun. It can be used in hundreds of different ways. Most of the shapes and fillings used for Danish pastry can be adapted. Other ideas for using puff paste can be found in Chapter 11, "Pastry Appetizers and Hors d'Oeuvres."

The best puff paste is made from bread flour, although all-purpose pastry flour can also be used. Bread flour, because it is made from hard wheat, is known as strong flour. Strong flour has the high gluten content necessary to achieve thin layers that won't collapse in the oven. All-purpose flour, fine for most other baking, is a blend of hard and soft wheat flour with a lower gluten content.

Gluten makes for elasticity in dough. When making the basic dough for puff paste, it is important to develop an elastic, rubbery dough so that the fat (preferably butter) will not break through the layers of dough when it is being rolled and re-rolled. When puff-paste dough is made from a soft flour (such as cake flour) the right consistency can never be reached. Even a dough made with strong flour must be well kneaded and worked or it won't acquire the necessary elasticity.

Butter for puff paste should be unsalted. Contrary to many recipes, unsalted butter doesn't need to be washed, and except for shaping it into a brick, the butter doesn't have to be worked in any way. The consistency of the butter, however, is important. If stone-cold when combined with the dough, it will break up under pressure of the rolling pin. If it is very soft, it will ooze out. It should be firm enough to be waxy, yet it should have approximately the same consistency as the dough, so that after the two are combined they can be rolled out together smoothly and easily.

After puff paste has been rolled out and folded a total of 5 times, it should be chilled in the refrigerator at least 3 hours before being finally rolled out, cut, and shaped. The shaped pastry must be chilled again before baking. Puff paste, well wrapped, can be kept in the refrigerator 3 to 4 days. Fresh puff paste can also be shaped and then frozen. Frozen pastries, baked as much as 3 months later, will be excellent.

Never throw away puff-paste trimmings. They are ideal for a number of little cakes. Trimmings should always be used for making any puff-paste pastry that expands horizontally instead of vertically, such as palmiers or papillons. Stack the trimmings evenly, one piece on top of another, folding thin, long ends carefully so that the layers of dough are disturbed as little as possible. The stacked trimmings should be pressed down with the hand and chilled before re-rolling.

Success with puff paste depends on knowing how to bake as well as how to make it. Most recipes for puff-paste pastries call for a very hot oven, 450 degrees or more. While the pastries rise well in such a hot oven, the bottoms are invariably too brown, and the centers of large pastries remain uncooked.

For that reason, a good deal of experimentation with temperatures was done for this book. A moderate oven of 350 degrees seems to be the ideal for puff paste. The pastries bake longer, but there is no danger of burned bottoms and raw insides.

Note: Don't try to make puff paste during hot weather unless your kitchen is air-conditioned.

PUFF PASTE

4 cups sifted bread flour
1 teaspoon salt
1 tablespoon lemon juice
1 1/3 cups water (approximately)
2 cups sweet butter

Set aside 3 tablespoons flour. Place remaining flour in a large bowl. Make a well in the center. Add salt, lemon juice, and 1 cup water. Using hand, work flour and liquid together to make a firm, slightly sticky dough. If necessary, add additional water gradually.

Knead the sticky ball of dough on a table for 15 to 20 minutes, or until dough is very elastic and smooth. It is almost impossible to overwork this dough. Pounding it on the table also helps achieve the right consistency. While working, dip fingers occasionally into water and dab a few drops into dough to prevent it from drying. Cover dough and let it rest for 10 minutes in refrigerator.

While dough is resting, make butter into shape of a brick approximately 3 x 5 x 1 1/2. Roll brick in the 3 tablespoons of flour, coating all sides well.

Place dough on a large, well-floured cloth. Sprinkle lightly with flour. Leaving the center a cushion about the size of the brick and 1/3 inch thick, roll out ball of dough on 4 sides, making 4 thinner "petals," about 1/4 inch thick. Brush off excess flour. Center butter on cushion. Stretch petals over butter, overlapping them and sealing so butter is completely enclosed. This will make a cushion of dough above and below the butter. Flour block of dough well. Wrap in aluminum foil. Chill for 20 minutes.

Roll out dough on well-floured cloth; roll evenly and gently into a rectangle 8 x 18 x 1/3. Be careful not to pound or squeeze dough. Use a firm, consistent rolling motion. Don't roll over ends. When rectangle is 18 inches long, lightly roll across dough (in the opposite direction) to flatten ends to same thickness as rest of sheet.

Brush off excess flour. Fold each end of rectangle to meet in center. Roll lightly. Again brush off excess flour. Then fold together again as though closing the pages of a book. There will be 4 layers of dough.

MAKING PUFF PASTE

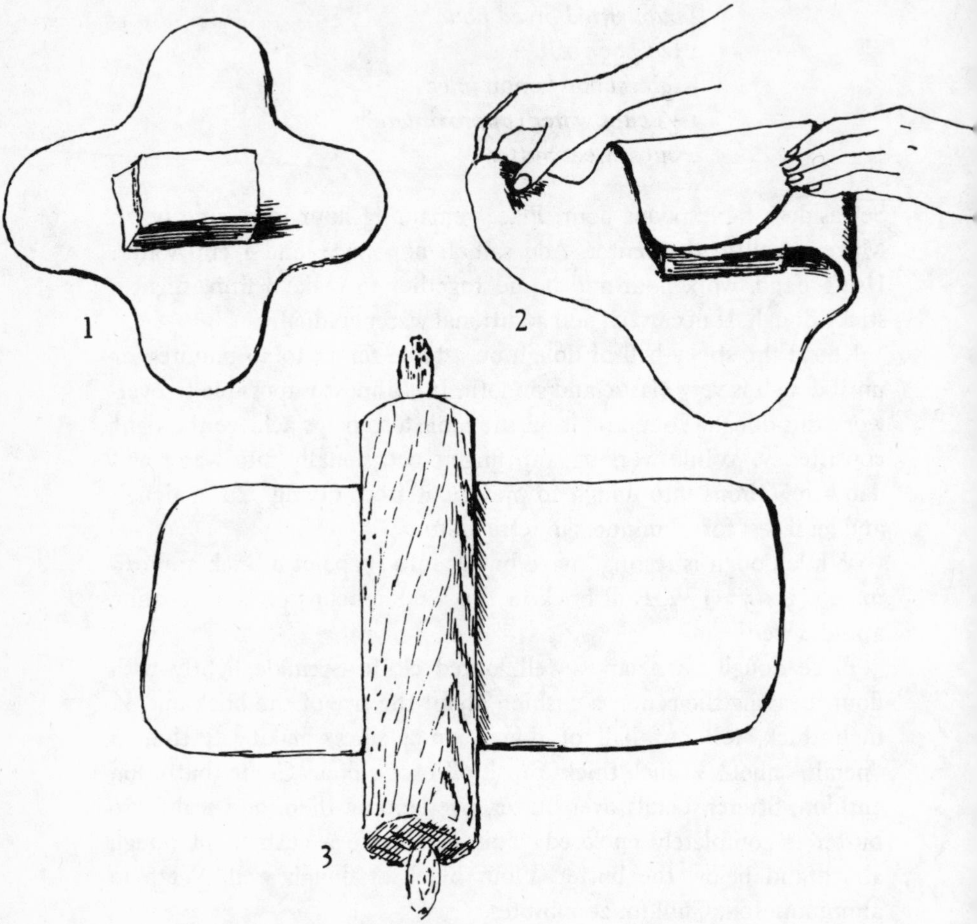

1. *Roll dough in clover shape. Put brick of butter in center.*

2. *Enclose butter in dough.*

3. *Roll dough (in which butter has been sealed) into rectangle 3 times longer than it is wide.*

4. *Fold ends of rectangle to meet in center.*

5. *Fold dough in half twice more, making 4 layers.*

6. *After chilling dough, roll out again.*

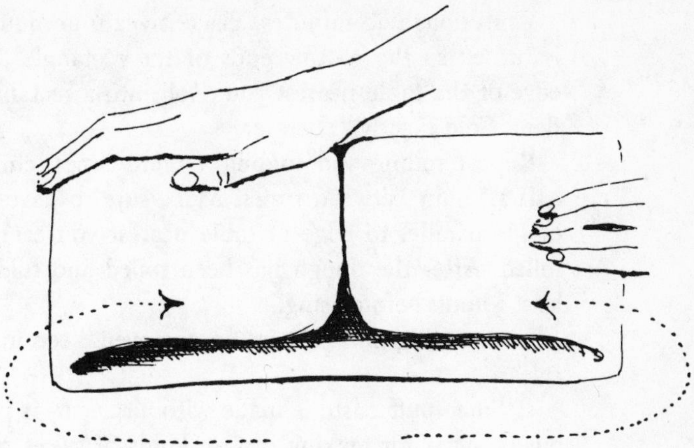

4

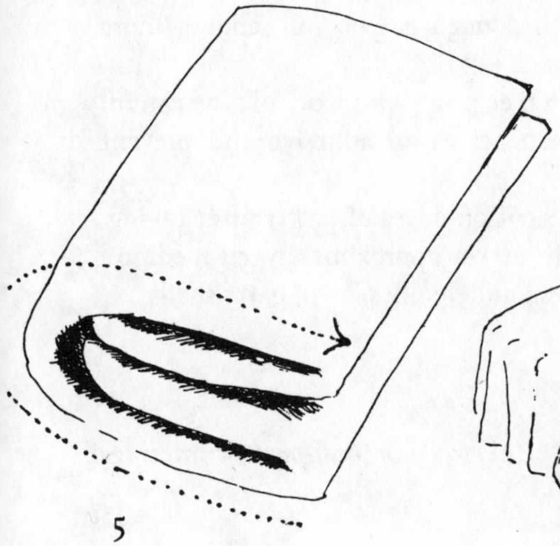

5

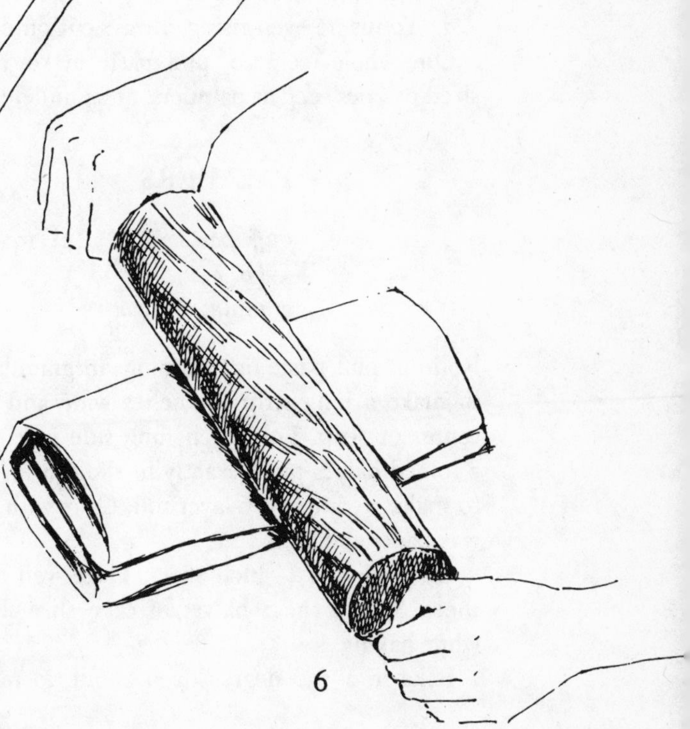

6

Chill dough 30 minutes. Place it again on floured cloth. Be sure it is turned so the narrow ends of the rectangle are parallel with the edge of the table nearest you. Roll into a rectangle. Brush off excess flour. Fold exactly as before.

Repeat rolling and folding 3 more times, chilling dough at least half an hour between times. Make sure to have narrow ends of rectangle parallel to edge of table nearest you each time the dough is rolled. After the dough has been rolled and folded 5 times, chill at least 3 hours before using.

In preparing puff pastries for the oven, keep in mind the following rules:

1. Since puff paste is made without sugar, it is necessary to roll it out in sugar for making certain kinds of sweet pastry. Sugar doesn't offer as much protection against sticking as flour does, so use plenty and keep checking underneath the dough as you roll, adding more sugar if there is any sign of stickiness.

2. In brushing pastry with beaten egg, egg white, or yolk, be careful not to drip on the sides. Egg can act as an adhesive and prevent pastry from rising in spots.

3. To insure even rising, always cut off edges of pastry after rolling.

One whole recipe of puff paste makes approximately 50 medium-sized pastries such as palmiers, or 24 millefeuilles, or 15 patty shells.

PALMIERS

puff paste recipe (*p.* 133) *or puff-paste trimmings* (*p.* 132)
granulated sugar

Roll out puff paste or trimmings in granulated sugar instead of flour, to make a long strip 10 inches wide and ⅛ inch thick. Determine center of strip. Fold each long side inward into thirds, so that the 2 folded halves meet exactly in the center. Then fold halves together to make a compact, 6-layer roll. Coat with additional sugar. Wrap in wax paper and chill.

Cut roll into ¼-inch slices. Place well apart on ungreased baking sheet. Spread the 2 halves of each slice slightly so they can expand while baking.

Bake in a 350 degree oven about 30 minutes, turning slices over once with a spatula after 25 minutes. Bake until cakes are caramelized and golden brown.

FOUR-FINGER PALMIERS

puff paste (*p.* 133) *or puff-paste trimmings* (*p.* 132)
granulated sugar

Roll out puff paste or trimmings in plenty of granulated sugar instead of flour, to make a sheet less than ⅛ inch thick. Trim edges and cut into long strips 5 inches wide.

Fold each strip so the 2 long ends meet in the center. Now fold in half the *opposite* way. Fold in half lengthwise once more, making a compact strip 1 ¼ inches wide composed of 4 double layers. Chill.

Slice across into ¼-inch slices. Place cakes flat on ungreased baking sheet, spread "fingers" slightly apart. Chill.

Bake in 350 degree oven about 25 minutes, turning cakes over once after 20 minutes, until they are golden brown.

PAPILLONS

puff paste (*p.* 133) *or puff-paste trimmings* (*p.* 132)
granulated sugar
1 *egg white mixed with*
1 *teaspoon water*

Roll out puff paste or trimmings ⅛ inch thick in granulated sugar instead of flour. Trim off edges. Divide remaining pastry into long strips 4 inches wide. Brush center of each strip lengthwise with egg-white mixture. Sandwich 4 strips together. Taking a long stick no thicker than a pencil, press down firmly along the center of top strip, lengthwise, to make an indentation. Fold in half using indentation as a guide. Cut into ¼-inch slices. Place slices flat on paper-lined baking sheet. Separate ends of each slice slightly so they can expand. Bake in a 350 degree oven 30 minutes, or until papillons are golden brown. Turn cakes over once after 25 minutes so they bake evenly on both sides.

PUFF PASTE SHAPES

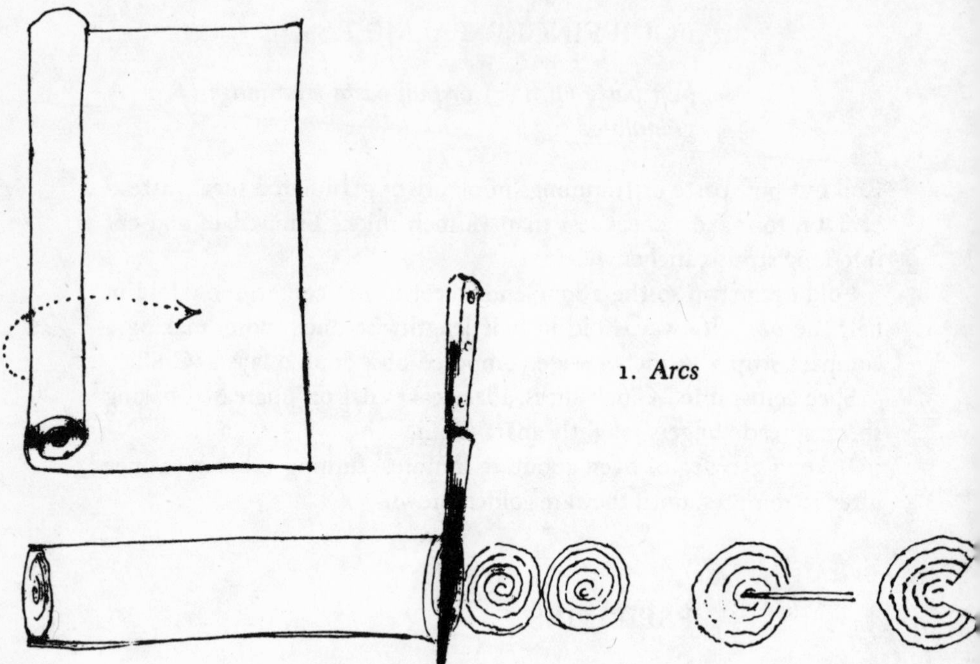

1. *Arcs*

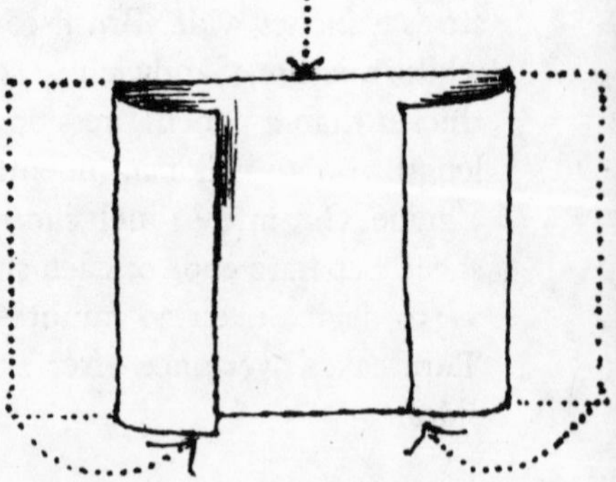

2. *Palmiers*

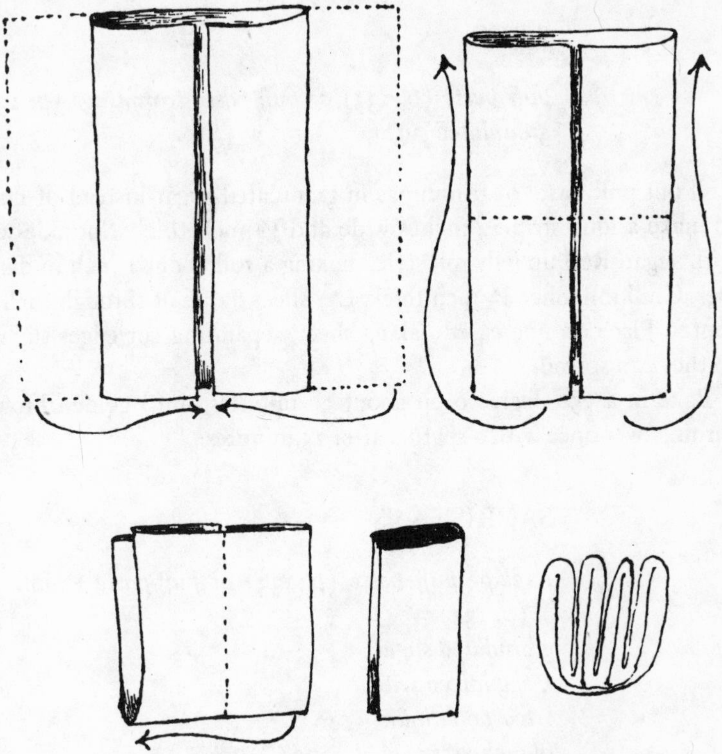

3. *Four-finger palmiers*

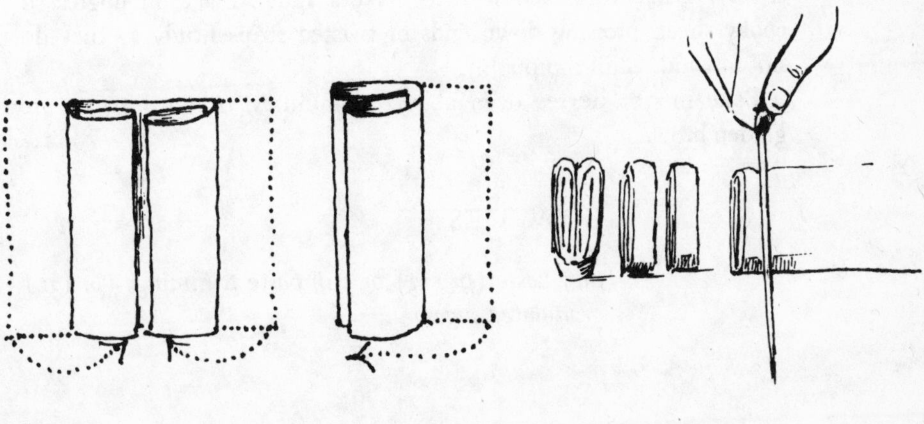

ARCS

puff paste (*p.* 133) *or puff-paste trimmings* (*p.* 132)
granulated sugar

Roll out puff paste or trimmings in granulated sugar instead of flour, to make a long strip 12 inches wide and 1/8 inch thick. Sprinkle well with sugar. Roll up jelly-roll style, making a roll about 1 inch in diameter. Chill roll. Slice 1/4 inch thick. Lay slices flat. Cut through each to center. Place on ungreased baking sheet, separating cut edges slightly so they can spread.

Bake in a 350 degree oven about 30 minutes, until golden brown, turning over once with a spatula after 25 minutes.

SACRISTANS

1 *recipe puff paste* (*p.* 133) *or puff-paste trimmings* (*p.* 132)
granulated sugar
1 *egg mixed with*
1 *teaspoon milk*
blanched, sliced almonds

Roll out puff paste or trimmings 1/8 inch thick in granulated sugar instead of flour. Trim off edges.

Brush trimmed pastry with beaten egg mixture. Sprinkle generously with blanched, sliced almonds and additional sugar. Cut dough into strips 1 x 4. Twist each strip to make a spiral. Place on ungreased cooky sheet, pressing down ends of twisted strips firmly so they do not unwind. Chill thoroughly.

Bake in 350 degree oven about 25 minutes, or until twists are golden brown.

BOW TIES

puff paste (*p.* 133) *or puff-paste trimmings* (*p.* 132)
granulated sugar

2 egg whites mixed with
2 teaspoons water
2 cups blanched, sliced almonds

Roll out puff paste ⅛ inch thick in granulated sugar. Trim edges. Cut into strips 2 x 4.

Brush lightly with egg-white mixture. Sprinkle with additional sugar and blanched, sliced almonds. Firmly twist each strip in the center so that a bow is formed and both nutted surfaces face upward. Place on ungreased baking sheet. Chill well. Bake in a 350 degree oven about 25 minutes or until twists are golden brown.

JELLY TARTS

1 recipe puff paste (*p.* 133)
granulated sugar
1 ½ cups thick jam (*approximately*)
2 egg whites mixed with
2 teaspoons water

Roll out puff paste in granulated sugar instead of flour, until ⅛ inch thick. Trim off edges.

Cut trimmed pastry into 3-inch squares. Put a small dab of thick jam in center of each square. Fold one corner over jam. Brush it with egg-white mixture. Fold opposite corner to overlap slightly, and press together firmly. Chill tarts.

Place on ungreased baking sheet. Bake in 350 degree oven about 30 minutes, or until tarts are golden brown.

LADY LOCKS (or CREAM HORNS)

½ recipe puff paste (*p.* 133)
2 egg whites mixed with
2 teaspoons water
crystallized sugar
3 cups heavy cream, whipped, sweetened, flavored with vanilla (*p.* 93)

To make this pastry you will need metal tubes or cornucopias. These are available in a variety of sizes.

Roll puff paste 1/8 inch thick. A metal tube measuring 5 1/2 inches long will require a strip of dough 3/4 inch wide and 30 inches long. Shorter strips are used when tubes are smaller.

Wind dough around each tube with edges slightly overlapping, starting at the narrowest end of the tube and rolling strips to within 1/2 inch of the top. This space is left uncovered so the tube can be easily removed later. Be careful not to stretch the pastry as it is rolled around the tube, or it will shrink and break in baking.

Chill pastry-covered horns. Brush with egg-white mixture, leaving a strip clear along one side, which will rest on cooky sheet. Roll egg-brushed pastry into granulated sugar or, for an even more special look, coarse crystal sugar.

Place tubes 1 inch apart on an ungreased baking sheet. (Do not stand on end.) Bake in a 350 degree oven for 40 to 50 minutes, or until pastry is golden. Remove tubes from pastry immediately by twisting them free.

Just before serving, fill each horn with sweetened, flavored whipped cream, using a pastry bag and tube to squirt it in.

APPLE TURNOVERS

1/2 recipe puff paste (p. 133)
granulated sugar
2 egg whites mixed with
2 teaspoons water
1/2 apple filling (p. 104)

Roll out puff paste 1/8 inch thick in granulated sugar instead of flour. Trim off edges. Cut remaining pastry into 4-inch squares. Brush each square lightly with egg-white mixture.

Drain apple filling. Put a scant teaspoon of filling in center of each square. Fold squares to make triangles, pressing dough firmly all around apple filling, without touching edges of pastry. Chill.

Place on ungreased baking sheet. Slash top of each turnover twice diagonally with a sharp knife to permit release of steam. Bake in a 350 degree oven about 40 minutes, or until pastries are golden brown.

OPEN-FACED APPLE SLICES

½ recipe puff paste (p. 133)
2 large apples, peeled, cored, and sliced thin
juice of 2 lemons
1 teaspoon vanilla
1 egg mixed with
1 tablespoon milk
½ cup currants
½ cup sliced, blanched almonds
1 teaspoon grated lemon rind
4 tablespoons cinnamon sugar (p. 44)
⅔ cup apricot glaze (p. 92)

Roll out puff paste ¼ inch thick. Trim edges. Cut into strips 3 ½ x 2. Place on ungreased baking sheet. Chill.

While pastry is chilling, soak sliced apples in lemon juice mixed with vanilla. Brush pastry strips with egg mixture. Arrange drained apples down center of each chilled strip, overlapping slices slightly. Sprinkle with currants, blanched sliced almonds, grated lemon rind, and cinnamon sugar. Bake in 350 degree oven about 35 minutes, or until strips are golden brown. While still hot, brush apples with apricot glaze. Note: Peaches, plums or cherries can be substituted for apples. Omit soaking other fruits in lemon juice. Omit currants. Use currant glaze (p. 92) for darker-colored fruits.

MILLEFEUILLES (NAPOLEONS)

puff paste recipe (p. 133)
3 cups cream, whipped, sweetened, flavored (p. 93)
or
half-and-half cream filling (p. 96)
vanilla sugar (p. 45)

Roll out puff paste ⅛ inch thick, to the same size as your baking sheet. Trim off edges. Transfer sheet of dough to ungreased baking sheet. Chill.

Prick dough all over with a heavy-pronged fork. Bake in a 350 degree oven about 55 minutes, or until pastry is well puffed and golden brown. Let cool. With a serrated knife trim off all edges. Split pastry horizontally through center. Place bottom slice on flat surface. Spread with flavored whipped cream or half-and-half cream filling.

Cover filling with top of pastry. Chill for an hour. With a serrated knife, cut into long strips 3 inches wide. Cut strips into 1 ½-inch slices. Dust with vanilla sugar.

VOL AU VENT

puff paste recipe (p. 133)
2 egg yolks mixed with
2 teaspoons cream

Roll out puff paste ½ inch thick. Cut out 3-inch rounds with a scalloped cutter. Using a slightly smaller plain cutter, press into center of each round only ⅔ through dough. Chill well. Brush tops with yolk-cream mixture. Place on ungreased baking sheet. Bake in 350 degree oven 40 to 50 minutes or until well puffed and golden brown. Use a small knife to loosen and remove center rounds. Scrape out any soft paste remaining in each shell. Fill as desired, using the little center round as a cap.

ALMOND-APRICOT BARS

½ recipe puff paste or puff-paste trimmings (pp. 133, 132)
½ recipe frangipane filling (p. 104)
⅔ cup apricot glaze (p. 92)

Roll out puff paste ⅛ inch thick. Trim off edges. Spread half of pastry thinly with frangipane filling. Fold remaining half over filling. Roll lightly over folded dough.

Cut into strips 12 x ½. Make a spiral of each strip by twisting ends in opposite directions. Place on ungreased baking sheet, pressing down ends so strips won't unwind. Chill.

Bake in 350 degree oven about 25 minutes or until strips are golden brown. Brush while still hot with apricot glaze.

NUT BARS

Follow recipe for almond-apricot bars, substituting nut filling (p. 102) for frangipane filling.

APRICOT HORNS

½ recipe puff paste (p. 133)
⅔ cup apricot jam
2 egg yolks mixed with
2 teaspoons cream
⅔ cup sliced filberts

Roll out puff paste just less than ⅛ inch thick. Trim edges. Cut into strips 3 inches wide. Divide strips into triangles. Place a scant teaspoon of thick apricot jam on widest side of each triangle. Roll toward opposite point. Bend slightly into a crescent shape.

Place crescent on ungreased baking sheet so that point of triangle rests on sheet. Chill well. Brush with egg yolk mixture. Sprinkle with sliced filberts. Bake in a 350 degree oven about 30 minutes or until golden brown.

MAKING A TART SHELL OF PUFF PASTE

½ recipe puff paste (p. 133)
2 egg yolks mixed with
2 teaspoons cream

An easy, attractive tart shell can be shaped from puff paste without using a flan ring or any kind of mold.

Roll out puff paste ⅛ inch thick. Trim off edges. Cut out a rectangle 6 x 14. Place on ungreased baking sheet. Brush with egg-yolk mixture. Cut four ½-inch-wide strips from remaining pastry, two 14 inches long, the remaining two 5 inches long. Place flat on rectangle to form a border. If a high shell is desired, cut the strips from thicker dough. Chill well. Prick bottom of shell all over with a fork. Brush rim with egg-yolk mixture. Bake in 350 degree oven about 45 minutes, or until shell is golden brown, pricking bottom of tart 3 or 4 times during first 15 or 20 minutes to prevent it from puffing up too much. Fill as desired with any of the fillings suggested for baked shells in chapter on tarts.

LARGE APPLE CHAUSSON

½ recipe puff paste (p. 133)
granulated sugar
apple custard filling (p. 105)
1 *egg white mixed with*
1 *teaspoon water*
¼ *cup sliced blanched almonds*

Roll out puff paste ¼ inch thick in granulated sugar instead of flour. Cut it into an oval 12 x 9. Spread apple custard filling lengthwise down center. Fold long side of oval over filling. Brush with egg-white mixture. Fold opposite side over. Being careful not to squeeze filling, press overlapping pastry together. Place on ungreased baking sheet.

Brush top with egg-white mixture. Sprinkle with sliced almonds and additional sugar. Bake in 350 degree oven about 1 hour, or until pastry is golden brown.

SAUTÉED APPLE CAKE

½ recipe puff paste (p. 133)
2 *egg whites mixed with*
2 *teaspoons water*
¼ *cup granulated sugar*
¼ *cup blanched sliced almonds*

Roll out puff paste slightly less than ⅛ inch thick. Trim edges. Divide into two 8-inch squares and 4 strips ½-inch wide. Place squares on baking sheet. Brush 1 of them with egg-white mixture. Arrange strips along edges to make a border. Chill both squares. Just before baking, brush plain square with egg-white mixture. Sprinkle it with granulated sugar and blanched, sliced almonds. Bake both squares in a 350 degree oven about 40 minutes, or until pastry is golden brown.

Fill bottom shell with the following sautéed apple filling:

SAUTÉED APPLE FILLING

4 pounds apples—preferably greenings—peeled, cored, and sliced or coarsely chopped
½ cup butter
2 to 3 tablespoons sugar
1 teaspoon grated lemon peel

Using a large skillet, sauté chopped apples over medium heat in approximately ½ cup butter, adding more if necessary. Sprinkle apples as they cook with 2 or 3 tablespoons granulated sugar and 1 teaspoon grated lemon peel. Turn them with a spatula occasionally so they brown lightly on all sides. Do not stir or apples will become mushy. When they are tender and lightly browned, remove from heat and cool. Pile into baked shell. Fit sugared square on top. Place in 300 degree oven for 15 minutes before serving. Serve with whipped cream.

PITHIVIERS

½ recipe puff paste (p. 133)
½ recipe almond cream filling or ½ recipe frangipane filling (p. 104)
1 egg mixed with
1 teaspoon cream
2 tablespoons confectioners' sugar

Roll out puff paste ¼ inch thick. Cut out two 8-inch circles, using a scalloped cutter, if possible. Place 1 circle on ungreased baking sheet. Spread with preferred filling to within ½ inch of outer edge. Using a small knife or a rolling pastry knife, score remaining circle with arcs radiating from center. Place scored circle over filling. Chill.

Brush top with egg mixture. Sprinkle with confectioners' sugar. Bake in a 350 degree oven about 1 hour, or until pastry is golden brown.

DARTOIS

½ recipe puff paste (p. 133)
2 egg yolks mixed with
2 teaspoons cream
apple custard filling (p. 105) or pastry cream (p. 95)
2 tablespoons confectioners' sugar

Roll out puff paste into a square ⅛ inch thick. Trim edges. Cut 3 strips ½ inch wide from 1 side of square, and cut remaining dough into 2 equal rectangles. Place rectangles on ungreased baking sheet. Brush them with egg-yolk mixture.

Place strips on 1 rectangle to form a border at edges, trimming as required.

Score remaining rectangle with a sharp knife, making diagonal lines. Brush with egg-yolk mixture.

Bake in a 350 degree oven about 40 minutes, or until pastry is lightly browned. Remove from oven. Fill shell with apple custard filling or pastry cream. Place scored pastry rectangle on top.

Dust with confectioners' sugar. Return to 350 degree oven, placing cake on highest rack so sugar will caramelize. Continue baking 15 to 20 minutes, or until pastry is golden brown.

THOUSAND LAYER CAKE

½ recipe puff paste (p. 133)
3 cups heavy cream, whipped, sweetened, flavored, gelatin added (p. 93)
⅔ cup white rum fondant (pp. 89-91)
½ ounce unsweetened chocolate or 1 tablespoon cocoa
2 ½ cups blanched, sliced, toasted almonds

Roll out puff paste less than ⅛ inch thick. Cut into three 7-inch circles, using a plate or pan for a pattern. Place rounds on ungreased baking sheet. Prick them all over with a fork. Chill.

Set oven at 350 degrees. Bake rounds in preheated oven about 40 minutes, or until golden brown. Cool. Sandwich together with half of whipped cream. Place the third circle bottom up to form top of cake.

Pour ¾ of rum fondant over cake to cover top. Flavor remaining fondant with chocolate. Place in a paper cornucopia. Cut a tiny hole in pointed end. Pipe lines of fondant 1 inch apart, across cake, working quickly so that fondant will not set. Marble top of cake by pulling the tip of a small knife across the piped lines, starting each time from the opposite side of cake.

Frost sides of cake with remaining whipped cream, then cover sides with toasted almonds.

MAKING STRUDEL

Why is strudel in the same chapter with puff paste? Following an idea of James Beard's, we once brushed thinly stretched strudel dough all over with melted butter and then carefully folded it into a small rectangle, brushing on additional butter before each fold. After chilling the dough very well, we rolled it out, cut it into shapes and baked them. They rose wonderfully well, bearing out the theory that strudel and puff paste are closely related.

Both pastries are crisp, light, and flaky after they are baked. Both are created from alternate layers of dough and fat, and in both pastries it is the fat that keeps the layers of dough from sticking together. In making puff paste, however, the dough and butter, after they are combined, are treated as one, while in strudel, the dough is first stretched paper-thin, then brushed all over with melted butter before being filled and folded.

Bread flour makes the best strudel because of its high gluten content. The dough itself is much softer than puff-paste dough. It must be worked, beaten, and slapped against the table until it no longer sticks to hand or table. This will give it enough elasticity so that it can be stretched and pulled to tissue-paper thinness.

Homemade strudel will remain crisp for several days after it has been baked. It is at its best when served slightly warm. Baked strudel can be frozen for a few weeks but should be reheated before serving. Unbaked dessert strudels should not be frozen because many uncooked fillings do not freeze well.

BASIC STRUDEL RECIPE

1 ½ cups flour (preferably bread flour)
¼ teaspoon salt
1 tablespoon lemon juice
2 egg whites
4 tablespoons peanut oil
¼ to ½ cup warm water
2 cups fine white bread crumbs sautéed in
⅔ cup butter
4 cups filling (approximately)

Place flour in a bowl. Make a well in the center. Add salt, lemon juice, egg whites, and peanut oil. Using hand, work ingredients together, adding enough water to make a very soft, sticky dough. Knead and beat well, slapping dough against table top or pulling it against bowl, whichever you find easier. If kneading on table, keep a spatula handy to push dough together when it spreads too far. When dough has been beaten at least 15 minutes and is very elastic and smooth, place it in an oiled bowl. Brush top with oil. Cover bowl with a plate, place in a pan of medium-hot water, and let dough become lukewarm. Turn dough in bowl once or twice. Warming will take 10 to 15 minutes.

Cover table top with a pastry cloth large enough to hang over the sides. Rub flour into the cloth, particularly in the center. Place dough on cloth. Sprinkle heavily with flour. Roll out thin to the size of a large handkerchief. Brush all over with oil.

Dip your fists into flour. Then by working fists under the dough (palms down), stretch dough, working from center out, until it is as thin as tissue paper. If it should begin to dry in spots before it is thin enough, brush with oil. If holes appear, ignore them. When dough is evenly stretched it may hang over edges of table. Let it dry about 10 minutes. Do not allow it to become brittle.

After it has dried slightly, pull or cut off thick edges. Brush remaining dough all over with melted butter. Sprinkle sautéed bread crumbs over dough. Arrange a 2-inch strip of filling across one end. Fold over flaps of dough to right and left of filling. Brush them with butter. Lift up end of cloth nearest filling and make the dough fold over on filling. By raising the cloth, continue this procedure until dough is completely rolled around filling. Flip onto greased pan. Bake in a 350 degree oven for 1 hour, basting occasionally with melted butter, until strudel is golden brown.

APPLE STRUDEL

stretched strudel dough (p. 150)
1 cup butter, melted
2 cups fresh bread crumbs sautéed lightly in butter
½ cup ground walnuts
4 cups peeled, sliced apples
1 cup raisins
1 teaspoon grated lemon rind
⅔ cup cinnamon sugar (p. 44)
vanilla sugar (p. 45)

Brush strudel dough generously with melted butter. Sprinkle all over with sautéed bread crumbs and ground walnuts. Place a 2-inch strip of sliced apples along one end of dough.

Brush apples with butter and sprinkle with raisins, grated lemon rind, and cinnamon sugar. Fold in flaps of dough at sides of filling. Brush them with butter. Lift up end of cloth nearest filling and make the dough fold over apples. By raising the cloth, continue to roll up apple filling until it is completely enclosed in the sheet of dough. Roll loosely.

Transfer strudel to lightly greased baking sheet, making a horseshoe shape if it is too long for the pan. Bake in a 350 degree oven for about 1 hour, basting occasionally with melted butter, until strudel is golden brown. Dust with vanilla sugar. Serve slightly warm.

MINCEMEAT STRUDEL

stretched strudel dough (p. 150)
1 cup butter, melted
2 cups fresh bread crumbs, sautéed lightly in butter
4 cups mincemeat filling (p. 109)

Follow directions given for apple strudel, substituting ingredients above.

MAKING STRUDEL

1. *Starting to roll warmed dough*
2. *Stretching the dough*
3. *Beginning to roll up the strudel*
4. *Flipping strudel onto baking sheet*

2

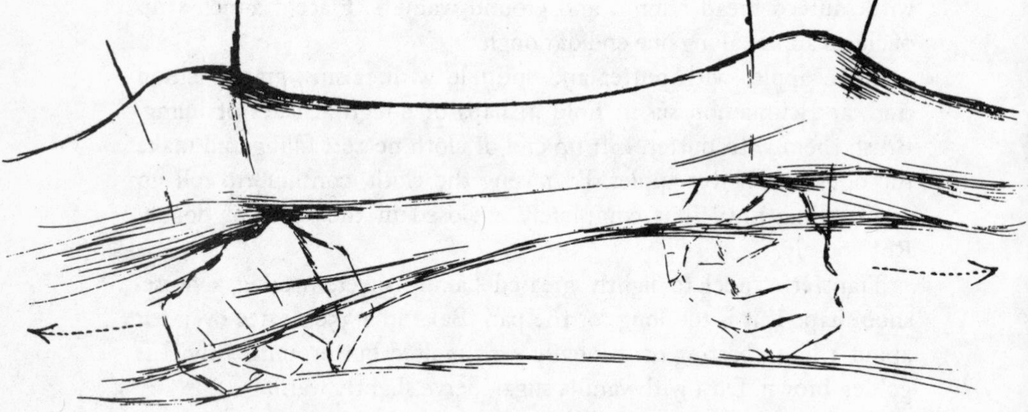

3

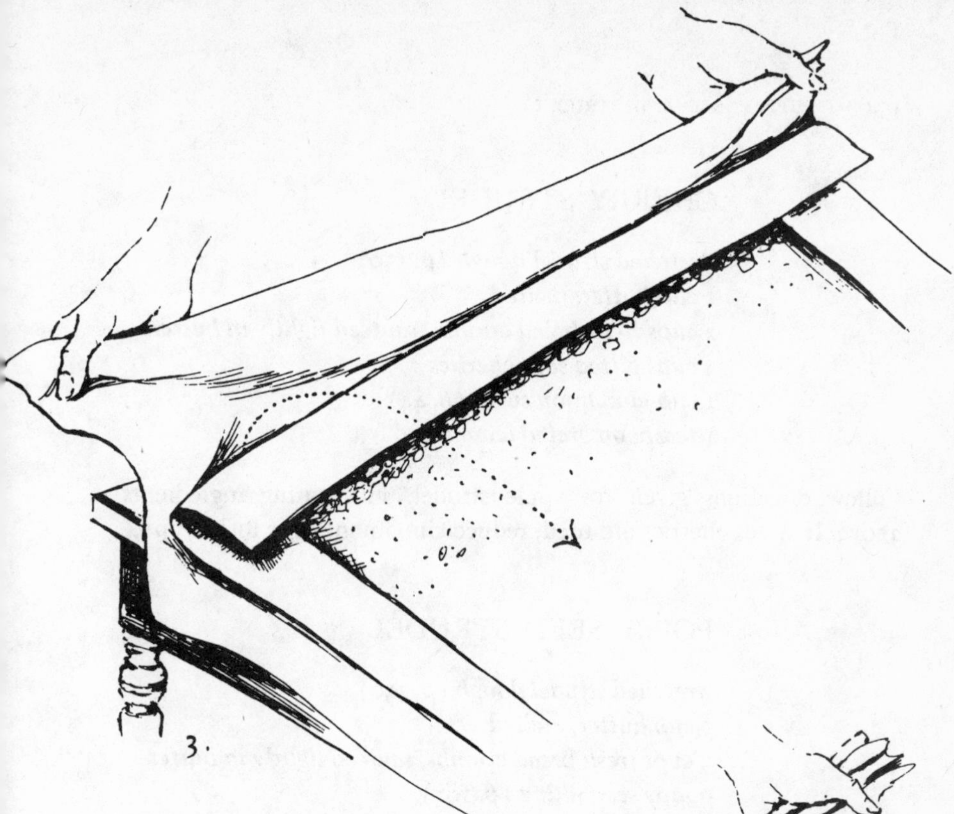

4

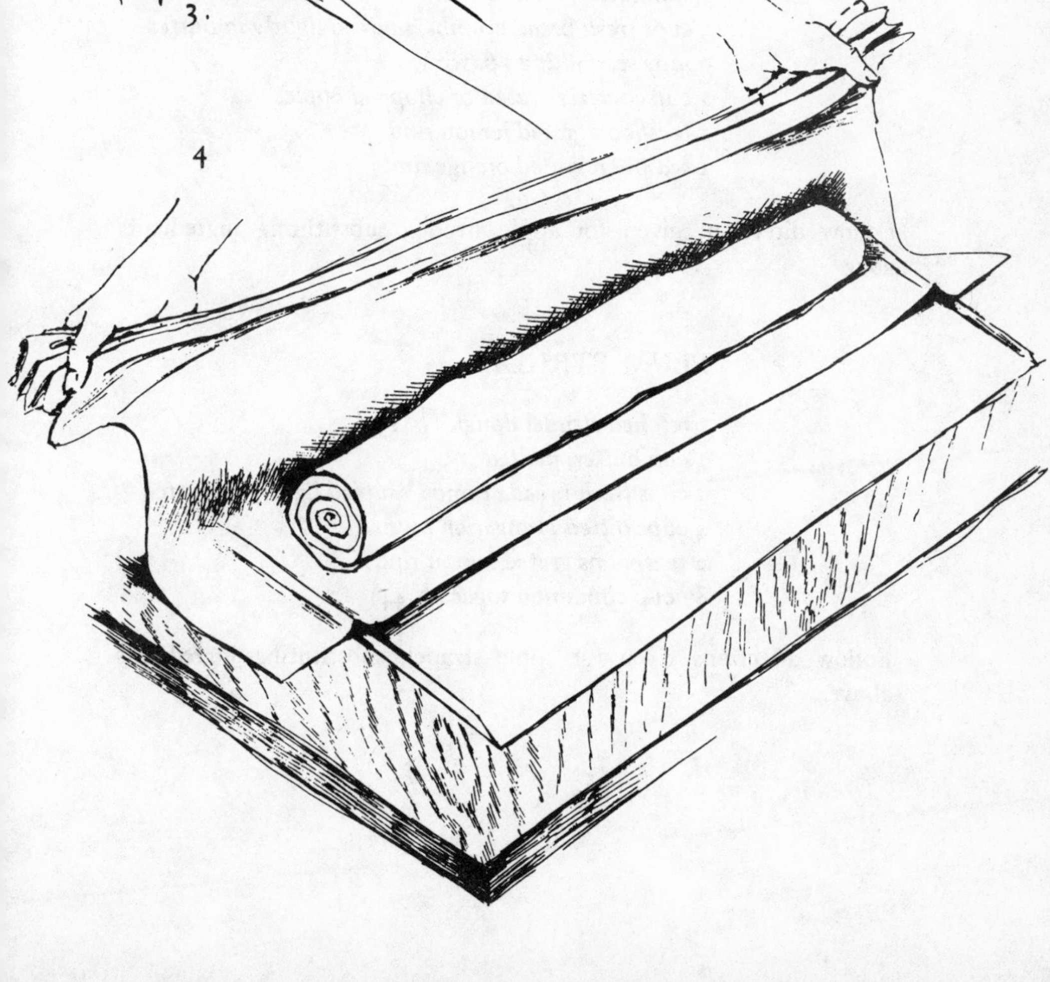

CHERRY STRUDEL

stretched strudel dough (p. 150)
1 *cup butter, melted*
2 *cups fresh bread crumbs, sautéed lightly in butter*
4 *cups pitted sour cherries*
1 *cup cinnamon sugar (p. 44)*
1 *teaspoon grated lemon rind*

Follow directions given for apple strudel, substituting ingredients above. If sweet cherries are used, reduce cinnamon sugar to ¼ cup.

POPPY SEED STRUDEL

stretched strudel dough (p. 150)
1 *cup butter, melted*
2 *cups fresh bread crumbs, sautéed lightly in butter*
poppy seed filling (p. 102)
1 *cup coarsely grated or chopped apples*
1 *teaspoon grated lemon rind*
1 *teaspoon grated orange rind*

Follow directions given for apple strudel, substituting ingredients above.

PLUM STRUDEL

stretched strudel dough (p. 150)
1 *cup butter, melted*
2 *cups fresh bread crumbs, sautéed lightly in butter*
4 *cups pitted Hungarian plums*
2 *teaspoons grated lemon rind*
⅔ *cup cinnamon sugar (p. 44)*

Follow directions given for apple strudel, substituting ingredients above.

CHEESE STRUDEL

stretched strudel dough (*p.* 150)
1 *cup butter, melted*
2 *cups fresh bread crumbs, sautéed lightly in butter*

FILLING

½ *pound cream cheese*
½ *pound large-curd, dry pot cheese*
½ *cup sugar*
2 *egg yolks*
¼ *cup heavy cream*
½ *teaspoon grated lemon rind*
1 *teaspoon vanilla*
½ *cup golden sultana raisins*

Cream all ingredients together until well blended.

Follow directions given for apple strudel, substituting cheese filling given above.

WALNUT AND RAISIN STRUDEL

stretched strudel dough (*p.* 150)
1 *cup butter, melted*
2 *cups fresh bread crumbs, sautéed lightly in butter*
1 *cup apricot or raspberry jam, warmed*
2 ½ *cups coarsely crushed walnuts*
1 ½ *cups sultana raisins*
½ *cup candied orange peel*
3 *tablespoons cinnamon sugar* (*p.* 44)

Brush stretched strudel dough with melted butter, then with warmed jam. Scatter bread crumbs evenly on top. Then sprinkle with crushed walnuts, raisins, candied orange rind, and cinnamon sugar. Filling should be spread over entire sheet of dough.

Roll up and bake strudel, following directions given for apple strudel.

Chapter 6

Gâteaux and Torten

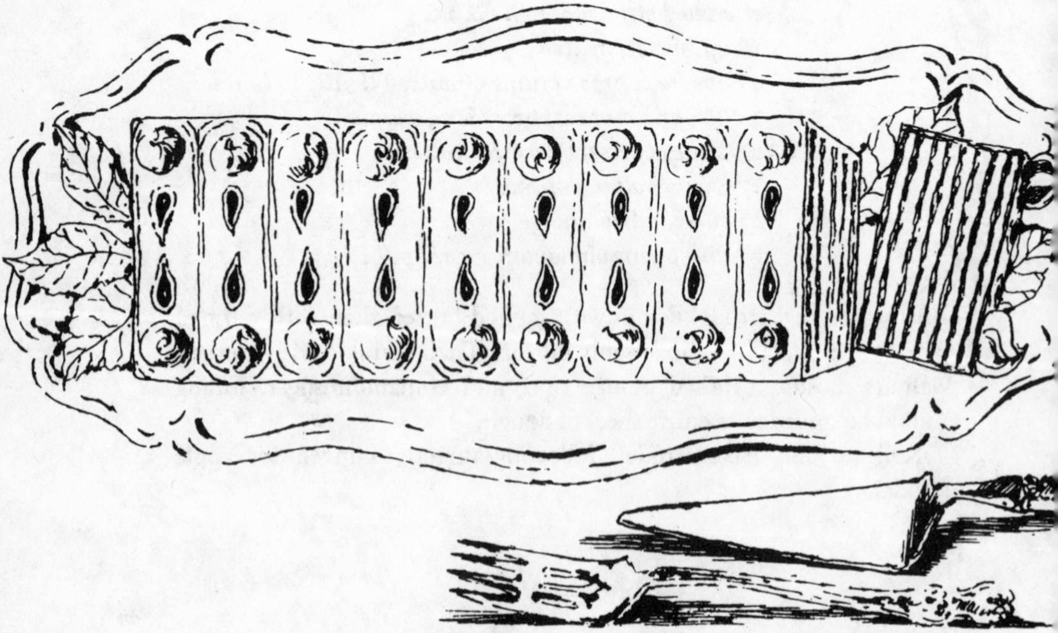

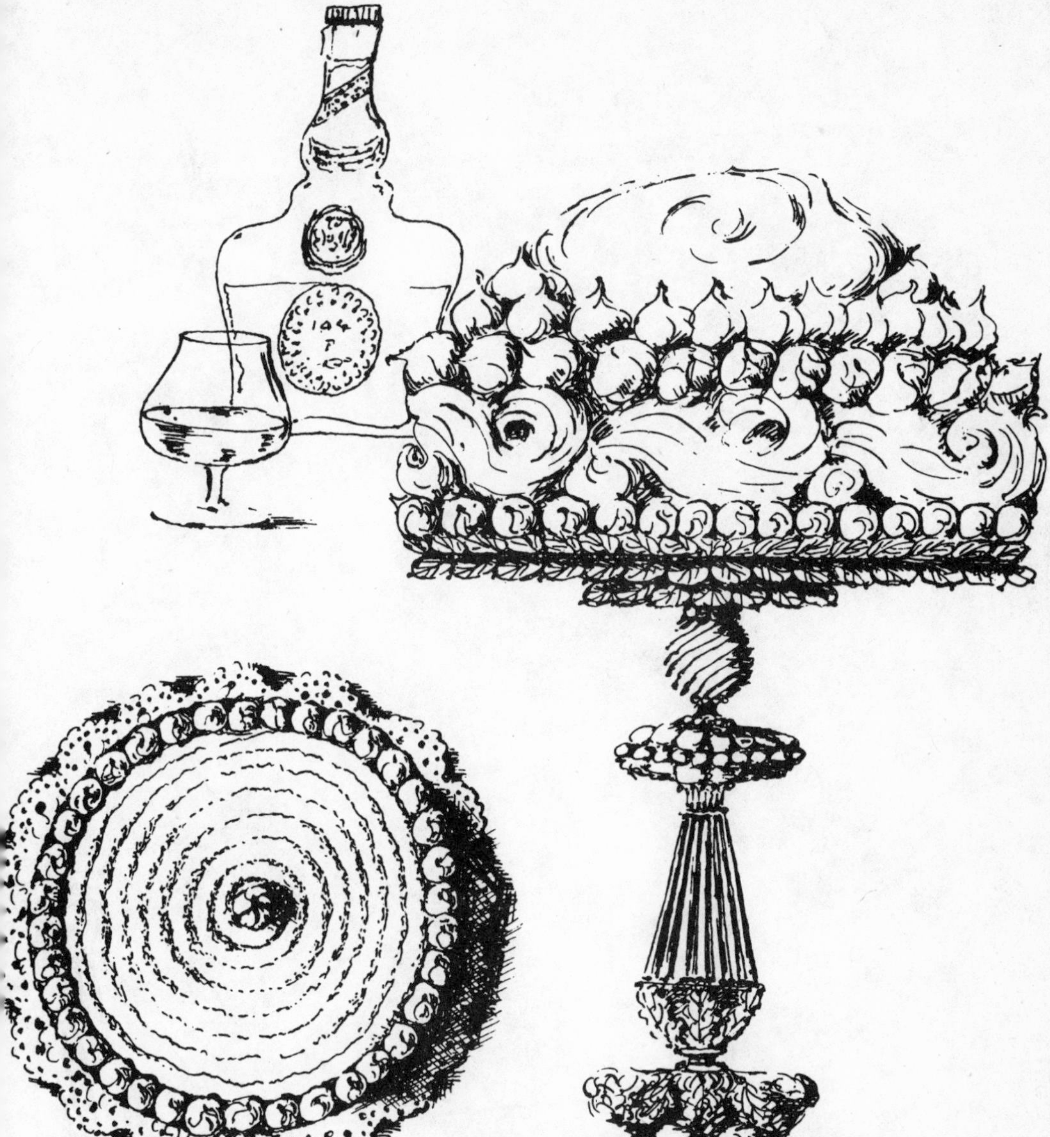

Gâteaux and Torten

These large, beautiful cakes, rich with butter creams, icings, and liqueurs, are in Paris and Brussels called *gâteaux;* in Vienna and Warsaw, *torten.*

They are truly luscious confections, scarcely everyday desserts. To make a holiday truly festive or a birthday a really special one, try one of these extra-beautiful cakes.

In making gâteaux and torten, learn to plan your work. Some of these recipes require, in addition to at least one basic cake, butter creams, preserves, and icings. It would be utter foolishness to prepare all these things on the day of a party. Butter creams can be made and refrigerated many days ahead. Some butter creams can even be frozen, and no harm is done if cake layers are baked and kept well wrapped a day or two. They can also be frozen for two months or more.

Many decorations, such as tiny balls of chocolate truffle, thin chocolate rounds, toasted almonds and filberts, can be made weeks ahead and kept refrigerated or frozen until needed.

With proper planning you can have party desserts as elaborate as gâteaux and torten always at hand.

BLACK BREAD TORTE

¼ cup rum
2 cups fresh pumpernickel crumbs
6 eggs, separated
pinch of salt
1 cup sugar
1 teaspoon vanilla
¼ cup walnuts, finely grated
¾ cup grated semisweet chocolate
1 ½ cups heavy cream, whipped, sweetened, flavored with rum (p. 93)

Set oven at 350 degrees. Grease bottom, but not the sides, of a deep, 9-inch tube pan.

Pour rum over bread crumbs. Set aside.

Beat egg whites with salt until they hold soft peaks. Add sugar, a tablespoon at a time, beating well after each addition. Beat for at least 5 minutes, or until egg whites are very firm.

Stir yolks with a fork to break them up. Add vanilla. Fold ¼ of the whites into the yolks. Pour these over remaining egg whites. Add bread crumb mixture, nuts and grated chocolate. Carefully fold all together. Pour into prepared pan.

Bake 50 to 60 minutes or until top of cake is brown and springy to the touch. Let cool in pan before removing. It will shrink quite a bit. Serve with sweetened whipped cream flavored with rum.

PARIS BREST

2 ½ recipes pâte à chou (p. 79)
1 egg mixed with
1 tablespoon cream
¾ cup blanched, sliced almonds
3 cups heavy cream, whipped, flavored with nougat powder (p. 93)
vanilla sugar (p. 45)

Set oven temperature at 375 degrees.

Lightly grease a cooky sheet. Form a 9-inch ring of pâte à chou 2 inches wide and ¾ inch high, using a spatula to shape it. Or a pastry bag can be used to form the ring. Brush all over with egg mixed with cream. Sprinkle with sliced almonds.

Bake 50 to 60 minutes, or until entire ring is well puffed and a delicate golden brown. Without removing cake from oven, stick a small sharp knife into 4 or 5 soft places in the sides. This will release the steam in the cake. Reduce oven to 325 degrees. Continue baking 10 to 15 minutes longer, or until cake seems completely crisp and dry.

Cool on a rack. Split ring in half. Pile bottom high with flavored whipped cream. Replace top. Dust with vanilla sugar before serving.

SWISS CRISPE TORTE

1 *9-inch layer almond butter cake* (*p.* 68)
¼ *cup cognac*
2 *thin 9-inch layers Swiss broyage* (*p.* 75)
1 *cup raspberry jam*
1 *cup chocolate butter cream* (*Chapter* 3)
1 ½ *cups blanched, sliced almonds, toasted*
vanilla sugar (*p.* 45)

Using fingers or spoon, sprinkle almond butter cake with cognac.

Place a layer of Swiss broyage on a plate. Spread it with ½ cup of raspberry jam. Set almond butter cake on top. Spread cake with remaining jam. Place second layer of Swiss broyage on top.

Spread sides of torte with butter cream and follow with a coating of toasted almonds. Decorate top of torte with a border of tiny chocolate butter cream rosettes. Dust with vanilla sugar before serving.

ROLLA TORTE

5 *thin 6-inch layers of Swiss broyage* (*p.* 75)
2 *cups coffee or chocolate butter cream* (*Chapter* 3)
vanilla sugar (*p.* 45)
1 ½ *cups blanched sliced toasted almonds*

Sandwich layers of Swiss broyage together with butter cream, spreading it thin. Leave top layer plain. Decorate with a lattice of vanilla sugar in the following way: Cut 4 strips of wax paper ¾ inch wide. Arrange paper strips on top layer, leaving even spaces between. Dust spaces heavily with vanilla sugar. Remove paper strips. Arrange them across top in opposite direction. Dust spaces again with sugar. Remove paper strips. Or place paper-lace doily on top layer, dust with vanilla sugar and remove doily.

Spread sides of torte with remaining butter cream and coat with toasted almonds. Refrigerate 24 hours before serving. The layers should soften slightly.

PUNCH TORTE

TORTE

old-fashioned spongecake batter (p. 69)
punch filling (p. 96)

FOR DECORATION

½ cup punch fondant icing (see Chapter 3, fondants)
1 cup punch butter cream (see Chapter 3, butter creams)

Bake old-fashioned spongecake batter in 3 thin 9-inch layers. Cool before removing from pans.

Cut out the center of 1 of the layers, leaving a ring 1 inch wide. Cut the center into small cubes. Make punch filling with cake cubes.

Spread 1 whole sponge layer thinly with raspberry jam. Place ring on top. Spoon punch filling into ring. Spread ring and filling thinly with jam. Place remaining cake layer on top. Pour warm punch fondant over top of torte.

When it has set (in 5 to 10 minutes), spread sides with punch butter cream. Refrigerate at least 6 hours before serving.

NOUGAT TORTE

2 layers nougat gênoise (p. 67)
⅔ cup hot nougat (p. 111)

2 cups nougat butter cream, flavored with rum (*see Chapter* 3)
2 cups sliced, blanched almonds, toasted

Place 1 layer gênoise on greased wax paper (this will make clean-up job easier). Pour hot nougat over top, spreading it thin with a greased spatula. Work fast, as nougat hardens rapidly. Before it has hardened, cut through nougat with an oiled knife, making serving-size wedges. This will help later in slicing the torte.

Spread remaining layer with about 1 1/3 cups of the butter cream. Place nougat-coated cake on top. Spread sides with remaining butter cream, followed by a coating of almonds.

PINEAPPLE TORTE

2 layers gênoise (*p.* 64)
3 cups heavy cream, whipped, sweetened, flavored with kirsch, gelatin added (*p.* 93)
1 cup well-drained pineapple preserves (*p.* 108)

Mince or chop 1/2 cup pineapple preserves fine. Fold into 1/4 of whipped cream. Use this pineapple-flavored whipped cream to sandwich gênoise layers.

Frost top and sides with remaining whipped cream, reserving enough to press through a large star tube to decorate torte. Arrange remaining pineapple around top edge of torte.

FROZEN STRAWBERRY CREAM TORTE

Swiss meringue (*p.* 73)
1/2 cup blanched, sliced almonds
2 1/2 cups heavy cream, whipped, unsweetened, gelatin added, flavored with rum (*p.* 93)
1 cup fresh strawberries, sliced and sweetened

Set oven at 250 degrees. Grease and flour 2 large baking sheets. Trace 4 circles in flour, each 6 inches in diameter.

Spread thin layer of Swiss meringue within each circle. Sprinkle 1 layer with sliced almonds.

Bake meringue layers in a 200 degree oven 30 to 40 minutes, or as slowly as possible, until they are completely crisp and dry, but still white.

Combine about 2 ⅓ cups of whipped cream with sweetened berries that have first been well drained, folding carefully together.

Working as quickly as possible to prevent meringue from softening, sandwich layers with whipped cream mixture. Place the almond-studded layer on top. Place in the freezer for 2 or 3 hours, or until cake is frozen.

Spread most of remaining whipped cream around sides. With a star tube, make a border of rosettes around top of torte with the last of the whipped cream.

Place again in freezer. When sides and border are frozen, the torte can be wrapped for freezer storage and kept up to 6 weeks. Serve frozen.

LINZER TORTE

This traditional Viennese cake looks more like a tart than a torte.

1 *cup unblanched almonds*
1 ¼ *cups sifted flour*
1 *cup soft butter*
2 *hard-cooked egg yolks, mashed*
2 *raw egg yolks*
½ *cup sugar*
2 *tablespoons dark, unsweetened cocoa*
⅛ *teaspoon ground cloves*
¼ *teaspoon cinnamon*
1 *teaspoon vanilla*
1 *teaspoon grated lemon rind*
1 *egg, beaten with*
2 *teaspoons light cream*
1 ½ *cups thick raspberry jam*

Set oven at 350 degrees. Lightly grease a cooky sheet.

Grate almonds fine. Mix flour and grated almonds together in a bowl. Make a well in the center. In well, place butter, mashed hard-cooked egg yolks, raw yolks, sugar, cocoa, spices, vanilla, and lemon rind. Combine these ingredients into a paste, gradually incorporating the flour and almonds to make a dough. If dough is very soft, chill it slightly.

Roll ½ the chilled dough between sheets of wax paper to a thickness of ½ inch (see p. 234). Using a plate or pan as a pattern, cut out a round of dough 6 inches in diameter. Place on prepared cooky sheet. Brush lightly with egg mixed with cream.

Roll out remaining half of dough into a rectangle ¼ inch thick between sheets of wax paper. Cut into strips ¼ inch wide. Make a border on circle with some of the strips, pressing to make certain they are set on firmly. Brush with egg.

Fill shell with 1 cup raspberry jam. Using most of remaining strips, make a lattice across top of the torte. The ends of each strip should rest on the border. Brush ends of strips with egg. Make a second border on top of first, using last of strips. Press down firmly with the tines of a fork. Chill torte (or you can freeze it for baking later).

Set oven at 350 degrees. Brush lattice and border with egg. Bake 40 to 50 minutes or until torte is lightly browned. Jam will have darkened in baking. While torte is still hot, use remaining jam for color to fill in between lattice strips.

DOBOSH TORTE

Real dobosh torte layers are crisp and should keep some of their crispness even after standing in the refrigerator several days.

basic sponge sheet batter (p. 72)
¾ cup sugar
1 teaspoon lemon juice
2 ½ cups chocolate butter cream (see Chapter 3)

Set oven at 350 degrees. Grease 2 large flat pans 11 x 16. Line with wax paper. Grease and lightly flour wax paper.

Divide batter between the 2 baking pans, spreading it thinly and evenly. Batter should be no more than ¼ inch deep in each pan. Bake 10 to 15 minutes or until cakes are golden brown.

Remove cakes from pans immediately. Strip off wax paper. Return to hot pans to prevent cakes from becoming crisp too fast. Before they are crisp, cut into strips 4 x 11. Two pans will make 8 layers. If cakes become crisp before all strips are cut, you may finish cutting with serrated knife, although this is a little more difficult. Remove layers from pan. If after cooling, layers still are not crisp, return them to a 300 degree oven to dry out. If they break, piece them together again.

Sandwich 7 layers together with 1 ½ cups chocolate butter cream. Place in refrigerator, keeping 8th layer separate.

Melt ¾ cup sugar with 1 teaspoon lemon juice in heavy skillet, stirring constantly until sugar is liquid and golden brown. Be careful not to let it burn. Place 8th layer on greased wax paper to make clean-up job easier. Pour caramelized sugar over top of cake, spreading it quickly before caramel hardens. With a greased knife, cut crosswise through the caramel at 1-inch intervals so cake can be sliced when caramel has set. As soon as it is completely cool, set the caramel-coated top layer on the torte. Trim sides to make them even.

Cover sides with remaining butter cream. Make some small butter cream rosettes around top. Refrigerate at least 12 hours before serving.

FILBERT TORTE

Pecans or walnuts may be substituted.

8 *egg whites*
pinch of salt
1 *cup sugar*
12 *egg yolks*
1 *teaspoon vanilla*
2 *cups filberts*
4 *tablespoons cognac*

FOR DECORATION

2 *cups coffee butter cream (see Chapter* 3)
1 *cup coffee fondant (see Chapter* 3)
12 *whole filberts, blanched and toasted*

Set oven at 350 degrees. Grease the bottoms of two 9-inch layer pans. Line with wax paper and grease again.

Grate filberts fine. Beat egg whites with salt until they hold soft peaks. Gradually add sugar, a tablespoon at a time, beating after each addition. Continue beating 5 more minutes, or until very stiff. Stir egg yolks with a fork to break them. Add vanilla. Fold ¼ of the egg whites into yolks. Pour mixture over remaining stiffly beaten egg whites, sprinkling grated filberts on top at the same time. Fold all together only until there are no lumps of egg white showing. Pour into prepared pans.

Bake 30 to 40 minutes, or until cake tops are springy to the touch. Let cakes cool before loosening sides and removing from pans. Sprinkle each layer with 2 tablespoons cognac. Sandwich layers with ¾ cup coffee butter cream, leaving top plain. Pour coffee fondant over top. When it has cooled and set, spread remaining butter cream over sides. Garnish top with a border of whole toasted filberts.

REGENT

gênoise cake batter (p. 64)
1 ½ *cups marron butter cream (see Chapter 3)*
1 ¼ *cups very thick, hot apricot glaze (p. 92)*

FOR DECORATION

candied orange peel
angelica
whole blanched almonds
2 ½ *cups rum fondant (see Chapter 3, fondants)*

Bake gênoise batter in three 9-inch tins, making 3 thin layers.

Sandwich layers together with marron butter cream, leaving top plain. Cover top and sides of cake with a thin coat of hot apricot glaze. Decorate top with the almonds and candied fruit, setting fruit into glaze before it has cooled. For example, a large piece of orange peel can be cut into petals and the green angelica into a stem, to make a daisy. Arrange almonds around the top as a border. Place cake on a rack.

Heat fondant slightly warmer than usual (to give it a translucent quality). Pour onto center of cake. It will spread over the daisy and run down the sides of the cake. Use a spatula to help it cover sides. Be sure there are no bare spots. Excess icing will drip under rack.

TOASTED ALMOND TORTE

1 cup blanched toasted almonds
6 eggs, separated
pinch of salt
1 cup sugar
1 teaspoon grated lemon rind
2 tablespoons lemon juice
½ teaspoon vanilla
½ teaspoon almond extract
½ teaspoon cinnamon
½ cup fine dry bread crumbs

FOR DECORATION

1 cup lemon butter cream (see Chapter 3, butter creams)
2 cups white lemon fondant (see Chapter 3, fondants)
12 whole blanched almonds, toasted

Set oven at 350 degrees. Grease the bottoms, but not the sides, of two 9-inch layer pans. Line bottoms with wax paper and grease again. Grate toasted almonds finely.

Add salt to egg whites and beat until whites hold soft peaks. Gradually add sugar, a tablespoon at a time, beating after each addition. Beat 5 minutes longer or until very stiff.

Break up egg yolks with a fork and stir in lemon rind, lemon juice, vanilla, almond extract, and cinnamon. Fold ¼ of the beaten egg whites into yolks. Pour mixture back over egg whites. Sprinkle grated almonds and bread crumbs on top. Fold all together.

When no more egg white shows, pour batter into prepared pans. Bake 30 to 40 minutes, or until tops of cakes are springy to the touch.

Let cool before removing from pans. Sandwich cakes with lemon butter cream. Pour lemon fondant over top and sides of cake. Arrange a border of whole blanched, toasted almonds around top.

CHEESE CAKE PUFF

1 recipe pâte à chou (p. 79)
cheese filling (p. 103)
1 tart apple, peeled, cored, and sliced thin
2 tablespoons cinnamon sugar (p. 44)
1 egg yolk mixed with
1 teaspoon cream
¼ cup sliced blanched almonds
vanilla sugar (p. 45)

Set oven at 375 degrees. Lightly grease and flour a baking sheet. Trace a 7-inch circle in flour on baking sheet, using a plate or pan for a pattern.

Spread a thin layer of pâte à chou about ¼ inch thick within the circle. Place remaining pâte à chou in a pastry bag fitted with a plain round No. 6 tube. Squeeze out small mounds of paste, one right next to the other, to make a low border around layer.

Pour cheese filling into center of shell. Spread evenly. Arrange sliced apples on top. Sprinkle with cinnamon sugar. Brush border with egg-yolk mixture. Sprinkle with almonds.

Bake in preheated oven 50 to 60 minutes, or until entire pastry is golden brown. Dust with vanilla sugar before serving.

ALMOND CREAM PUFF

pâte à chou (p. 79)
almond cream filling (p. 104)

Follow recipe for making cheese cake puff, substituting almond cream filling for cheese filling.

MANON

1 recipe savarin dough (p. 80)
⅔ cup (approximately) kirsch or any fruit-flavored liqueur
1 cup chocolate pastry cream (p. 96)
1 cup vanilla pastry cream (p. 95)
2 cups apricot glaze (p. 92)
2 cups blanched, sliced almonds, toasted
vanilla sugar (p. 45)

Bake savarin dough in a well-greased 1-quart mold. Use a round charlotte tin or a deep metal bowl.

When cake has cooled, cut it into 5 thin layers. Brush both sides of each layer with kirsch. (Kirsch may be diluted slightly with water if desired.)

Sandwich cake together, using alternating layers of vanilla pastry cream and chocolate pastry cream. Brush cake all over with hot apricot glaze. Cover glaze with sliced almonds. Before serving, dust with vanilla sugar.

WALNUT TORTE

Black walnuts are a delicious substitute for English walnuts in this recipe.

2 layers walnut gênoise (p. 67)
1 ½ cups apricot glaze (p. 92)
2 cups walnut rum butter cream (see Chapter 3)
1 cup white rum fondant (see Chapter 3)
some whole walnut halves

Spread both layers walnut gênoise thinly with apricot glaze. Sandwich them together, using ⅔ cup butter cream.

Spread top with remaining apricot glaze. Pour warm rum fondant over, covering top only.

When icing has set, spread sides with remaining butter cream. Make a border around top of torte with pieces of walnut.

CHOCOLATE VELVET

1 *basic sponge sheet* 11 x 16 (*p.* 72)
1 ½ *pounds semisweet chocolate*
3 *egg yolks*
½ *cup strong coffee*
½ *cup Grand Marnier*
6 *egg whites*
pinch of salt
¼ *cup sugar*
1 *cup heavy cream, whipped*

FOR DECORATION

2 *cups heavy cream, whipped, unsweetened, flavored with Grand Marnier, gelatin added* (*p.* 93)
1 *crystallized violet*

Completely line a round 1-quart mold with basic sponge sheet by cutting out a round to fit the bottom of mold; then, from remaining cake, cut out one long or two short strips to cover the sides. Reserve any sponge sheet left to make into a top later on.

Melt chocolate. Add egg yolks, coffee, and Grand Marnier. Stir all together until smooth.

Beat egg whites with salt until they hold soft peaks. Add sugar, a tablespoon at a time, beating well after each addition. Continue beating 5 more minutes, or until very stiff.

Fold unsweetened whipped cream and very stiffly beaten egg whites together. Pour chocolate mixture over top. Fold in gently but thoroughly.

Pour into sponge-lined mold. Place in refrigerator for 2 hours or until filling is firm. Cover top with remaining sponge sheet, fitting together any bits and pieces if there isn't a single piece large enough. Loosen sides of mold with a sharp knife. Turn out upside down on a plate. Frost all over with whipped cream, reserving some for decorating top. Place reserved whipped cream in a pastry bag fitted with medium star tube No. 4. Press tiny rosettes all over top of cake, very close together. Place a crystallized violet in the center.

Chill if not to be served immediately. Chocolate velvet may be frozen (before frosting and decorating), if necessary.

ORANGE TUBE TORTE

old-fashioned spongecake batter (p. 69)
2 tablespoons orange juice
1 teaspoon grated orange rind
⅔ cup orange butter cream, flavored with Grand Marnier (see Chapter 3, butter creams)
½ cup orange fondant, flavored with Grand Marnier (see Chapter 3, fondants)
⅔ cup coarsely crushed pecans

Follow directions for making old-fashioned spongecake, adding orange juice and grated orange rind to egg yolks.

After cake is cool, remove from pan. Slice in half to make two layers. Sandwich together with orange butter cream.

Pour warm orange fondant over top only, allowing a little to drip down over sides. Before glaze has dried, scatter crushed pecans on top.

CHEESE CAKE

1 package zwieback, made into crumbs
1 cup finely grated walnuts or pecans
⅓ cup butter, melted
1 cup sugar
1 ¼ pounds soft cream cheese
¼ teaspoon salt
1 ½ teaspoons vanilla
1 teaspoon grated lemon rind
4 eggs, separated
1 cup heavy cream, whipped
½ cup sifted flour
vanilla sugar (p. 45)

Set oven temperature at 325 degrees. Lightly grease bottom and sides of a 9-inch spring-form pan. Combine zwieback crumbs, grated nuts, melted butter, and 2 tablespoons sugar. Mix together with finger tips until ingredients are blended. Spread crumb mixture on bottom of spring-form pan. Press down firmly.

Mix cream cheese with half of remaining sugar, salt, vanilla, and grated lemon rind. Beat in egg yolks.

Beat egg whites until they hold soft peaks. Add remaining sugar a tablespoon at a time, beating well after each addition. Beat until very firm. Pour whipped cream on top of stiffly beaten whites. Add cream cheese mixture. Sprinkle flour on top. Fold all together gently.

Pour into prepared pan. Bake for 1 hour and 15 minutes. Do not open oven door until a full hour of the baking time has elapsed. When cake is a light golden brown, turn off oven heat. Let stand in oven 3 or 4 hours. Cake may crack slightly, but this is unimportant. Chill cake before serving. Dust with vanilla sugar. Cheese cake can be kept frozen for 4 to 6 weeks after baking.

MOCHA TORTE

2 thin 9-inch layers chocolate gênoise (p. 67)
¼ cup cognac
⅔ cup apricot jam
1 ½ cups mocha butter cream (see Chapter 3, butter creams)
16 thin 2-inch chocolate rounds (p. 110)

Sprinkle layers with cognac. Sandwich them together with apricot jam. Spread sides and top smoothly with butter cream, reserving some for decoration.

Arrange chocolate rounds next to each other flat against side of torte. Save 3 chocolate rounds to cut into quarters. Set quarters flat in the butter cream around the top of the cake. Decorate torte with remaining butter cream pressed through a medium star tube.

TRUFFLE CAKE

2 9-inch layers chocolate gênoise (p. 67)
4 tablespoons rum
1 cup apricot jam
2 cups chocolate butter cream (see Chapter 3)
bitter chocolate glaze (p. 93)
1 cup chocolate broyage crumbs (p. 110)
or grated semisweet chocolate
12 small chocolate truffles (p. 110)

Sprinkle chocolate gênoise layers with rum. Spread both with apricot jam and cover 1 layer with ¾ cup chocolate butter cream. Place the other layer on top with apricot jam facing down. Chill cake.

Pour bitter chocolate glaze over top of cake. When glaze has cooled and set, spread sides smoothly with remaining butter cream and coat them with chocolate broyage crumbs or grated chocolate. Make a border of chocolate truffles around top of cake.

VACHERIN SHELL

2 recipes Swiss meringue (p. 73)
2 cups sweetened berries or sliced peaches
2 cups heavy cream, whipped, unsweetened (p. 93)

Set oven temperature as low as possible. Grease and flour 2 large cooky sheets. Trace 5 circles in flour, each 7 inches in diameter.

Spread meringue within 1 of the circles, making a layer ¼ inch thick.

Fit a pastry bag with a large round No. 8 tube. Fill bag with meringue. Pipe a meringue ring around each of the remaining circles, making certain the meringue rests exactly within the traced circle. You will have one layer and four rings.

On another part of the cooky sheet, form about sixteen 1-inch balls (or rosettes) of meringue. Reserve about ¼ of meringue mixture.

Bake circles and rosettes as slowly as possible, in a 200 degree oven about 40 minutes, or until they are firm and almost entirely dry. Cool. Loosen from baking sheets. Spread a little unbaked meringue around edge of solid layer. Set 1 of the rings on top. Spread it lightly with a little more meringue. Add another ring. Continue until all the rings are used.

If the remaining unbaked meringue now seems loose, beat it until it stiffens. Coat the outside of the vacherin so the rings are concealed, reserving a teaspoon of meringue mixture for use later.

Place in a very slow oven and bake until shell is totally dry, though still white. Remove from oven but leave oven on. Arrange most of the little balls or rosettes around top of shell, using final bit of uncooked meringue to hold them in place. Now turn oven heat off and leave vacherin in oven several hours, even overnight if possible.

Just before serving, fold whipped cream and sweetened fruit together. Fill shell. Decorate top of cream with remaining meringue balls. Serve immediately.

LEMON TORTE

2 *9-inch layers Swiss broyage (p. 75)*
2 *9-inch layers lemon gênoise (p. 66)*
2 *cups lemon cream or lemon butter cream (see Chapter 3)*
vanilla sugar (p. 45)

Sandwich 1 layer of Swiss broyage between 2 lemon gênoise layers, using 1 cup of lemon filling. Leave top plain. Spread remaining filling around sides of cake.

Crush second layer of Swiss broyage to make fine crumbs, or grind in blender. Coat sides of cake heavily with crumbs. Dust top with vanilla sugar just before serving.

MAESTRO GÂTEAU

½ *basic sponge sheet, 5 ½ x 16 (p. 72)*
1 ½ *cups apricot jam*
1 *9-inch layer filbert gênoise (p. 66)*
3 *tablespoons rum*
2 *cups rum butter cream (see Chapter 3)*
1 ½ *cups sliced toasted filberts*

Spread sponge thinly with ½ cup apricot jam. Roll up tightly to make a long, thin jelly roll. Sprinkle filbert gênoise with rum. Spread top with ¾ cup butter cream. Cut jelly roll into ½-inch slices and place them flat to cover entire top of gênoise.

Heat remaining apricot jam to make a glaze. Pour and spread over jelly-roll slices. When glaze has set, spread sides of cake with remaining butter cream, and coat with sliced filberts.

CHOCOLATE RING

6 eggs
⅔ cup sugar
1 teaspoon vanilla
1 cup ground almonds
7 tablespoons dark, unsweetened cocoa
⅓ cup butter, melted and cooled to lukewarm
4 tablespoons cognac
2 cups heavy cream, whipped, sweetened, flavored with cocoa and vanilla (p. 93)

Set oven at 350 degrees. Grease the bottom, but not the sides, of a deep 9-inch tube pan. In a large bowl, stir eggs and sugar together for 1 minute. Set bowl on a saucepan of warm water and heat. (See directions for gênoise, p. 64.) When eggs are warm, beat them until they are cool, fluffy, and tripled in bulk. Beat in vanilla.

Combine ground nuts with cocoa. Sprinkle on top of beaten eggs. Fold in gently, adding the cooled melted butter at the same time. As soon as there is no further trace of butter, pour batter into prepared pan.

Bake 50 to 60 minutes or until top of cake is springy. Let ring cool before removing it from the pan. Sprinkle with cognac. Frost with chocolate whipped cream.

IMPERIAL

2 9-inch layers walnut gênoise (p. 67)
1 cup walnut rum butter cream (see Chapter 3)
1 9-inch layer chocolate gênoise (p. 67)
4 tablespoons rum

FOR DECORATION

1 cup rum fondant (see Chapter 3)
1 cup chocolate butter cream (see Chapter 3)
12 walnut halves

Spread 1 layer of walnut gênoise thinly with ½ cup walnut rum butter cream. Sprinkle chocolate gênoise with rum and place on top of frosted walnut gênoise. Spread with remaining walnut rum butter cream and cover with second walnut gênoise layer.

Warm fondant. Pour over top of cake. Spread chocolate butter cream smoothly around sides. Arrange walnut halves around top.

CHOCOLATE ROLL

chocolate pastry (*pp.* 77-78)
1 *cup heavy cream, whipped, unsweetened, flavored with cognac* (*p.* 93)
¾ *cup sifted cocoa* (*approximately*)

Place chocolate pastry on a sheet of wax paper large enough to extend at least 1 inch on all sides of pastry. Spread pastry with flavored, unsweetened whipped cream. Now, lifting one long side of wax paper, make pastry roll inward. Continue to lift wax paper while pastry rolls up, jelly-roll style. Roll will crack, but cracks can be covered with additional sifted cocoa before serving. Twist wax paper firmly around chocolate roll to help give it shape, and chill before serving. If you want to make a spectacular dessert for a large party, you can join two or more chocolate rolls together on a long board, decorated with green leaves or any way you like. Sift plenty of cocoa over the places where they are joined together.

Chapter 7

Petits Fours Glacés and Small Dessert Cakes

7 *Petits Fours Glacés and Small Dessert Cakes*

Homemade petits fours are a real delicacy. Any small filled, decorated cakes—tiny cream puffs, éclairs, tartlets, even very tiny babas au rhum—can be served in an assortment as petits fours glacés.

Just as some larger cakes become petits fours when made in miniature, a number of petits fours can be made a little larger and served as individual dessert pastries. A delightful tidbit may become too much of a mouthful when served in a larger size, however. Your own taste is the best guide in judging which petits fours can be adapted for this purpose most successfully.

Almost all petits fours freeze well before they are iced. If you have a freezer, you may be able to serve an assortment of fifteen or twenty different kinds, most of which have been made ahead of time, although iced on the day of serving. Not all petits fours require an icing glaze, but a traditional assortment always includes some which are glazed with fondant. This is tricky to make and use. A detailed recipe for making and using fondant can be found in Chapter 3. There you will also find a recipe for a fondant-like icing, which is much simpler. While the second recipe doesn't have the long-keeping quality of fondant, it gives fine results on pastries which will be eaten within a few days. Traditionally, petits fours are served in small, individual paper cases.

PETITS FOURS GLACÉS
(Basic Recipe)

almond butter cake (p. 68) or gênoise for petits fours (p. 67), baked in an 11 x 16 jelly-roll pan
1 cup apricot jam, raspberry jam or butter cream (see Chapter 3)
1 cup apricot glaze (p. 92)
3 cups fondant or mock fondant (see Chapter 3)
2 teaspoons vanilla or any liqueur
1 tablespoon strong coffee (approximately)
2 ounces unsweetened chocolate, melted

To make the little iced geometric cakes most people think of as petits fours, bake a sheet of almond butter cake or gênoise for petits fours in an 11 x 16 jelly-roll pan. The baked sheets of cake should not be more than ¾ inch high. If possible, bake the cake a day ahead so it can be cut more easily.

Cut the cake in half, making 2 layers, each 8 x 11. Spread 1 layer with a thin layer of apricot or raspberry jam. (If desired, any butter cream may be substituted for jam.) Place second layer on top of first. If butter cream is used, chill cake slightly.

Brush top with hot apricot glaze. Trim off all crisp edges. Allow glaze to dry for a few minutes. Then, using a long knife with a serrated edge, cut cake into even 1-inch shapes: cubes, rectangles, triangles, etc. A ruler may be used for making cakes of equal size. Rounds can be cut with a cooky cutter, although there is much waste. Wipe knife edge off with a damp sponge after each slice.

Place ⅓ of the little cakes on a cake rack, leaving some space between them. Set rack in a shallow pan.

Warm the fondant or mock fondant. Flavor it with vanilla or a liqueur. When lukewarm, spoon or pour plenty of icing in the center of each cake so that it will run down and coat sides. Excess will drip into pan under rack.

Scrape up drippings and return them to pan of vanilla fondant. Add coffee to flavor fondant. Reheat what is now coffee fondant to lukewarm. If necessary, thin it with a little syrup or water.

Arrange another third of the cakes on a second cake rack. Place rack in shallow pan. Cover tops and sides of the little cakes with coffee fondant. Scrape icing up and return it to pan.

Flavor remaining coffee fondant with chocolate. The chocolate flavor and color will now dominate. Place remaining cakes on a third rack and cover with chocolate fondant.

Allow all the cakes to dry about 10 minutes. Loosen from racks with a spatula. Place each in a tiny paper case and, if desired, decorate.

Simple decorations can be very beautiful: crushed bits of crystallized violets or green pistachio nuts; or prepare an additional ½ cup of fondant, coloring it as you like. It should be a little thicker than the fondant used for pouring. Fill a paper cornucopia with the colored fondant and cut a tiny hole in the pointed end. Make dots, lines, scrolls; a variety of patterns can be improvised. Each little cake needs no more than the tiniest bit of decoration.

Yield: approximately 90.

KIRSCH CUBES

1 recipe almond butter cake batter (p. 68)
3 tablespoons kirsch
¼ cup chopped liquored cherries (p. 108)
or preserved cherries, well drained
1 cup kirsch butter cream (see Chapter 3)
whole preserved or liquored cherries
2 cups white kirsch fondant (see Chapter 3)

Bake almond butter cake in an 11 x 16 jelly-roll pan. Divide cooled cake, making 2 equal layers 5 ½ x 16. Sprinkle them with kirsch.

Mix drained, chopped cherries into kirsch butter cream. Sandwich layers together with butter cream, leaving top plain. Chill until butter cream is firm.

Trim edges so cake is even. Cut into 1-inch cubes, wiping off knife after each slice. Put a whole liquored or preserved cherry in center of each cube.

Place squares on a cake rack. Cover tops and sides thinly with kirsch fondant after heating the fondant until it is a little warmer than usual. It will then be translucent and the cherry will show through.

Yield: approximately 90.

MONETTES

1 recipe chocolate pastry (pp. 77-78) baked in 11 x 16 jelly-roll pan
½ basic sponge sheet 5 ½ x 16 (p. 72)
1 cup bourbon-flavored butter cream (see Chapter 3)
dark, unsweetened cocoa

Divide chocolate pastry in half, making 2 equal layers 5 ½ x 16. Sandwich sponge-sheet layer between chocolate layers, icing the 2 lower layers with bourbon butter cream. Leave top plain. Chill until butter cream is firm.

Dust top generously with cocoa. Trim edges. Divide cake into 4 equal strips. Cut strips into small triangles, wiping knife off after each slice.

Yield: approximately 85.

HEAVENLY CHOCOLATE CUBES

1 recipe chocolate pastry (pp. 77-78) baked in an 11 x 16 jelly-roll pan
2 cups mocha butter cream flavored with cognac (see Chapter 3)
dark, unsweetened cocoa

Divide chocolate pastry in half to make 2 equal layers 8 x 11. Spread 1 layer with butter cream, ¾ inch thick. Carefully place remaining layer on top. Chill until butter cream is very firm.

Dust top heavily with cocoa. Cut cake into 1-inch cubes, wiping knife off after each slice. Dip sides of each square into cocoa, coating them well.

Yield: approximately 90.

NOUGAT TRIANGLES

½ recipe filbert gênoise (p. 67) baked in an 11 x 16 jelly-roll pan
3 tablespoons rum
1 ¼ cups nougat butter cream (see Chapter 3)
crushed nougat or nougat triangles (p. 111)

Cut filbert gênoise into 3 equal strips 16 inches long. Sprinkle each lightly with rum. Sandwich them together with nougat butter cream, covering top smoothly. Chill until butter cream is firm.

Divide sandwiched cake equally in half, making 2 thin strips. Cut each strip into small triangles, wiping off the knife with a damp sponge after each slice. Sprinkle top of each triangle with a little crushed nougat or place a small nougat triangle flat in the center of each cake.

Yield: approximately 32.

ORANGE SLICES

1 recipe basic sponge sheet (p. 72), baked in an 11 x 16 jelly-roll pan
1 ½ cups orange marmalade
2 cups orange butter cream, flavored with Grand Marnier (see Chapter 3)
blanched almonds, halved and toasted

Divide sponge sheet equally into 4 strips 16 inches long. Sandwich strips together with orange marmalade, leaving top and sides plain. Trim edges if they are uneven. Frost top and long sides with butter cream, reserving some.

Chill until butter cream is firm. Cut each strip into ¾-inch slices, wiping knife off after each slice. Decorate top of each slice with a border of small butter cream rosettes, made with a No. 2 b tube. Place a toasted almond half in center of each slice.

Yield: approximately 20.

CHESTNUT PEAKS

½ recipe almond short pastry (p. 231)
double recipe marron butter cream (see Chapter 3)
2 cups white rum fondant (see Chapter 3)
crystallized violets, crushed

Roll out almond short pastry ¼ inch thick. Cut into rounds 1 inch in diameter. Scraps may be re-rolled. Bake on a lightly greased cooky sheet in a 350 degree oven about 8 minutes or until lightly browned.

Fit a large pastry bag with a plain round No. 3 tube. Fill bag with marron butter cream. Press cream out on each cooky, spiraling it around and around to form a tall peak. Or hand-mold peaks by using 1 tablespoon marron cream for each cake. Dip hands into confectioners' sugar to prevent cream from sticking to them. Chill peaks.

Arrange chestnut peaks on cake rack. Pour or spoon rum fondant which is *barely* warm over each one, covering it entirely. Press a bit of violet into the top of each cake.
Yield: approximately 24.

VIENNESE BALLS

basic sponge sheet batter (p. 72)
¼ cup cognac
¾ cup apricot jam
1 ½ cups heavy cream, whipped, unsweetened, flavored with cognac (p. 93)
creamy chocolate glaze (p. 92)
liquored cherries (p. 108)

Set oven at 400 degrees. Fit a large pastry bag with a large, round No. 7 tube. Fill bag with basic sponge sheet batter. Press rounds of batter 1 ¼ inches in diameter on a well-greased baking sheet, making rounds high. The rounds may also be shaped with 2 spoons in the manner of drop cookies. Bake in preheated oven about 12 minutes or until cakes are lightly browned.

When cakes have cooled, cut out some of the soft inside from the flat bottom of each one, leaving a ¼-inch shell. Brush inside of shells with cognac, then with apricot jam. Fill shells with whipped cream. Put cakes together in pairs to form balls. Chill well, or even freeze the filled cakes for at least 1 hour.

Arrange cakes on rack. Spoon or pour cooled, creamy chocolate glaze over each one, covering sides as well as tops. Garnish each with a liquored cherry.
Yield: approximately 12.

COFFEE CREAM BALLS

basic sponge sheet batter (p. 72)
¾ cup apricot jam
1 ½ cups heavy cream, whipped, sweetened, flavored with coffee and cognac (p. 93)
2 cups coffee fondant or mock fondant (see Chapter 3)
walnut halves

Follow recipe for Viennese balls (p. 188). Fill centers with sweetened coffee-flavored whipped cream. Glaze tops and sides with coffee fondant. Garnish each cake with a walnut half.
Yield: approximately 12.

CHOCOLATE CREAM BALLS

basic sponge sheet batter (p. 72)
¾ cup apricot jam
1 ½ cups heavy cream, whipped, sweetened, flavored with cocoa and cognac (p. 93)
creamy chocolate glaze (p. 92)
crystallized violets

Follow recipe for Viennese balls (p. 188). Fill centers with whipped cream. Glaze tops and sides with creamy chocolate glaze. Decorate each with a crystallized violet.
Yield: approximately 12.

PUNCH BALLS

basic sponge sheet batter (p. 72)
¾ cup raspberry jam
punch filling (p. 96)
2 cups heavy cream, whipped, unsweetened, flavored with vanilla, gelatin added (p. 93)
¾ cup shaved chocolate

Follow recipe for Viennese balls (p. 188). Make punch filling with centers taken from cakes. Refill shells with punch filling. Frost tops and sides generously with whipped cream. Garnish with shaved chocolate.
Yield: approximately 12.

LEMON LOGS

1 *basic sponge sheet* 11 x 16 (*p.* 72)
1 ½ *cups lemon cream or lemon butter cream* (*see Chapter* 3)
1 *cup blanched, sliced almonds, toasted and crushed slightly*
vanilla sugar (*p.* 45)

Cut sponge roll in half to make 2 long rectangles. Spread each thinly with lemon filling. Roll up jelly-roll style, making 2 long, thin rolls. Trim ends. Cut into 2-inch lengths. Spread the ends of each little roll with remaining lemon filling. Dip ends into toasted almonds. Dust with vanilla sugar.
Yield: approximately 14.

PUNCH SLICES

1 *basic sponge sheet*, 11 x 16 (*p.* 72)
punch filling (*p.* 96)
3 *tablespoons rum*
1 *cup liqueur-flavored butter cream* (*see Chapter* 3) *or* ⅔ *cup raspberry jam*
1 *cup punch fondant* (*see Chapter* 3) *or creamy chocolate glaze* (*p.* 92)
sliced, toasted almonds
liquored cherries (*p.* 108)

Cut basic sponge sheet in half to make 2 rectangles 16 inches long. Prepare punch filling with 1 of these, using only enough punch to moisten cake cubes.

Sprinkle remaining half with rum and spread with punch butter cream or raspberry jam. Mold punch filling into a thin roll lengthwise along center of cake. Roll cake around filling, resting it on seam.

Pour punch fondant or creamy chocolate glaze over roll, covering top and sides. Coat sides with sliced, toasted almonds. Chill. Trim ends. Slice ¾ inch thick, wiping knife after each slice. Decorate each slice with a liquored cherry.
Yield: approximately 16.

CHOCOLATE CHESTNUT SLICES

1 basic sponge sheet 11 x 16 (p. 72)
4 tablespoons cognac
1 cup chocolate butter cream (see Chapter 3)
chestnut cream center (see below)
1 cup apricot glaze (p. 92)
1 ½ recipes bitter chocolate glaze (p. 93)
crystallized violets, crushed

CHESTNUT CREAM CENTER

1 can whole chestnuts
½ cup soft butter
¾ cup sifted confectioners' sugar
1 ounce unsweetened chocolate, melted
¼ cup cognac

Heat chestnuts in their liquid. Drain well. Mash to a fine purée. Cool. Cream chestnut purée with butter. Add confectioners' sugar, melted chocolate and cognac. Chill until firm enough to mold.

Cut sponge sheet in half lengthwise, making two rectangles 16 inches long. Sprinkle both with cognac and spread with chocolate butter cream. Shape chestnut cream into two rolls, each 16 inches long and no more than 1 inch in diameter. If cream is very soft, use wax paper to help mold it.

Place rolls of chestnut cream in center of cakes. Roll cakes around chestnut centers, turning seams to the bottom. Brush rolls with hot apricot glaze. Place them on a cake rack. Pour rich bitter-chocolate glaze over top and sides. Chill. Cut into ¾-inch slices, wiping knife after each slice. Decorate each slice with a bit of crystallized violet.
Yield: approximately 32.

Note: Marron butter cream may be substituted for chestnut cream center.

CURRANT ARKS

1 basic sponge sheet 11 x 16 (*p.* 72)
4 tablespoons cognac
⅔ cup currant jam
1 cup chocolate butter cream (*see Chapter* 3)
creamy chocolate glaze (*p.* 92)

Cut off ⅓ of baked sponge sheet crosswise. Set aside to use later. Sprinkle remaining cake with half of cognac. Spread with thin layer of currant jam. Roll cake tightly jelly-roll style. Using a knife with a serrated edge, split jelly roll in half lengthwise.

Now cut reserved sponge sheet into 2 rectangles to fit the flat sides of halved jelly rolls. Sprinkle rectangles with remaining cognac and spread a ¼-inch layer of chocolate butter cream on each. Place halved jelly rolls, flat side down, on iced rectangles. Chill until butter cream is firm.

Place cakes on racks. Coat each with creamy chocolate glaze, pouring glaze generously to cover sides as well as tops. Chill again. Cut into ½-inch slices, wiping off knife after each slice.
Yield: approximately 40.

ROLLA TORTLETS

2 recipes Swiss broyage (*p.* 75)
2 cups chocolate butter cream (*see Chapter* 3)
1 ½ cups sliced, toasted almonds, slightly crushed
vanilla sugar (*p.* 45)

Shape and bake Swiss broyage in rounds 2 inches in diameter.

Sandwich cookies together by threes, using chocolate butter cream between layers. Leave top plain. Cover sides with butter cream. Roll cakes in toasted almonds which have been slightly crushed.

Fill a pastry bag fitted with a No. 2 b tube with remaining butter cream. Make a border of tiny rosettes around top of each cake. Dust with vanilla sugar.
Yield: approximately 18.

MOCHA CRISPS

1 recipe chocolate broyage (p. 77)
2 cups mocha butter cream (see Chapter 3)
vanilla sugar (p. 45)

Using a pastry bag fitted with a large star tube, make doughnut-shaped rings of chocolate broyage 2 inches in diameter. Bake in a 325 degree oven about 20 minutes, or until crisp.

When cool, put rings together in pairs, using butter cream between. Place remaining butter cream in a pastry bag fitted with a No. 6 star tube. Press out a high rosette in center of each cake. Dust with vanilla sugar.

Yield: approximately 14.

CHOCOLATE BROYAGE BALLS

1 recipe chocolate broyage (p. 77)
1 cup apricot jam
1 ½ cups chocolate butter cream (see Chapter 3)
shaved chocolate
vanilla sugar (p. 45)

Using a pastry bag or two spoons, shape and bake even, high mounds of chocolate broyage 1 inch in diameter.

Sandwich cakes together in pairs with apricot jam to make balls. Spread chocolate butter cream all over each cake. Roll in shaved chocolate.

Before serving, dust with vanilla sugar. Make these at least 24 hours ahead to allow broyage to mellow.

Yield: approximately 14.

PUNCH PYRAMIDS

½ recipe chocolate broyage (p. 77)
1 cup raspberry jam
⅔ cup toasted, blanched filberts, coarsely crushed
punch filling (p. 96)
creamy chocolate glaze (p. 92), or 1 ½ cups chocolate fondant (see Chapter 3)
about 15 whole roasted filberts

Shape and bake round chocolate broyage cookies 1 inch in diameter. When cool, spread each thinly with raspberry jam.

Add toasted filberts to punch filling. Do not make punch filling too wet; use only enough punch to moisten cake. Form punch filling by hand into 3-sided pyramids, using about 1 ½ tablespoons of filling for each. Set pyramids on cookies.

Arrange on a cake rack. Spoon or pour chocolate glaze or chocolate fondant over each pyramid. Decorate the top of each with a whole filbert, the bottom of which has first been dipped into hot raspberry jam.
Yield: approximately 18.

NOUGAT SANDWICHES

1 recipe Swiss broyage (p. 75)
3 cups nougat butter cream (see Chapter 3)
2 cups filberts, toasted and ground, or nougat powder (p. 111)
liquored cherries (p. 108) or nougat rounds (p. 111)

Shape and bake Swiss broyage in rounds 2 inches in diameter. Sandwich pairs together with a ¼-inch layer of butter cream. Chill until butter cream is firm. Spread top and sides of each cake thinly with remaining butter cream. Scatter praline powder or ground filberts generously over top and sides of each cake. Garnish centers with well-drained liquored cherries or with a tiny round of nougat. If possible, make these 24 hours ahead of serving to allow broyage to mellow.
Yield: approximately 14.

CRISPE TORTLETS

1 recipe almond butter cake (p. 68) baked in an 11 x 16 jelly-roll pan
2 recipes Swiss broyage (p. 75)
1 cup raspberry jam
1 ½ cups chocolate butter cream (see Chapter 3)
2 cups sliced, blanched almonds, toasted
vanilla sugar (p. 45)

Cut almond butter cake into rounds 2 inches in diameter. Shape and bake Swiss broyage in rounds 2 inches in diameter. Follow directions for Swiss crispe torte (*see p.* 161), making small tortlets instead.
Yield: approximately 28.

CHOCOLATINES

chocolate gênoise (p. 67) baked in an 11 x 16 jelly-roll pan
1 ¼ cups apricot jam
3 cups chocolate butter cream (see Chapter 3)
2 ½ cups blanched, sliced almonds, toasted

Cut chocolate gênoise in half to make 2 pieces 8 x 11. Sandwich them together with apricot jam. Frost top with some of chocolate butter cream. Chill until butter cream is firm.

Trim edges. Cut into 2-inch squares with a serrated knife, wiping knife after each slice. Frost sides of each square with butter cream, then dip sides into sliced, toasted almonds.

Decorate the top of each square with a border of tiny butter cream rosettes, pressed through a bag fitted with a No. 2b star tube.
Yield: approximately 20.

MOCHATINES

Follow recipe for chocolatines, using mocha or coffee butter cream.

TINY TARTLETS

Using almond short pastry (p. 231), line and bake extra-small tartlet shells in special tins, which are available at baking specialty shops.

After pastry is cool, remove from tins. Use a tiny dab of any pastry cream (see Chapter 3) in each shell. Arrange one or two small bits of attractively cut fruit on top. Small fruits such as raspberries, strawberries, and currants can be used whole and are especially appropriate. Brush with apricot glaze (p. 92) if light-colored fruit is used, or currant glaze (p. 92) if red fruit is used.

LINZER SLICES

See recipe for linzer torte (p. 164). Instead of a round torte, make a long, rectangular torte only 2 inches wide. Make strips ⅛ inch thick for the border and for the lattice top. After filling, baking, and cooling the torte, cut it into 1-inch slices. Dust with vanilla sugar (p. 45). Yield: approximately 32.

ROYAL EGG SQUARES
(*A very delicate Mexican pastry*)

8 *egg yolks*
1 *teaspoon grated orange rind*
1 *cup sugar*
½ *cup water*
stick cinnamon
4 *tablespoons light sultana raisins or currants*
4 *tablespoons pine nuts*
¼ *cup sherry*

Set oven temperature at 350 degrees. Grease bottom of 8-inch square pan.

Beat egg yolks until very thick and fluffy. Add grated orange rind. Pour into prepared pan. Cover with sheet of aluminum foil. Bake in a pan of water about 45 minutes, or until egg yolks are puffy and firm. They will not be brown. Remove foil. Cool this egg sponge in pan.

While egg sponge is baking, make a syrup of sugar and water. Stir over low heat until sugar has completely dissolved. Add cinnamon stick and boil until syrup spins a thread (230 degrees). Remove from heat. Add raisins and pine nuts. Cool. Remove cinnamon and add sherry. Pour over cooled egg sponge. Cut into 1-inch squares. Let stand at least 1 hour.
Yield: approximately 64.

BUTTER CREAM PUFFLETS

tiny cream puffs (p. 80)
2 *cups coffee or chocolate butter cream (see Chapter 3)*
1 *cup chocolate or coffee fondant (see Chapter 3)*
¼ *cup contrasting color fondant*

Make tiny cream puffs. Cool.

Fit a pastry bag with plain tube No. 3 and fill with coffee or chocolate butter cream. Push the pointed end of the tube into the side of each puff and squirt in butter cream. Dip top of each filled puff into warm coffee or chocolate fondant.

Fill a small paper cornucopia with a contrasting color fondant (coffee for chocolate, mocha for coffee). Make a small hole in the pointed end of cornucopia and press fondant through, forming a spiral around top of each pufflet.
Yield: approximately 60.

CREAM PUFFS

Shape and bake large cream puffs (p. 79).

Fill with one of the following: pastry cream (p. 95), whipped cream (pp. 93, 94), half-and-half cream filling (p. 95), or chocolate whipped cream (p. 94). Either cut puffs in half to fill or squirt filling in through a hole, as for butter cream pufflets. Dust puffs with vanilla sugar (p. 45). Do not fill cream puffs until just before serving or they may become soggy.
Yield: approximately 16.

ÉCLAIRS

Éclairs, large or small, are made by pressing cream puff paste (p. 79) through a pastry bag, fitted with a plain No. 7 tube, into the shape of flattened fingers, slightly wider at the ends. They are baked and filled like cream puffs. Glaze tops with rich chocolate glaze or chocolate fondant.

DOBOSH SLICELETS

Tiny dobosh slices make especially appealing petits fours. See recipe for dobosh torte (p. 165). Divide baked sponge sheets into long rectangular strips less than 2 inches wide. Use 4 strips of sponge for each whole cake. Sandwich strips together with butter cream. Glaze top with caramelized sugar, following directions in recipe for dobosh torte. Make indentations in the caramelized top ½ inch apart.

Chill strips thoroughly. Cut into slices, using indentations as guide. Yield: approximately 90.

BABAS AU RHUM

1 *recipe savarin dough* (*p.* 80)
1 *cup basic simple syrup* (*p.* 44)
½ *cup rum*
1 *cup apricot glaze* (*p.* 92)
whipped cream, sweetened and flavored (*optional*)
crystallized violets

Set oven at 400 degrees.

Grease 24 small baba or savarin tins. Fill halfway with savarin dough. Let dough rise almost to the top of tins. Place all the tins on a single baking sheet and bake for 10 minutes in preheated oven. Reduce heat to 350 degrees. Continue baking about 10 minutes longer, or until cakes are golden brown.

Several hours before serving, place little cakes in rum syrup or spoon syrup over them to soak thoroughly. Brush cakes with hot apricot glaze.

If savarin rings are used, fill center of each cake with sweetened whipped cream, pressed through a large star tube. Decorate whipped cream with bits of crystallized violets.
Yield: approximately 24.

Chapter 8

Cookies and Petits Fours Secs

8 Cookies and Petits Fours Secs

DROP COOKIES

Langues du chat, macaroons, and a number of traditional French petits fours secs are really drop cookies—a good indication that drop cookies need not be the shapeless, uneven little cakes they frequently are when made at home.

The teaspoon method of shaping cookies is clumsy and inefficient. It is much faster and easier to form cookies with a pastry bag fitted with a large, plain round tube (Nos. 7 and 9 are good sizes).

Fill a large pastry bag ⅔ full with batter. Twist the top of the bag to seal in batter. Holding the bag vertically, the end of the tube about ½ inch away from the cooky sheet, press out rounds of batter. A little practice will teach you to make cookies of any size. It's a simple matter to get the knack of dropping even amounts of batter for each cooky.

When baking a great many cookies, line the baking sheets with Baking Pan Liner Paper. Then cut several extra paper liners and press out all the remaining cooky batter onto the liners. As each sheet of cookies is baked, remove the old liner and slip a new sheet of unbaked cookies in its place. Remove baked cookies from baking-pan liner at once.

In making cookies of any kind—drop, rolled, or molded—never work or beat the dough after flour has been added, or the cookies will be tough.

CATS' TONGUES (LANGUES DU CHAT)

½ cup sugar
½ cup butter
3 egg whites
1 cup sifted flour
pinch of salt
½ teaspoon vanilla

Set oven at 400 degrees. Grease and flour baking sheets.

Cream butter and sugar together. Beat in unbeaten egg whites, a little at a time, beating very well after each addition. Fold in flour, salt, and vanilla.

Fit a pastry bag with a plain No. 3 tube. Fill ⅔ full of cooky batter. On prepared baking sheets, press out pencils of batter about 2 inches long. Leave 1 inch between cookies for spreading.

Bake about 7 minutes, or until edges of cookies are golden brown. Centers should remain light. Remove cookies from baking sheet at once.
Yield: approximately 50.

LEMON WAFERS

1 cats' tongues recipe (above)
2 teaspoons grated lemon rind
1 tablespoon lemon juice

Follow recipe for cats' tongues. Add grated lemon rind and lemon juice. Fit a pastry bag with a plain No. 7 tube. Press out small rounds of batter 1 inch apart. Bake in a 400 degree oven until edges of cookies are golden brown. Remove cookies from baking sheet at once.
Yield: approximately 50.

CRISP MACAROONS

1 cup unblanched almonds, ground
1 cup sugar
2 to 3 egg whites

½ teaspoon almond extract
½ teaspoon vanilla
blanched almond halves

Set oven at 400 degrees. Grease and flour a baking sheet.

Combine ground almonds with ⅔ cup sugar. Gradually add egg whites a little at a time, using enough to make a consistency slightly softer than mashed potatoes. Beat hard for 3 minutes. Add almond extract and vanilla.

Using a pastry bag fitted with a plain No. 7 tube, pipe rounds 2 inches in diameter, spaced 1 inch apart, on prepared cooky sheet. Sprinkle each with remaining sugar. Press a blanched almond half into each cooky. Bake about 15 minutes, or until tops are crackled and lightly browned.
Yield: approximately 16.

FLORENTINES

½ cup sugar
⅓ cup heavy cream
⅓ cup honey
2 tablespoons butter
¼ cup candied orange peel, finely chopped or ground
1 ½ cups blanched, sliced almonds
3 tablespoons sifted flour
8 ounces semisweet chocolate
1 tablespoon vegetable shortening

Set oven at 400 degrees. Grease baking sheets very well.

Combine sugar, cream, honey, butter in a heavy saucepan. Stir over low heat until sugar is dissolved. Raise heat and boil without stirring until a ball forms when a bit of mixture is dropped into cold water, or until mixture registers 238 degrees on a candy thermometer. Cool slightly.

Stir in orange peel, nuts, and flour. Drop small rounds of batter on prepared cooky sheets, leaving at least 2 inches between cookies. Flatten each cooky with a fork dipped in milk.

Bake 8 to 10 minutes, or until cookies are golden brown. They will spread in baking. Therefore, immediately upon removing them from the oven, pull each one back into shape with a round, greased 3-inch cutter. Using the cutter will insure their final roundness.

When cookies are firm, remove them from cooky sheet and finish cooling on a rack.

Melt semisweet chocolate. Stir in shortening. Coat underside of each cooky thinly with melted chocolate. Place in refrigerator long enough to set chocolate.
Yield: approximately 16.

CRACKLED CHOCOLATE DROPS

8 *ounces semisweet chocolate, melted*
8 *egg yolks*
½ *cup sugar*
1 *teaspoon vanilla*
1 *cup blanched almonds, grated*
⅞ *cup sifted flour*
pinch of salt

Set oven at 350 degrees. Grease and flour a baking sheet.

While chocolate is melting, beat egg yolks and sugar together until light and fluffy. Add vanilla. Stir in melted chocolate, grated almonds, and flour mixed with salt.

Drop or pipe small rounds of batter on prepared cooky sheet, leaving 1 inch between cookies. Bake about 25 minutes, or until cookies are crackled and dry.
Yield: approximately 30.

NUT WAFERS

1 *cup butter*
¾ *cup sugar*
2 *eggs*
1 *cup grated pecans or walnuts*
1 *teaspoon vanilla*
1 ½ *cups sifted flour*

½ teaspoon salt
1 cup coarsely cut pecans or walnuts

Set oven at 375 degrees. Grease and flour baking sheets.

Cream butter and sugar together. Beat in eggs, grated nuts, and vanilla. Stir in flour mixed with salt.

Fit a pastry bag with a plain No. 7 tube. Drop small rounds of batter on cooky sheets, leaving 2-inch space between cookies. Place a piece of nut meat in the center of each cooky. Bake about 10 minutes, or until edges are golden brown.
Yield: approximately 36.

ALMOND DROPS

¼ cup almond paste
⅓ cup butter, melted and cooled
pinch of salt
5 egg whites
¾ cup sugar
½ cup flour
½ cup blanched, slivered almonds

Set oven at 450 degrees. Grease and flour baking sheets.

Cream almond paste with melted butter. Beat egg whites with salt until they hold soft peaks. Add sugar, a tablespoon at a time. Continue beating until meringue is very firm. Fold into almond-paste mixture, adding flour and slivered almonds.

Fit a pastry bag with a plain No. 7 tube. Drop small rounds of batter on prepared cooky sheets, leaving 1 inch between cookies. Bake for 5 to 8 minutes, or until edges of cookies are golden brown.
Yield: approximately 30.

MADELEINES

These are a kind of drop cake, but the batter is "dropped" into special shell-shaped molds. Madeleines are very delicate and need no embellishment.

4 eggs
1 ½ cups sugar
1 teaspoon grated lemon rind
1 teaspoon vanilla
2 cups flour
1 ½ cups butter, melted and clarified (p. 35)

Set oven temperature at 450 degrees. Grease madeleine molds well.

Combine eggs, sugar, and lemon rind in a large bowl. Heat over hot water (see directions for making gênoise, p. 64). When eggs are warm, remove from stove and beat in mixer at high speed until they are light, fluffy, and tripled in bulk. Add vanilla. Fold in flour, then melted butter. Be careful not to beat after flour is added.

Fill a bag, fitted with a large plain round tube, with batter. Squirt batter into madeleine molds, filling them ⅔ full. Bake about 10 minutes, or until tops of cakes are golden. Remove from molds immediately. Grease molds again; refill with batter and bake. Continue until all batter is used.

Yield: approximately 48 medium-size madeleines.

COOKY BARS

Cakes which can be cut into bars after they are baked are easy and quick to make. A sharp knife and a firm hand are the only essentials for cutting the cakes neatly.

Cut cooky bars after cooling cake slightly. Crisp edges can be left (many people like them), or they can be cut away. If your eye is uncertain, a ruler should be used to mark off even squares.

Most cookies look and taste better when they are made small. Cut 1-inch squares or 1 x 2-inch bars. Cooky bars can be frozen.

PLAIN MAZURKA

Mazurka is a Polish cooky bar. There are many ways to make it. It is sometimes filled. Here is one simple and delicious version.

1 3/4 cups butter
1 3/4 cups sugar
8 hard-cooked egg yolks, mashed
1 teaspoon vanilla
4 cups sifted flour
1/2 teaspoon salt
1 egg white
1 teaspoon water
2 cups blanched, sliced almonds

Lightly grease an 11 x 16 jelly-roll pan.

Cream butter with sugar. Add mashed hard-cooked egg yolks and vanilla. Gently stir in flour mixed with salt. Press dough into prepared pan. Chill until dough in pan is firm.

Set oven at 350 degrees.

Mix egg white lightly with water and brush over top of dough. Sprinkle with almonds. Bake almost 1 hour, then cool slightly before slicing into small bars.

Yield: approximately 96.

VADIS BARS

2 recipes rich tart dough (p. 230)
1 recipe butter crunch topping (p. 106)

Set oven at 350 degrees.

Press dough into lightly greased 11 x 16 jelly-roll pan. Chill.

Bake in preheated oven about 45 minutes, or until dough is almost completely baked. Remove from oven. Spread with butter crunch topping. Return to oven, placing pan on a high rack. Bake 10 to 15 minutes longer or until top is bubbling. Cool slightly before cutting with a greased knife into small bars.

Yield: approximately 140.

POPPY SEED BARS

1 ¼ cups butter
1 cup sugar
1 teaspoon vanilla
1 ½ cups grated almonds (unblanched)
3 cups sifted flour
¼ teaspoon each cinnamon, ginger, and mace
1 egg, beaten
½ cup poppy seeds

Set oven at 375 degrees.

Lightly grease an 11 x 16 jelly-roll pan.

Cream butter and sugar together. Add vanilla and grated almonds. Gently stir in flour mixed with spices. Press dough into prepared pan. Chill until dough is firm. Brush top with beaten whole egg. Sprinkle with poppy seeds. Bake about 25 minutes, or until golden brown. Cool slightly before cutting into small squares or bars.
Yield: approximately 96.

CROQUETS AUX FILBERTS

½ cup butter
1 cup sugar
1 teaspoon grated orange rind
1 teaspoon grated lemon rind
1 teaspoon vanilla
1 egg
1 ½ cups blanched filberts, toasted and sliced or coarsely chopped
1 ¼ cups flour
½ teaspoon salt
1 egg white
1 teaspoon water

Set oven at 375 degrees. Lightly grease a baking sheet. Cream butter and ½ cup sugar together. Add orange and lemon rind, vanilla, egg, and 1 cup filberts. Gently stir in flour mixed with salt. Chill slightly.

Divide dough in half. Form each half into a long, slim loaf about 2 inches wide. Place loaves well apart on prepared baking sheet.

With a knife, score each loaf with crisscross lines. Brush with egg white mixed with water. Sprinkle with remaining sugar and sliced filberts. Bake about 25 minutes, or until loaves are golden brown. Cool slightly.

Cut diagonally into slices ½ inch thick. Replace slices in a 300 degree oven for 10 minutes, or until they are lightly toasted and dry. Yield: approximately 44.

MACAROON JAM SLICES

1 ½ cups nuts (almonds, walnuts, filberts)
⅓ cup sugar
1 to 2 egg whites, unbeaten
1 ½ cups thick, hot jam or preserves (raspberry, strawberry, apricot)

Set oven at 350 degrees. Grease a baking sheet well. Grate or grind nuts fine.

Mix ground nuts with sugar. Add only enough egg white, a little at a time, to bind mixture together into a paste firm enough to be shaped.

Form into a long roll 1 ½ inches in diameter. Place on prepared baking sheet. Using index finger dipped in water, make a deep trench down the center of the roll.

Bake 15 to 20 minutes, or until nut roll is lightly browned.

Meanwhile heat some jam until it is thick and boiling hot.

Immediately upon taking nut roll from the oven, fill trench with hot jam. Cool slightly. Loosen from cooky sheet. When completely cool, cut diagonally into ½-inch slices.

Yield: approximately 30.

BERLIN STICKS

1 recipe rich tart dough (p. 230)
½ cup raspberry jam

CHOCOLATE ALMOND TOPPING

2 egg whites
¼ cup sugar
1 teaspoon vanilla
¼ cup almonds, ground
2 ounces semisweet chocolate, melted
½ cup sliced, blanched almonds

Set oven at 350 degrees. Grease square 9-inch baking pan.

Roll or pat dough to fit bottom of pan. Bake about 20 minutes or until dough is more than half cooked. Remove from oven. Spread with jam. Cover jam with the following chocolate-almond topping: Beat egg whites until they hold soft peaks. Add sugar, a little at a time, beating after each addition. When firm, fold in vanilla, ground almonds, and melted chocolate.

Sprinkle topping with sliced, blanched almonds. Place pan in oven. Bake 15 to 20 minutes longer, or until top looks crisp. Cool slightly before cutting into small squares or bars.
Yield: approximately 72.

BROWNIES

6 ounces baking chocolate
¾ cup butter
6 eggs
3 cups sugar
2 teaspoons vanilla
1 ½ cups flour
½ teaspoon salt
1 ½ cups walnuts, coarsely chopped

Set oven at 325 degrees. Grease and lightly flour an 11 x 16 jelly-roll pan. Melt chocolate and butter together. Set aside to cool slightly.

Beat eggs and sugar together unil fluffy. Add vanilla. Stir in chocolate mixture, then the flour, salt, and nuts. Mix only until combined.

Pour into prepared pan, bake about 25 minutes, or until top looks dry. Cool before cutting into squares or bars.

Yield: approximately 75.

ROLLED COOKIES

Holiday cookies are often made from dough which is rolled out and then cut with special cutters to form the shapes we associate with Christmas, Easter, and other special occasions.

To successfully roll and cut cookies, dough must not be too soft. Neither must too much flour be added. Too much flour makes the dough easier to handle, but the baked cookies are virtually inedible. If the dough is first chilled, then rolled out on a *floured cloth* or between sheets of waxed paper, there will be no need to use excess flour.

When a large amount of dough is made, divide it into 2 or 3 pieces. Wrap each piece in wax paper. Chill until firm enough to roll. Extra long chilling, however, will make most high-fat doughs difficult to roll.

Some rich rolled-cooky doughs, before they are chilled, can be forced through a pastry bag and tube to make various shapes. If the dough is to be shaped in this way, it is often necessary to withhold a little of the flour—about ¼ of the total amount—so the dough won't be too firm.

When cutting out cooky shapes, cut them as close to each other as possible. Unless the dough is very soft and sticky, the cutters need not be floured. If you have been careful not to get the dough floury, it is perfectly all right to re-roll and use the scraps.

Rolled cookies can be frozen either before or after baking.

SCANDINAVIAN CHRISTMAS COOKIES

1 cup butter
⅔ cup brown sugar
⅓ cup light corn syrup
⅔ cup maple syrup or honey
1 teaspoon grated lemon rind
1 teaspoon dark rum
4 ½ cups sifted flour (approximately)
1 teaspoon salt
1 teaspoon soda
1 teaspoon ginger
½ teaspoon cloves
1 teaspoon cinnamon

Cream butter with sugar. Add syrups, lemon rind, and rum. Mix well. Add flour mixed with salt, soda, and spices. This should make a soft dough.

Chill dough until firm enough to roll.

Set oven at 350 degrees. Grease and flour baking sheets.

On a well-floured cloth, roll dough very thin (less than ⅛ inch, if possible). Cut into desired shapes. Transfer cookies to baking sheets with a spatula. Bake 8 to 10 minutes, or until cookies are puffed and lightly browned.

Yield: approximately 9 dozen.

CREAM COOKIES

1 cup soft butter
2 ¾ cups sifted flour
½ teaspoon salt
1 ½ cups finely sliced, blanched almonds
½ cup heavy cream
granulated sugar
2 cups thick raspberry jam

Cream butter together with flour, salt, almonds, and heavy cream, adding cream alternately with flour. Chill until dough is firm enough to roll.

Set oven at 350 degrees. Grease and flour baking sheets.

Roll dough ⅛ inch thick on pastry cloth generously sprinkled with granulated sugar. (Use no flour for rolling this dough.) Cut out cookies, using a 1-inch round cooky cutter. With a slightly smaller cutter, cut out the centers of half the cookies, leaving rings. (The small rounds cut from centers can be baked as small extra cookies, or re-rolled.)

Transfer cookies to baking sheets. Bake 7 to 10 minutes. Remove from sheet and cool on rack.

Sandwich pairs of cookies together with raspberry jam; the top one should be a ring-shaped cooky. Fill in centers with a little more jam. Yield: approximately 36.

APRICOT LEAVES

½ cup almond paste
1 egg, separated
½ cup butter
¼ cup sugar
½ teaspoon vanilla
1 lemon, grated rind and juice
1 cup plus 1 tablespoon flour
½ teaspoon salt
1 teaspoon water
2 cups blanched, sliced almonds
½ cup thick apricot jam

Cream almond paste with egg yolk until soft. Beat in softened butter, a little at a time, then add sugar, vanilla, lemon rind, and juice. Gently stir in flour mixed with salt. Chill.

Set oven at 375 degrees. Grease and flour baking sheets.

Roll dough ⅛ inch thick on well-floured cloth. Cut out cookies with a round, scalloped cutter. Transfer to baking sheets with a spatula.

Beat egg white slightly with a teaspoon of water. Brush each cooky with egg white. Coat generously with blanched, sliced almonds. Bake

10 minutes, or until cookies are a light golden brown. Immediately upon taking cookies from oven, pipe a tiny dab of hot, thick apricot jam in the center of each one. Cool on a rack.
Yield: approximately 24.

POLISH BUTTER COOKIES

1 cup butter
¾ cup sugar
5 hard-cooked egg yolks, sieved
1 teaspoon vanilla
2 cups sifted flour
½ teaspoon salt
1 whole egg mixed with 1 teaspoon milk

FOR TOPPINGS

finely chopped nuts
cinnamon sugar (p. 44)
poppy seeds

Cream butter and sugar. Stir in sieved hard-cooked egg yolks, vanilla and then flour mixed with salt. Chill dough.

Set oven at 350 degrees. Lightly grease cooky sheets.

Roll out cooky dough ¼ inch thick on a floured cloth. Cut cookies with cutters into small crescents, stars, or other shapes. Transfer to cooky sheet, leaving a little space between cookies. Brush with beaten whole egg. Leave cookies plain or sprinkle with one of the following: finely chopped nuts, cinnamon sugar, poppy seeds. Bake about 12 minutes, or until cookies are lightly browned.
Yield: approximately 48.

CHOCOLATE CRESCENTS

1 cup butter
¼ cup sugar
1 teaspoon vanilla
⅔ cup grated semisweet chocolate
1 cup grated pistachio nuts

2 ¼ cups sifted flour
½ teaspoon salt
¾ cup orange fondant (see Chapter 3)

Cream butter and sugar. Add vanilla. Stir in grated chocolate and nuts. Add flour mixed with salt. Chill.

Set oven at 350 degrees. Lightly grease and flour baking sheets.

Roll out dough ⅛ inch thick on a well-floured cloth. Cut out cookies with a crescent-shaped cutter. Place on cooky sheet, spacing slightly apart. Bake 10 minutes, or until cookies are dry and firm.

When cookies are cool, brush each one with a thin coating of warm orange fondant.

Yield: approximately 60.

VIENNESE POCKETS

1 ¼ cups butter
⅔ cup sugar
2 hard-cooked egg yolks, mashed
1 raw egg yolk
1 teaspoon grated orange rind
2 teaspoons vanilla
2 ½ cups sifted flour
½ teaspoon salt
thick jam or preserves
2 egg whites
2 teaspoons water

Cream butter with sugar. Stir in sieved hard-cooked egg yolks, raw yolk, orange rind, vanilla. Gently add flour mixed with salt. Chill dough.

Roll out ⅛ inch thick. Cut into 2-inch squares. Place a small dab of thick jam on each square. Fold in half to make triangles. Pinch edges together. Chill again.

Set oven at 350 degrees. Lightly grease and flour baking sheets. Prick top of each cooky with a fork. Brush with egg white slightly beaten with water.

Bake 10 to 15 minutes, or until cookies are lightly browned.

Yield: approximately 40.

FROSTED SHORTBREADS

1 cup butter
¾ cup sifted confectioners' sugar
1 teaspoon vanilla
2 cups sifted flour
½ teaspoon salt
6 ounces semisweet chocolate
1 teaspoon vegetable shortening

Cream together butter, sugar, and vanilla. Gently stir in flour mixed with salt. Chill.

Set oven at 300 degrees.

Roll ½ inch thick on a lightly floured cloth. Cut into rounds with a scalloped cutter. (Dough can also be shaped into a roll, chilled, and sliced ½ inch thick.)

Bake on an ungreased cooky sheet for 20 to 25 minutes, or until cookies are dry but not brown. Cool on a rack.

While cookies cool, melt chocolate. Stir in vegetable shortening. Dip one end of each cooky into chocolate. Place in refrigerator briefly to harden chocolate.

Yield: approximately 28.

LECKERLI

These should be made at least a week, preferably 2 or 3 weeks, before using, to enable Leckerli to mellow. In an airtight box, these will keep well for many months.

½ cup honey
1 cup sugar
¾ cup candied orange peel, finely chopped
1 teaspoon grated lemon rind
1 cup blanched, sliced almonds
2 ¼ cups sifted flour
½ teaspoon cloves
1 teaspoon nutmeg
1 teaspoon cinnamon

1 teaspoon soda
¼ cup water

Place honey and ½ cup sugar in a saucepan. Cook, stirring over low heat, until mixture boils. Remove from heat. Add candied orange peel and grated lemon rind. Cool to lukewarm. Stir in sliced almonds, then the flour mixed with spices and baking soda. Cover dough and let mellow at room temperature for at least 2 days.

Set oven at 325 degrees. Grease and flour baking sheets. On a well-floured cloth, roll out dough ⅓ inch thick. Cut into bars 1 ½ x 3 inches. Place on baking sheets. Bake approximately 25 minutes, or until cookies are lightly browned.

Cook remaining sugar with ¼ cup water until it spins a thread (230 degrees). Brush each cooky with hot syrup. When completely cool, store in airtight box.

Yield: approximately 56.

POLISH CHRUST

6 egg yolks
¼ teaspoon salt
⅓ cup sugar
¼ cup heavy cream
⅛ teaspoon mace
2 to 2 ½ cups sifted flour (approximately)
shortening for deep frying
vanilla sugar (p. 45)

Beat yolks with salt and sugar until light and fluffy. Stir in cream and mace. Add enough flour to make a soft dough. *Do not knead dough.* Kneading will result in hard, tough cookies. Chill.

Heat shortening to 375 degrees in a deep pan.

Roll out dough as thin as possible, half at a time, on well-floured cloth. Cut into strips 1 x 3 inches. Make a slit down the center of each strip. Turn one end of strip in through slit. Fry, a few strips at a time, in preheated shortening, turning them once. They are done when lightly brown on both sides.

Drain on paper towels. When cool, dust with vanilla sugar.

Yield: approximately 50.

MOLDED COOKIES

Molded cookies are among the most festive of cookies in appearance. Their texture is often similar to rich shortbread.

This type of cooky, which invariably contains a great deal of butter, can be shaped by several different methods. The simplest is to form the dough into a long roll or a square 1 or 2 inches thick. The roll should next be wrapped securely in wax paper, well chilled, then sliced, thick or thin, with a sharp knife, or with a serrated potato slicer, if desired. These cookies can be placed less than an inch apart on a cooky sheet since they hardly spread at all.

Another method of handling these shortbread-like doughs is to press them either through a cooky press or through a pastry bag. Dough pressed through large pastry tubes can be formed quickly and easily into rings, rosettes, and ribbons. The flour in dough which is to be handled in this way must sometimes be reduced by about ¼ the total quantity. The dough must be soft enough to be forced through a tube, yet firm enough to keep its shape during baking.

Still another method of shaping molded cookies consists of hand-shaping each into a tiny crescent, ball, log, or ring. Although it takes longer, this method makes very attractive cookies.

Molded cookies can be frozen baked or unbaked. In freezing unbaked cookies, place them one next to the other on a wax-paper lined cooky sheet. When the cookies are solidly frozen, peel them from the wax paper. Pack into containers which can be tightly covered.

CHOCOLATE PUFFS

1 *cup butter*
¼ *cup sugar*
1 *egg yolk*
1 *tablespoon cognac*
1 *teaspoon vanilla*
1 *cup walnuts, grated*
3 *ounces baking chocolate, melted*
2 ⅔ *cups sifted flour*

Set oven at 325 degrees. Grease baking sheets lightly.

Cream butter and sugar. Add egg yolk, cognac, vanilla, grated nuts, and cooled, melted chocolate. Stir in flour. Chill until firm. Roll dough into small balls the size of a large cherry.

Roll each ball in granulated sugar. Press a piece of walnut into each cooky. Place balls slightly apart on prepared baking sheet. Bake 15 to 20 minutes, or until cookies are crackled and dry.
Yield: approximately 48.

GINGER SLICES

1 cup butter
1 cup sugar
½ cup molasses
1 tablespoon ginger
1 teaspoon cinnamon
½ teaspoon cloves
1 teaspoon soda
2 cups sliced almonds
3 ¼ cups flour

Cream butter and sugar. Add molasses, spices, baking soda, and almonds. Stir in flour. Form dough into 4 or 5 long rolls 1 inch in diameter. Chill.

Set oven at 350 degrees. Lightly grease baking sheets.

Slice rolls ¼ inch thick. Place slices on prepared cooky sheet 1 inch apart. Bake 8 to 10 minutes, or until cookies are firm.
Yield: approximately 60.

OAT CRISPS

⅔ cup butter
½ cup sugar
2 cups old-fashioned oats
1 cup grated cocoanut
½ teaspoon cinnamon
1 teaspoon vanilla
1 teaspoon lemon rind
1 teaspoon orange rind
½ teaspoon salt

Cream butter with sugar. Add all remaining ingredients. Mix well. Form into a long roll 1 inch in diameter. Wrap in wax paper. Chill until completely firm.

Set oven at 325 degrees.

Cut roll into ¼-inch slices. Place cooky slices 1 inch apart on an ungreased baking sheet. Bake 15 to 20 minutes, or until cookies are lightly browned. Cool before removing from cooky sheets.

Yield: approximately 30.

Note: Quick-cooking oats may be substituted, but the cookies will be less chewy and somewhat less distinctive.

ORANGE BUTTER RINGS

Polish butter cooky dough (*p.* 214)
2 *teaspoons grated orange rind*
¼ *cup heavy cream*
⅔ *cup ground nuts*
½ *cup granulated sugar*

Set oven at 350 degrees. Lightly grease baking sheets.

Follow recipe for Polish butter cookies, adding 2 teaspoons grated orange rind to creamed butter and sugar. After dough has been chilled, pinch off pieces of dough the size of a large cherry. Roll into pencil-thin sticks 3 inches long. Turn each stick into a ring, pinching the ends together. Place on lightly greased baking sheets.

Brush cookies with cream. Sprinkle with a mixture of finely ground nuts and granulated sugar. Bake in oven for 10 to 15 minutes, or until cookies are golden.

Yield: approximately 48.

ALMOND CRESCENTS

1 ¼ *cups almonds, unblanched*
1 *cup butter*
½ *cup sugar*
1 *teaspoon vanilla*

½ teaspoon salt
2 cups sifted flour
additional granulated sugar for decoration

Grate or grind almonds fine. Cream butter and sugar together. Stir in ground almonds, vanilla, salt, and flour. Chill dough till firm.

Set oven at 350 degrees. Lightly grease baking sheets. Break off walnut-size pieces of dough. Roll pieces into sticks ½ inch thick. Bend sticks into little crescent shapes. Place on prepared baking sheets, leaving slight space between crescents.

Bake 15 to 20 minutes, or until crescents are dry but not brown. Cool slightly. Roll each cooky in granulated sugar.
Yield: approximately 36.

PECAN BALLS

1 ¼ cup pecans
almond crescent recipe (p. 220), omitting almonds
vanilla sugar (p. 45)

Grate or grind pecans finely.

Follow recipe for almond crescents, substituting ground pecans for almonds. Pinch off small pieces of dough and roll into balls the size of a large cherry. Bake 15 to 20 minutes. Roll warm cookies in vanilla sugar.
Yield: approximately 48.

PRALINE BALLS

⅔ cup butter
¼ cup brown sugar
½ cup nougat powder (p. 111)
1 teaspoon vanilla
½ teaspoon salt
1 ½ cups sifted flour
vanilla sugar (p. 45)

Cream butter and sugar. Stir in nougat powder, vanilla, salt, and flour. Chill dough until firm.

Set oven at 350 degrees. Lightly grease cooky sheets.

Pinch off pieces of dough the size of a large cherry. Roll into balls. Place on baking sheet, leaving slight space between cookies. Bake 15 to 20 minutes. Roll warm cookies in vanilla sugar.

Yield: approximately 36.

NUT CRISPS

This recipe requires no flour.

1 ½ cups nuts (almonds, walnuts, filberts)
½ cup butter
⅓ cup sugar
pinch of salt
1 teaspoon vanilla

Grate or grind nuts fine.

Cream butter and sugar. Stir in ground nuts, salt, and vanilla. Form dough into a long roll, 1 inch in diameter. Wrap in wax paper. Chill until firm.

Set oven at 350 degrees.

Cut into thin slices. Place slices on ungreased baking sheet.

Bake about 7 minutes, or until cookies are lightly brown. Watch carefully to prevent burning. Place cookies on paper towels to absorb excess fat, if any.

Yield: approximately 36.

GINGER SHORTBREADS

⅔ cup butter
⅔ cup sugar
¼ cup dark molasses
vanilla
½ teaspoon cinnamon
¼ teaspoon cloves

1 ½ *teaspoons ginger*
½ *teaspoon nutmeg*
1 *teaspoon soda*
2 *cups sifted flour*

Cream butter and ⅓ cup sugar together. Add molasses, vanilla, spices, and soda. Stir in flour. Chill until firm.

Set oven at 375 degrees. Grease cooky sheets lightly.

Pinch off small pieces of dough. Roll into small balls the size of a large cherry. Roll balls in remaining granulated sugar. Flatten balls slightly. Place on cooky sheets, leaving a space between cookies. Bake 12 to 15 minutes or until cookies are crackled and dry.

Yield: approximately 48.

WHITE SPRITZ COOKIES

1 *cup butter*
⅔ *cup sugar*
1 *teaspoon vanilla*
3 *egg whites*
2 *to* 2½ *cups flour*
¼ *teaspoon salt*

Set oven at 375 degrees. Lightly grease a baking sheet.

Cream butter and sugar together. Add vanilla, then egg whites, beating them in well. Gently stir in flour mixed with salt.

Press out small shapes (stars, sticks, rings) through a pastry tube, or use a cooky press.

Bake 8 to 10 minutes, or until edges of cookies are golden brown.

Yield: approximately 60.

SPRITZ COOKIES

¾ cup butter
½ cup sugar
1 teaspoon vanilla
2 egg yolks
2 to 2¼ cups flour
¼ teaspoon salt

Set oven at 375 degrees. Lightly grease baking sheets. Cream butter and sugar together. Beat in vanilla and egg yolks. Stir in flour mixed with salt.

Press out small shapes (stars, sticks, rings) through a pastry tube, or use a cooky press.

Bake 8 to 10 minutes or until edges of cookies are golden brown.
Yield: approximately 48.

RASPBERRY SPRITZ BARS

spritz cooky dough (above)
2 cups hot, thick raspberry jam

Form ½ of dough into a long strip ¼ inch thick by 1 ½ inches wide. Place on cooky sheet.

Fit a pastry bag with star tube No. 4. Fill with remaining dough. Force dough through tube along each side of strip to make a border, leaving the center hollow.

Bake 15 to 20 minutes, or until bar is a light golden brown. Immediately fill center with hot raspberry jam. Cool before cutting diagonally into bars with a sharp knife.
Yield: approximately 36.

SOFT FILBERT MACAROONS

3 cups ground filberts
⅔ cup granulated sugar
1 teaspoon vanilla
⅛ teaspoon ground cloves
¼ teaspoon cinnamon
⅛ teaspoon allspice
3 to 4 egg whites
30 blanched whole filberts (approximately)

Set oven at 350 degrees. Grease a cooky sheet well.

Combine ground filberts, sugar, vanilla, and spices in a bowl. Add enough egg white to make a medium-firm dough. Pinch off pieces slightly smaller than a walnut. Roll into balls.

Place on prepared baking sheet. Flatten balls slightly. Stick a whole filbert into center of each cooky.

Bake 15 to 20 minutes, or until tops of cookies are firm.

Yield: approximately 30.

Chapter 9

Tarts

9 *Tarts*

A tart is not a pie. It is a delicious, delicate pastry shell filled with cooked or raw fruit and sometimes custard. To some, a pie might also fit this description. However, there are many important differences.

A tart is never, as most pies are, completely covered by a top crust. Tart pastry—even the bottom—is crisp and stays so for days. The tops of tarts are colorful and bright with fruit glaze. A fruit tart is a light dessert, in contrast to the heaviness of most double-crusted pies.

Pie pastry at its best is light, flaky, and tender. This, even for experienced cooks, is not easily achieved. The nature of piecrust demands that it be eaten almost immediately after baking. A pie which has stood around only an hour or two often has a soggy bottom crust.

Tart pastry, even for the beginner, is easy to make because there is little danger in overhandling. Its consistency after being baked is not flaky; it is short, crisp, and delicate—comparable to a rich cooky dough. The crust of a tart may even outlast the edibility of its filling. Even after being kept for several days it will usually remain crisp and delicious.

For shaping tarts, flan rings give the best results, although pie tins can be used. Flan rings are available in rectangular, square, and round shapes. They are so simple in appearance that they sometimes present a puzzle to those who have never used them. A flan ring is merely a metal hoop, with no top and no bottom, usually about 1 inch high. Various sizes are available.

A cooky sheet serves as the bottom of a flan ring. This has a number of advantages. The most important is that the pastry, especially the bottom, bakes through better.

A tart baked in a flan ring is easily transferred from cooky sheet to serving plate by gently sliding it off the sheet while it is still in the ring. Since baked pastry always shrinks a little, the flan ring can then be lifted off without difficulty, leaving the tart standing free.

Unbaked tart pastry can be frozen for several months, and it will taste even better because of the extra chilling. The easy way to do this is to line several flan rings at the same time. If a doubled piece of heavy aluminum foil is placed under each ring (to serve as a bottom), the pastry-lined rings can be frozen without using up all the baking sheets in the kitchen. After the pastry has frozen solid, the entire ring should be well wrapped for storage. Frozen pastry should be transferred directly from freezer to oven. It should never be thawed first.

Baked tart shells can also be placed in the freezer. However, a certain fresh taste is sacrificed.

In baking tarts, their oven position is extremely important. This is especially so when filling and pastry are baked together. *Always bake a filled tart shell on the lowest rack so maximum heat will be directed to the bottom of the pastry.* Bake until fruit fillings bubble. A custard filling should be baked until it is just firm. Some people prefer to half-bake pastry shells before filling them with custard mixtures.

Unfilled tart shells should be baked slightly higher—on the center rack, rather than on the lowest in the oven.

The same rules apply to baking small tartlets, filled or unfilled. Tarts large and small are baked in a 350 degree oven.

RICH TART PASTRY

2 *cups sifted flour*
3 *tablespoons sugar*
¾ *cup butter*
½ *teaspoon salt*
2 *teaspoons grated lemon rind*
3 *hard-cooked egg yolks, mashed*
2 *raw egg yolks*

Place flour in a bowl. Make a well in the center. Add all ingredients to well. The butter should not be ice cold, nor should it be so soft that it is oily.

With finger tips, make a paste of center ingredients, gradually incorporating flour to form a smooth, firm ball of dough. Work quickly so the butter does not become oily. When sides of the bowl are left clean, the pastry is finished. Wrap it in wax paper and chill until dough is firm enough to roll.

Roll pastry between sheets of wax paper.

This is enough pastry for one 9-inch flan ring, with some left over for a lattice top; or for approximately 2½ dozen tartlet shells.

Note: To make pastry which is less fragile and crisper in texture, substitute 2 egg whites for the raw egg yolks.

ELECTRIC MIXER METHOD FOR MAKING TART PASTRY

Place flour in largest bowl of electric mixer. Make a well in center. To it add remaining ingredients. Turn mixer on to low speed. Keep mixer running until ingredients are all combined, pushing flour from sides into center with a spatula. As soon as flour is completely incorporated, stop machine. Make pastry into a ball. Wrap in wax paper and chill until firm enough to roll.

ALMOND SHORT PASTRY

½ cup almond paste
3 egg yolks, raw
⅔ cup unblanched almonds
1 ¼ cups sifted flour
⅓ cup sugar
½ teaspoon salt
1 teaspoon grated lemon rind
½ cup butter
pinch of cloves
¼ teaspoon cinnamon
2 egg yolks, hard-cooked and sieved

Cream almond paste with raw egg yolks until soft.

Grate or grind almonds.

Mix flour and ground almonds together and place in a bowl, making a well in the center. In well, place sugar, salt, lemon rind, softened butter, spices, hard-cooked yolks, and almond-paste mixture.

With finger tips, combine center ingredients, gradually incorporating flour and nuts to make a smooth, firm ball of dough. Chill until firm enough to roll between sheets of wax paper. Use as a substitute for sweet tart dough.

This is enough pastry for one 9-inch flan ring or approximately 2 dozen tartlet shells.

Note: To mix in electric mixer, follow directions given in recipe for rich tart pastry, adding almond paste to well after it has been creamed with egg yolks.

LINING A FLAN RING

Place flan ring on an ungreased baking sheet. Roll out tart pastry (p. 230) between sheets of wax paper, loosening both sheets occasionally while rolling, to allow dough to spread. (See pp. 23-24 on how to roll out dough.) When rolled, dough should be slightly less than ¼ inch thick and 1 inch larger in diameter than flan ring.

Peel off top paper. Use undersheet to help pick up pastry and invert over flan ring. Center pastry. Carefully peel off paper. Ease pastry down into ring, pressing it along the sides and bottom. Try not to stretch pastry, since stretching will cause it to shrink in the oven. Press overlapping pastry into sides to make sides slightly thicker than bottom of shell.

Cover pastry-lined ring with paper. Run rolling pin across the top to cut off excess pastry. Keep excess for making tartlets or lattice tops.

Flute edges of pastry-lined ring (see illustration, p. 236). Chill well, preferably in freezer, before baking.

LINING AND BAKING TARTLET SHELLS

All the recipes for large tarts can be adapted to tartlets.

Arrange 12 or more shallow tartlet tins, touching one another, in rows of 4 or 6.

Roll out rich tart pastry (p. 230) or almond short pastry (p. 231) ¼ inch thick, between sheets of wax paper to a size slightly larger than the total combination of tartlet tins. Peel off top sheet of paper. Invert pastry over tartlet molds. Peel off the remaining sheet of paper. Let pastry stand for ten minutes to settle into the little tins. This natural stretching won't harm pastry. Cover pastry-lined tins with wax paper. Run rolling pin over the tops. This will cut the pastry to the exact size of the tartlet tins. Gather up surplus pastry. From it, pinch off a small ball the size of a walnut. Dip ball into flour. Use floured ball to press pastry firmly into the tins.

Chill lined tins well, preferably in the freezer, before baking.

To bake tartlet shells, unfilled, place all of them on a baking sheet. Bake in a 350 degree oven, on the second rack from bottom, about 10 minutes, or until shells are light brown.

Prick each shell 2 or 3 times with a fork during first 5 minutes of baking when air bubbles appear. Cool baked pastry slightly before removing from tins. If pastry should stick, use the point of a small knife to loosen one side.

To bake filled tartlets, fill them ¾ full. Place on a baking sheet and bake on lowest oven rack in a 350 degree oven about 20 minutes, or until pastry is golden and filling is set.

BAKING AN UNFILLED TART SHELL

Set oven at 350 degrees. Place baking rack at second level from bottom of oven. Place chilled pastry in oven, taking it directly from freezer or refrigerator so it is as cold as possible. Prick bottom all over with a fork. Prick 3 or 4 times during first 10 minutes of baking to prevent bottom of pastry from puffing up.

If sides of pastry should sink down during first 10 minutes of baking, simply press them back with a fork.

Bake a total of 25 minutes, or until shell is golden brown.

A HOMEMADE FLAN RING

If you find it impossible to locate a flan ring in any store in your community, here is how to improvise one.

To make a 9-inch ring, cut a piece of heavy aluminum foil 18 x 26.

LINING A FLAN RING

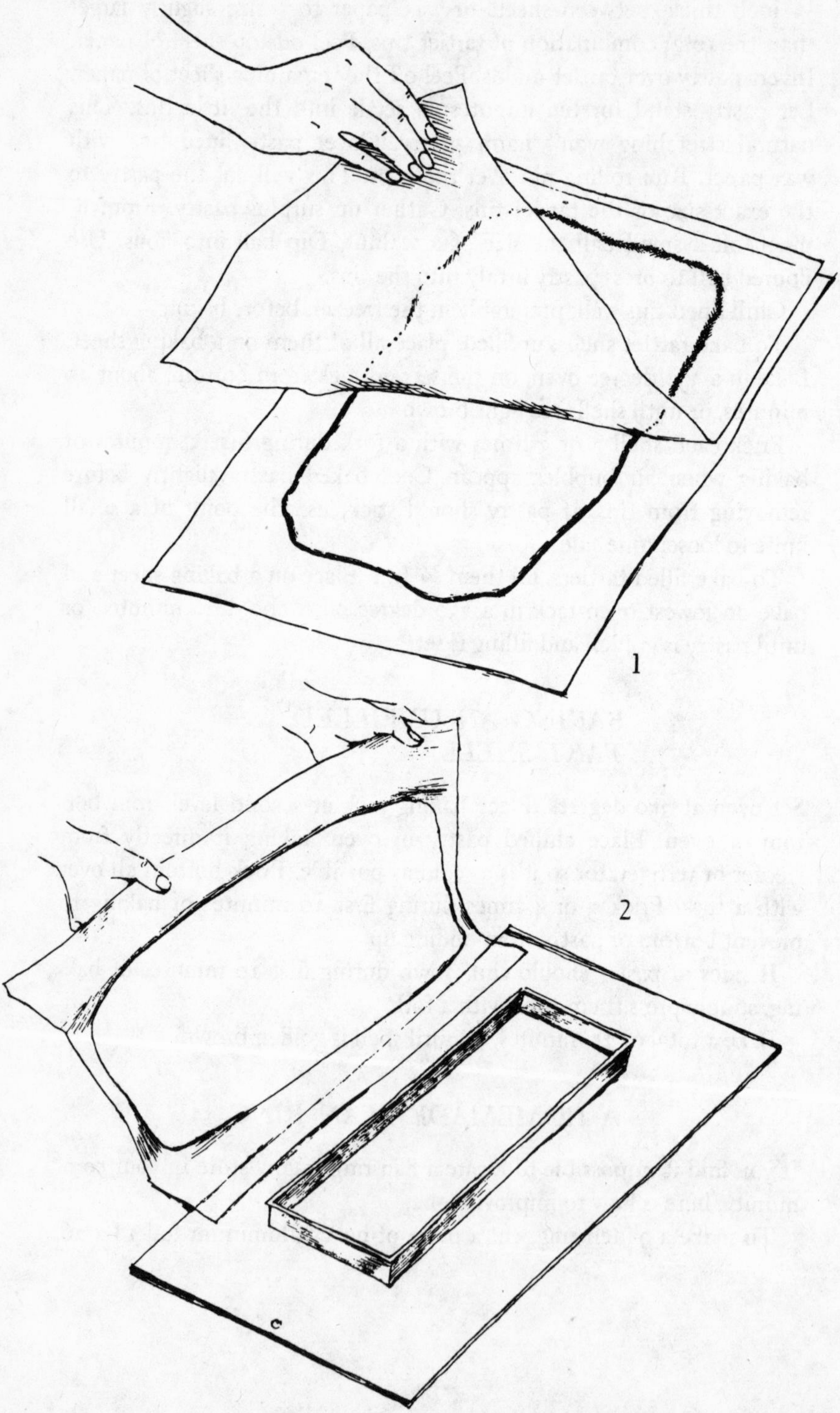

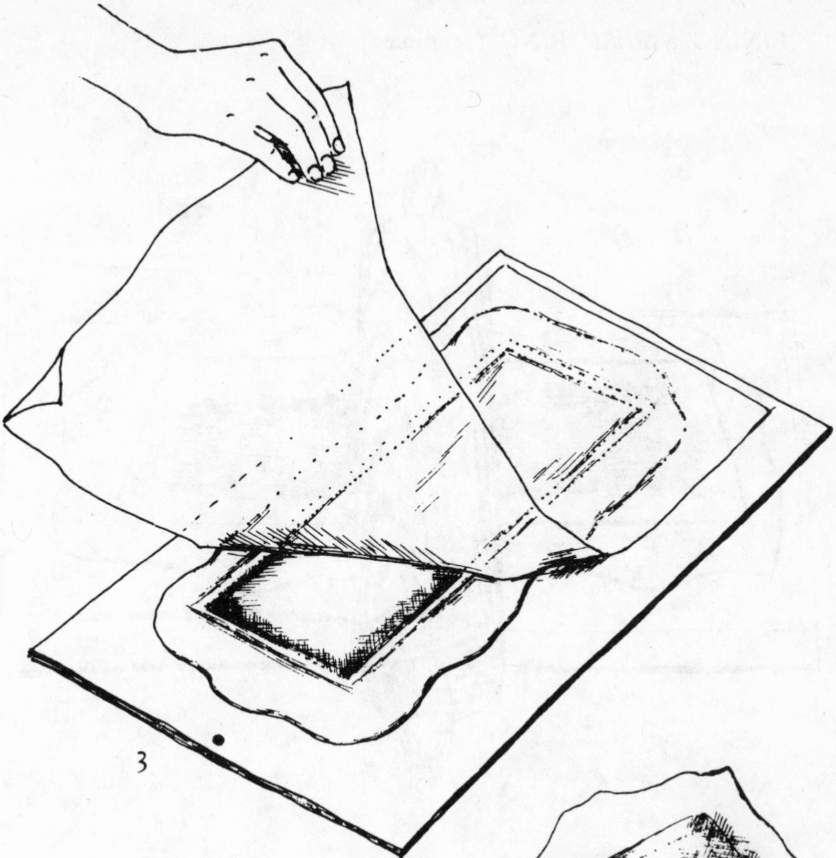

3

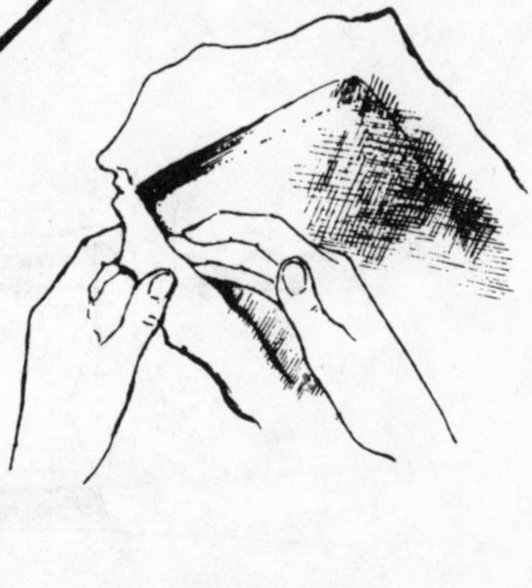

4

1. *Peeling off top sheet of wax paper from rolled-out tart dough*

2. *Inverting pastry over flan ring which has been placed on a baking sheet*

3. *Peeling second sheet of wax paper from dough*

4. *Fitting dough into flan ring*

(*Continued overleaf*)

LINING A FLAN RING (*continued*)

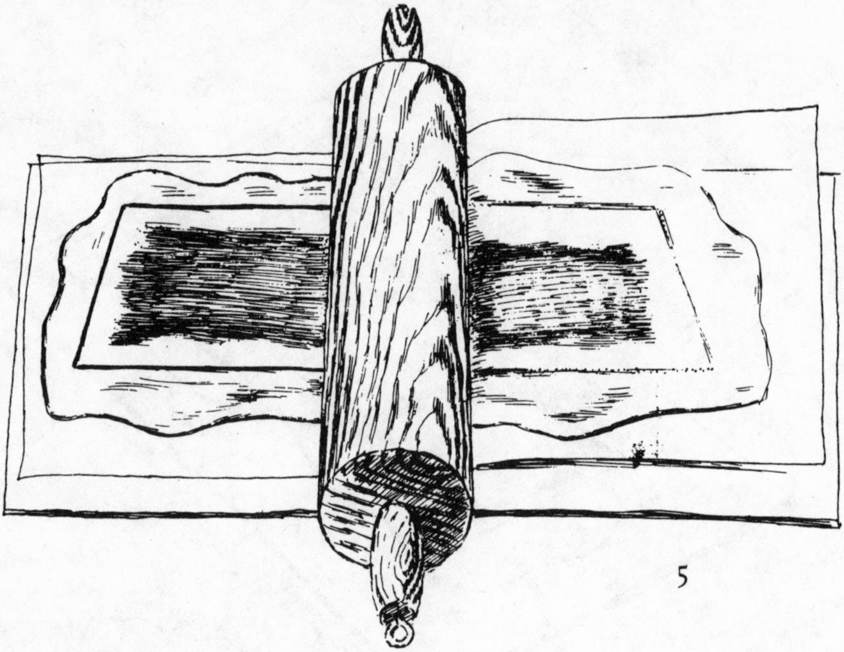

5

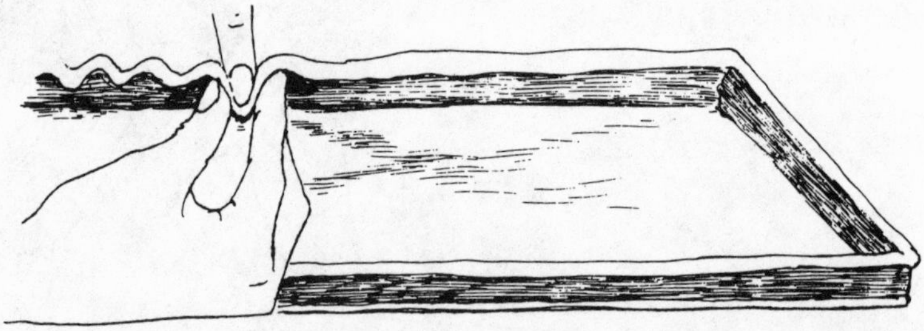

6

5. *Rolling off excess pastry*

6. *Fluting edge of pastry*

LINING TARTLET SHELLS

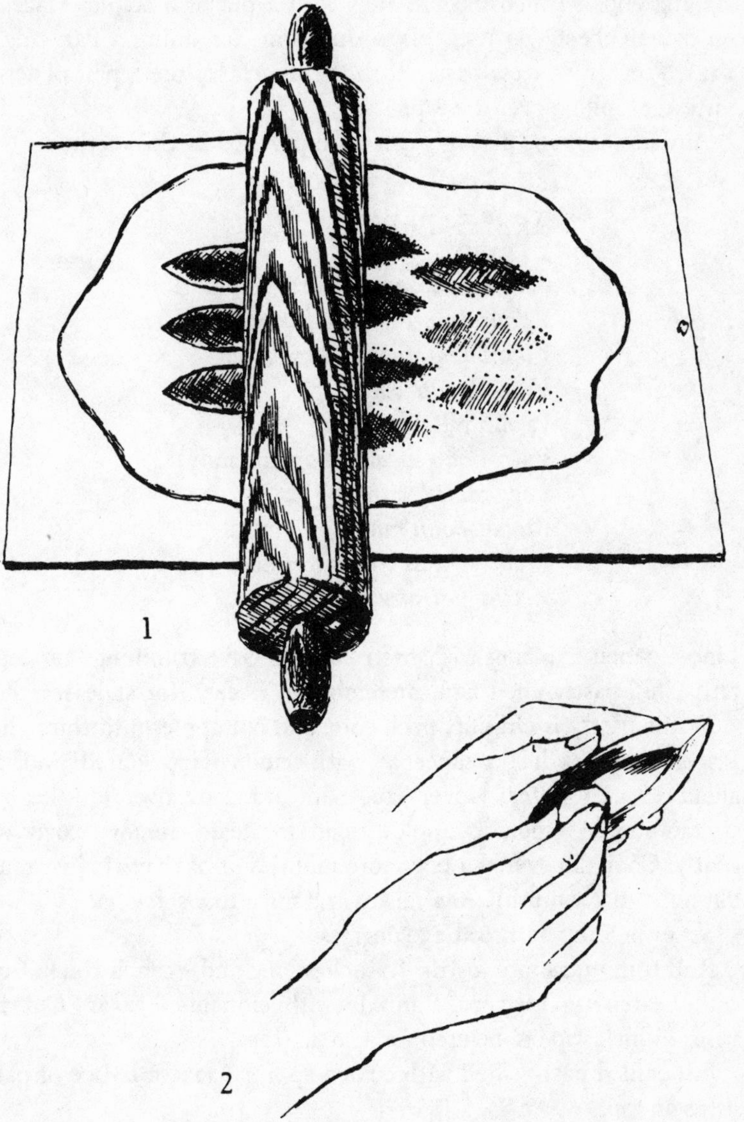

1. *Cutting through pastry* (*which has been inverted over tartlet tins*) *with a rolling pin*

2. *Pressing dough down into tartlet tins with a small ball of dough*

Fold foil lengthwise until you have a heavy strip 26 x 1. Pull strip through your fingers to give it flexibility. Shape it into a ring, overlapping ends ½ inch. Secure ends with a pin or a staple. Place ring on baking sheet. To use, follow directions for lining a flan ring (p. 232). Pinch off excess pastry with the fingers, or use a pair of scissors instead of rolling over the top.

Any size or shape flan ring can be improvised by this method.

APPLE TART I

rich tart pastry (p. 230)
3 pounds tart apples, preferably greenings
1 lemon, grated rind and juice
½ to ¾ cup water
½ cup yellow raisins
½ to 1 cup sugar (approximately)
1 egg mixed with
1 tablespoon milk
2 tablespoons cinnamon sugar (p. 44)
½ cup apricot glaze (p. 92)

Line a 9-inch flan ring with pastry dough. Save trimmings for top of tart. Chill pastry-lined flan, preferably in freezer, for at least 1 hour.

While pastry is chilling, peel, core, and cut apples into thick slices. Place them in a heavy saucepan with lemon juice, grated rind, and about ½ cup water. Cover saucepan and cook over low heat for 10 minutes. As soon as apples begin to steam, remove cover. Stir gently. Cook uncovered a few more minutes until they are just tender but not entirely mushy. Add raisins and sugar to taste. Cool.

Set oven temperature at 350 degrees.

Roll trimmings into a strip 10 inches long and ¼ inch thick. Brush with beaten-egg mixture. Sprinkle with cinnamon sugar. Cut into strips ¼ inch wide to be used for a lattice top.

Fill chilled pastry shell with cooled apples. Make a lattice of pastry strips on top.

Place on lowest rack of oven. Bake about 1 hour and 15 minutes, or until apple filling bubbles slightly in the center of tart. If necessary, raise tart to a higher rack during the last 15 minutes of baking so the lattice will brown.

While tart is still hot, brush apple filling showing through lattice with hot apricot glaze.

Note: Cooked apple filling can be frozen.

APPLE TART II

apple tart I
2 large apples
juice of 2 lemons
1 teaspoon vanilla
⅔ cup apricot glaze (p. 92)

Follow directions for apple tart I, omitting beaten egg and cinnamon sugar.

Instead of making a lattice top, peel, core, and slice thin 2 large apples. Soak them for 20 minutes in the juice of 2 large lemons and 1 teaspoon vanilla. Drain apples. Arrange them overlapping each other neatly on top of apple filling. Brush top with apricot glaze after baking.

RHUBARB TART

rich tart pastry (p. 230)
1 beaten egg mixed with
1 tablespoon milk
2 tablespoons cinnamon sugar (p. 44)
1 cup ground walnuts, filberts, or pecans
3 tablespoons flour
1 cup sugar
3 to 4 cups rhubarb, sliced in 1-inch pieces
½ cup currant glaze (p. 92)

Line a 9-inch flan ring with pastry. Save trimmings for top of tart. Chill pastry-lined flan, preferably in a freezer, for at least 1 hour.

Set oven temperature at 350 degrees.

Roll pastry trimmings into a strip 10 inches long and ¼ inch thick. Brush with beaten egg mixture. Sprinkle with cinnamon sugar. Cut into strips ¼ inch wide to be used for a lattice top.

Press ground nuts into bottom of pastry shell. Mix together flour, sugar, and rhubarb. Fill pastry shell. Make a lattice of pastry strips on top.

Place tart on lowest rack of oven. Bake 1 hour and 15 minutes, or until juices bubble in tart. If necessary, raise tart to a higher rack during last 15 minutes of baking so top browns.

While tart is still hot, brush currant glaze over rhubarb filling showing through lattice.

GLAZED FRUIT TART

(Made with uncooked fruit baked in an uncooked pastry shell.)

rich tart pastry (*p.* 230)
⅛ *teaspoon cinnamon*
¾ *cup ground almonds, pecans, or walnuts*
½ *cup sugar* (*approximately*)
3 *to* 4 *cups raw, pitted fruit, such as cherries, plums, pears, or peaches*
½ *cup apricot glaze or*
½ *cup currant glaze* (*p.* 92)

Line a 9-inch flan ring with pastry. Chill, preferably in freezer, for at least 1 hour.

Set oven at 350 degrees.

Add cinnamon to nuts. Sprinkle nuts over bottom of unbaked pastry shell, pressing them in gently but firmly.

Sprinkle sugar over prepared fruit. Toss lightly together. Place fruit neatly in unbaked shell, arranging top slices to form a design.

Place on lowest rack in preheated oven. Bake 1 hour and 10 minutes, or until fruit bubbles slightly in the center.

While tart is still hot, brush light-colored fruit, such as peaches, with apricot glaze and dark-colored fruit, such as cherries and plums, with currant glaze.

PLUM TART

Follow recipe for glazed fruit tart, using pitted, unpeeled plums. If plums are large, they should be quartered. Otherwise, cut them in half.

PEACH TART

Follow recipe for glazed fruit tart. Slice pitted, peeled peaches thin or cut into quarters or eighths.

CHERRY TART

Follow recipe for glazed fruit tart, using pitted cherries. If cherries are very sour, increase sugar to 1 cup.

PINEAPPLE TART I

1 nine-inch baked tart shell (*p.* 233)
1 ½ cups pastry cream (*p.* 95)
1 cup preserved pineapple (*p.* 108)
½ cup apricot glaze (*p.* 92)

Spread pastry cream in bottom of tart shell. Arrange well-drained pineapple pieces on top of pastry cream. Brush pineapple with apricot glaze.

PINEAPPLE TART II

1 nine-inch baked tart shell (*p.* 233)
1 cup ground walnuts or pecans
2 cups preserved pineapple (*p.* 108)
½ cup apricot glaze (*p.* 92)
1 cup heavy cream, whipped, unsweetened, flavored with brandy (*p.* 93)

Sprinkle ground nuts in bottom of tart shell. Arrange well-drained pineapple on top. Brush pineapple with apricot glaze. Serve with unsweetened, flavored whipped cream.

STRAWBERRY TART I

1 cup cold pastry cream (*p.* 95)
1 nine-inch baked tart shell (*p.* 233)
2 cups perfect strawberries, hulled
½ cup currant glaze (*p.* 92)

Spread pastry cream in bottom of baked tart shell, making a thin layer. Arrange strawberries on top, close together, using largest ones in center. Strawberries should cover pastry cream.

Spoon or lightly brush currant glaze over berries.

Refrigerate until serving time.

STRAWBERRY TART II

⅔ cup finely ground walnuts, pecans, or almonds
1 nine-inch baked tart shell (p. 233)
4 cups strawberries
1 cup currant glaze (p. 92)

Strawberries should be perfectly free of surface moisture. If they must be washed, be sure they are then thoroughly dried on paper towels.

Scatter ground nuts in bottom of baked tart shell. Press them in gently but firmly.

Slice 2 cups strawberries. Choose the least perfect ones for slicing. Pour half of hot currant glaze over slices. Toss gently. Spoon into pastry shell.

Arrange remaining whole berries on top, setting them close together. Spoon or brush remaining currant glaze over berries.

BLUEBERRY TART

4 cups blueberries
⅜ cup sugar
grated rind and juice of ½ lemon
½ teaspoon cinnamon
1 nine-inch baked tart shell (p. 233)

In a heavy saucepan, combine 1 ½ cups blueberries, sugar, lemon rind and juice, and cinnamon. Cook over low heat, stirring until sugar is dissolved. Raise heat and boil rapidly about 8 minutes, or until blueberries thicken and acquire the consistency of jam. Cool.

Combine raw blueberries with cooled jam, mixing gently. Spoon into baked tart shell.

Note: 1 cup pastry cream may be spread on bottom of baked tart shell before the blueberry mixture is added, if desired.

FRESH GRAPE TART

1 nine-inch baked tart shell (p. 233)
1 ½ cups apricot glaze (p. 92)
2 cups grapes of assorted colors, halved and seeded

Brush bottom of baked tart shell with apricot glaze. Fill shell ⅔ full with mixed, seeded grapes. Pour half of glaze over them. Arrange remaining grapes on top, making a design with the various colors (circles, triangles, etc.). Brush with apricot glaze.

GERMAN SPONGE TART

rich tart pastry (p. 230)
1 cup well-drained fruit preserves, such as cherry, peach, plum
⅔ cup walnuts, pecans, or filberts
1 tablespoon cinnamon sugar (p. 44)
4 eggs, separated
½ cup sugar
1 teaspoon vanilla
¼ cup sifted flour
¼ cup sifted cornstarch

Line a 9-inch flan ring, 1 inch deep, with pastry. Chill, preferably in freezer, for at least 1 hour.

Set oven at 375 degrees.

Grind nuts finely. Mix with cinnamon sugar. Press into bottom of well-chilled pastry shell. Spread preserves on top of nuts.

Separate eggs. Beat egg whites until they hold soft peaks. Add sugar gradually, a tablespoon at a time, beating very well after each one.

Stir egg yolks with a fork to break them up. Add vanilla. Fold about ¼ of the beaten egg whites thoroughly into egg yolks. Pour yolk mixture back over remaining stiffly beaten egg whites. Sprinkle flour and cornstarch lightly on top. Fold all gently together.

Pour sponge mixture into prepared tart shell.

Bake on lowest rack in preheated oven, 40 to 50 minutes, or until pastry is golden brown and sponge is puffed and a deep golden brown. Test sponge by inserting a toothpick into center. If toothpick is clean when it is withdrawn, remove tart from oven. If sponge shows signs of moisture, continue to bake as long as necessary. If top browns too rapidly, cover it with a piece of brown paper or a paper towel.

Cool tart before serving. Do not refrigerate.

MINCEMEAT TART I

rich tart pastry (p. 230)
1 *whole egg mixed with*
1 *tablespoon milk*
2 *tablespoons cinnamon sugar (p. 44)*
1 ½ *cups mincemeat filling, drained (p. 109)*
1 ¼ *cups peeled, chopped apple*
½ *cup apricot glaze (p. 92)*

Line a 9-inch flan ring with tart pastry. Save trimmings for top of tart. Chill, preferably in freezer, for at least 1 hour.

Set oven at 350 degrees.

Roll trimmings into a strip 10 inches long and ¼ inch thick. Brush with egg mixture. Sprinkle with cinnamon sugar. Cut into strips ¼ inch wide.

Combine mincemeat with chopped apples. Fill unbaked pastry shell. Make a lattice on top with pastry strips.

Place tart on lowest oven rack. Bake in preheated oven for 1 hour and 15 minutes, or until the filling bubbles. If necessary, raise tart to a higher rack during final 15 minutes of baking so lattice will brown.

While tart is still hot, brush apricot glaze over mincemeat filling showing through lattice.

MINCEMEAT TART II

mincemeat tart I
2 *large apples*
juice of 2 lemons
1 *teaspoon vanilla*
½ *cup apricot glaze (p. 92)*

Follow recipe for mincemeat tart I, omitting beaten egg mixture and cinnamon sugar.

Instead of making a lattice top, peel, core and thinly slice 2 large apples. Soak apples for 20 minutes in juice of 2 lemons and 1 teaspoon vanilla. Drain apples. Arrange them, overlapping each other, on top of mincemeat filling.

Glaze sliced apple top, after baking, with apricot glaze.

FRANGIPANE TART

rich tart pastry (p. 230)
2 recipes frangipane filling (p. 104)
½ cup apricot glaze (p. 92)
¼ cup coarsely chopped pistachio nuts

Line a 9-inch flan ring with pastry. Chill, preferably in freezer, for at least 1 hour.

Set oven at 350 degrees.

Fill pastry shell almost to the top with frangipane filling. Bake on lowest rack in oven until tart is golden brown, nearly 1 hour.

Brush tart, while still hot, with apricot glaze. Sprinkle with chopped pistachio nuts.

This recipe is especially delicious when made as tartlets.

LEMON PUFF TART

4 egg whites
pinch of salt
¼ cup sugar
¾ cup lemon cream (p. 101)
1 nine-inch baked tart shell (p. 233)

Set oven at 350 degrees.

Beat egg whites with salt until they hold soft peaks. Gradually beat in sugar, a tablespoon at a time. Continue to beat until whites are very stiff.

Fold egg whites into lemon cream. Pour into baked tart shell. Bake in a 350 degree oven about 15 minutes, or just long enough to set filling and lightly brown the top of tart.

CUSTARD TART

rich tart pastry (p. 230)
5 eggs
⅔ cup sugar
2 cups light cream
1 teaspoon vanilla
1 cup ground walnuts, filberts, or pecans
½ cup apricot glaze (p. 92)

Line a 9-inch flan ring with pastry. Roll pastry slightly thicker than usual to prevent seepage before custard is set. Chill pastry-lined flan ring, preferably in freezer, for at least 1 hour.

Set oven temperature at 350 degrees.

Beat eggs and sugar together for 3 minutes. Stir in cream and vanilla. Press ground nuts firmly into bottom of pastry shell. Pour egg mixture on top.

Bake on lowest rack of preheated oven about 1 hour, or until custard is set and lightly browned on top. While still hot, brush with apricot glaze. Chill before serving.

Note: Fresh fruit (berries, peaches, grapes, plums) can be arranged in a design on top of baked custard and glazed with apricot or currant glaze. Or, if preferred, fruit preserves, well drained, may be placed in bottom of an unbaked shell and the custard mixture poured on top.

LEMON CREAM TART

1 nine-inch baked tart shell (p. 233)
1 cup lemon cream (p. 101)
2 cups heavy cream, whipped, unsweetened, flavored with vanilla, gelatin added (p. 93)

Fold together lemon cream and 1 cup unsweetened whipped cream. Fill baked shell. Using pastry bag fitted with a medium star tube, make a lattice top with remaining whipped cream. Chill before serving.

APPLE CUSTARD TART

rich tart pastry (p. 230)
1 *cup cream*
3 *egg yolks*
1 *teaspoon vanilla*
1 *cup sweetened apple sauce*
nutmeg
vanilla sugar (p. 45)

Line a 9-inch flan ring with pastry. Chill, preferably in freezer, for at least 1 hour.

Set oven at 350 degrees.

Combine cream, yolks, and vanilla. Stir into apple sauce.

Pour into unbaked tart shell. Sprinkle with nutmeg.

Bake on lowest rack in preheated oven about 45 minutes, or until apple custard is set and crust is golden. Dust with vanilla sugar just before serving.

SOUR CREAM CUSTARD CHERRY TART

This can also be made with peaches or apricots.

rich tart pastry (p. 230)
3 *eggs*
⅓ *cup sugar*
¾ *cup sour cream*
½ *teaspoon vanilla*
2 *cups pitted sweet cherries*

Line a 9-inch flan ring with pastry. Chill, preferably in freezer, for at least 1 hour.

Set oven at 350 degrees.

Beat eggs with sugar, sour cream, and vanilla.

Arrange pitted cherries in unbaked tart shell. Pour egg mixture over them. Bake about 45 minutes on lowest rack of oven, or until custard is firm and crust is brown. Serve chilled.

Chapter 10

A Few Breads,

Many Coffeecakes

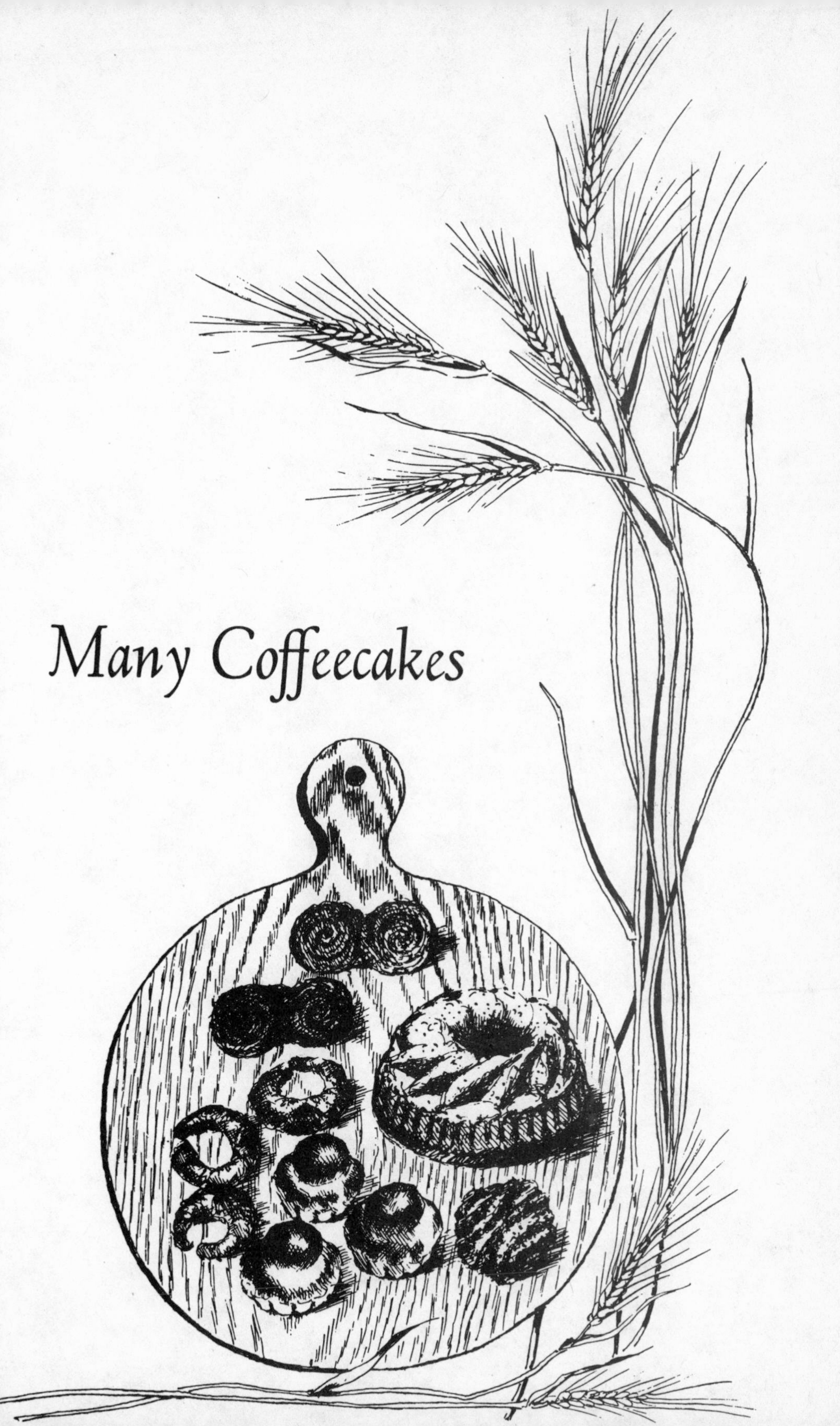

10 A Few Breads, Many Coffeecakes

The aroma of home-baked bread is probably the most delicious smell in the world. Furthermore, baking breads at home is fun. There is a lifelike quality to yeast dough as it is transformed in your hands from a sticky mass into satin-smoothness. A well-worked piece of yeast dough truly feels like satin—so smooth to touch you won't want to stop kneading it—and after the dough has been allowed to rise, it can be twisted, braided, or shaped to suit any fancy. Shaping yeast breads is much of the fun. The illustrations in this chapter show the various ways in which this can be done.

YEAST

Yeast is the beneficial living bacteria which leavens bread and gives it its characteristic flavor. Yeast is generally available in two forms: as fresh yeast which has been compressed into blocks or small cakes and as granulated, dry yeast.

Fresh yeast, although difficult to purchase in some areas, is preferable. Fortunately, even in large cities, pieces of fresh yeast can often be bought from small bakeries. Seeking a source of supply in your community is definitely worth while.

Two-ounce cakes of fresh yeast may be stored in the refrigerator for two weeks or more; larger pieces of yeast, even longer. A 1-pound cake will keep up to six weeks in the refrigerator. The dry brown edges which may form after yeast has been stored for a while can be cut away.

Four packages of granulated dry yeast equal 2 ounces of fresh yeast.

When using dry yeast, follow package directions for dissolving it in warm water. Subtract the water used for dissolving dry yeast from the total liquid in the recipe.

Since the action of yeast can be completely destroyed by extreme heat, the ingredients used in yeast dough should never be warmer than lukewarm. Ideally, yeast dough needs a temperature of around 80 degrees to rise. But this does not mean you can't bake with yeast if your kitchen is cool. Here is one solution that always works:

To raise yeast dough in a cool room, double the quantity of yeast in the recipe. Be sure that none of the ingredients is ice cold. They should be at room temperature, except for milk, which should be heated to lukewarm. After the dough has been mixed and kneaded, *set it to rise in the warmest spot in your kitchen. Near or on the stove, if it isn't hot, is a good place. On unheated oven is also fine, since it is at least draft-free.*

Using some additional yeast has no adverse effect on the taste of bread. On the other hand, as little as ½ ounce of yeast can be used for 4 cups of flour—but the dough will take several hours to rise.

Yeast must always be broken down into a liquid so that it can be mixed evenly through a dough. With fresh yeast this is usually done by crumbling it into a little lukewarm milk or water. Another method is to cream the yeast with the sugar and salt in a recipe. This creates a syrup which is easily combined with other ingredients and is an especially good method for recipes using cold milk, such as croissants or Danish pastry.

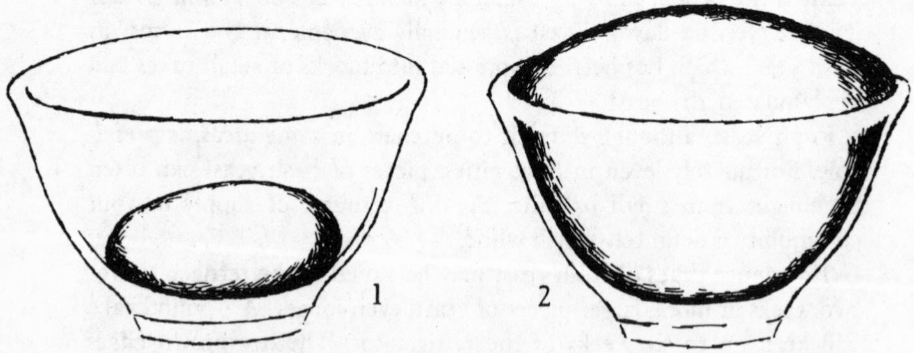

1. *Yeast dough before it has risen . . .*

2. *. . . after it has doubled in bulk*

OTHER INGREDIENTS

In most breads and coffeecakes, either all-purpose or bread flour can be used. Bread-flour doughs rise to a slightly greater volume and make breads which are a little lighter in texture. With all-purpose flour, yeast dough will, at best, double its bulk in rising; a bread-flour dough may rise 2½ to 3 times its original size. A dough has risen sufficiently if it no longer springs back when poked lightly in the center with two fingers—that is, when it holds the indentations.

Flours vary in their abilities to absorb moisture and develop gluten. This is why it is impossible to give an exact flour measurement for yeast doughs.

Milk, sugar, eggs, butter, and salt give color, richness, flavor, and texture to breads. The amounts of these ingredients also are variable. Bread which is excellent in both taste and appearance can be made from only flour, yeast, water, sugar, and salt. When shortening and milk are omitted, however, bread will have limited keeping quality.

KNEADING AND SHAPING YEAST DOUGHS

Kneading develops the gluten in flour, which in turn helps dough to stretch evenly, giving bread its characteristic light, airy texture. Doughs made from bread flour contain more gluten and require more kneading than doughs made from all-purpose flour.

Dough has been kneaded enough when it is smooth and satiny and loses its rough, sticky quality.

The well-kneaded dough should be placed in a large bowl, dusted with flour or lightly brushed with fat, covered, and allowed to rise until it has at least doubled its size.

Coffeecake doughs are not generally as firm as bread doughs. Babka, kugelhopf, and a number of other coffeecakes are made from heavy batters. These soft doughs should be especially well worked. They are beaten, rather than kneaded. This is best done in a bowl with the bare hand. The actual motion is a pulling one (see illustrations, page 20). Very soft dough has been worked sufficiently when it is satiny smooth and has many surface blisters.

After yeast dough has risen sufficiently, it must be punched down and lightly kneaded to remove all air. It can then be shaped.

Most shaped breads and coffeecakes should be permitted to rise again on a baking sheet or in pans until they have risen to almost double their original bulk. There are some exceptions, which will be noted in specific recipes.

Braids and twists should always be allowed to completely double in size before they are baked. If baked before having risen sufficiently, they will burst open at the seams while baking and lose attractiveness.

GLAZING YEAST BREADS

Some breads and most coffeecakes should be lightly brushed with an egg mixture just before baking to make a shiny brown crust.

Egg wash may be:

1. *Whole egg* beaten with 1 teaspoon cream or milk, which gives a shiny, medium-brown glaze.
2. *Egg yolk* beaten with 1 teaspoon cream or milk, which gives the shiniest, brownest glaze.
3. *Egg white* beaten with 1 teaspoon water, which gives shine without brownness.

Plain bread and rolls are usually brushed with whole egg or egg-white mixture. Elaborate coffeecakes and twists should be glazed with an egg-yolk wash.

BASIC WHITE BREAD

4 *packages dry yeast or* 2 *ounces fresh yeast*
2 *tablespoons salt*
3 *tablespoons sugar*
2 ¼ *cups lukewarm milk, water, or potato water* (*p.* 42)
6 *to* 8 *cups flour*
3 *tablespoons soft butter*

If dry yeast is used, follow directions on package. If fresh yeast is used, cream it with salt and sugar. Add liquid. Add enough flour to make a stiff dough. Add soft butter.

Knead (see p. 20), adding more flour if necessary, until dough is smooth and elastic—about 10 minutes.

Place dough in bowl. Flour it lightly. Cover and let rise in a draft-free place until it has doubled in bulk (30 to 45 minutes). Punch down. Knead again briefly, to remove all air. Return to bowl. Cover and let rise a second time until it has almost doubled in bulk.

Set oven temperature at 425 degrees. Grease two 9 x 5 x 3 loaf pans.

Divide dough in half. Mold dough into 2 compact loaves which are higher and rounder in the centers. Place in greased pans, filling them ⅔ full. Cover and let rise until dough reaches tops of pans.

Bake on lowest rack in preheated oven 30 to 40 minutes, or until loaves are golden brown. Remove bread from pans. Cool on a rack.

Brush loaves with an egg wash (see p. 254) before baking if a shiny crust is desired. To make a loaf of bread with a soft crust, brush with melted butter while bread is still hot. Makes 2 large loaves.

WHOLE WHEAT BREAD

basic white bread recipe (*above*), *made with*
1 *tablespoon sugar*
3 *tablespoons dark molasses*
(*substitute flour measurement as follows:*)
3 *to* 4 *cups flour*
3 *to* 4 *cups whole wheat flour*

Follow recipe for basic white bread, using only 1 tablespoon sugar. Add three tablespoons dark molasses. Substitute flour proportions given above.

CUBAN BREAD

Cuban bread is a crusty, delicious water bread. It was popularized by James Beard in his cooking classes, where students particularly enjoy making it because it is so quickly and easily learned.

Since it is a water bread without any shortening, it can be kept only for a day or two. However, it freezes as well as any other bread.

4 packages dry yeast or 2 ounces fresh yeast
2 tablespoons salt
1 tablespoon sugar
2 ½ cups warm water
7 to 8 cups flour
½ cup cornmeal
3 tablespoons sesame seeds (optional)

If dry yeast is used, follow directions on package. If fresh yeast is used, cream with salt and sugar to make a syrup. Add lukewarm water. Stir in enough flour to make a stiff dough. Knead dough well, until it is completely smooth and elastic, adding more flour if necessary.

Place dough in bowl. Dust top with flour. Cover bowl. Let rise in a draft-free place until dough has doubled in bulk, about 40 minutes.

Punch it down. Divide into 3 or 4 pieces. Shape by stretching and rolling each piece of dough into a long sausage about 1 ½ inches in diameter. Place loaves, well apart, on ungreased baking sheet which has been sprinkled with cornmeal.

Slash each loaf diagonally across top 3 or 4 times. Brush with water. Sprinkle with sesame seeds if desired.

Place on lowest rack in a cold oven. Turn oven on and set at 350 degrees. Bread will rise in oven. Bake 1 hour to 65 minutes, or until it is a deep, golden brown.

Makes 3 medium-size loaves.

WHOLE WHEAT CUBAN BREAD

Follow preceding recipe for Cuban bread. Substitute 3 to 4 cups whole wheat flour for the same amount of white flour, still using 6 to 8 cups in all.

ITALIAN PEPPER TWIST

Cuban bread dough (p. 255)
1 cup crisp pork cracklings
  or crisp, cooked sausage bits
1 tablespoon cracked black pepper
3 tablespoons lard (left from cooking pork)

Follow recipe for Cuban bread. After dough has risen, knead in cracklings and cracked pepper.

Divide dough into 6 equal pieces. Roll each piece into a long, thin sausage shape. Twist dough strips together in pairs, making 3 twisted loaves. Press ends of each loaf firmly together.

Set oven temperature at 425 degrees. Grease a baking sheet. Place twists well apart on lightly greased baking sheet. Let rise until almost double in bulk. Brush with melted lard.

Bake in preheated oven about 50 minutes, or until golden brown.

ROLLS

All the roll shapes shown below can be made from any bread dough. Basic white bread, Cuban bread, or even a *firm* brioche dough can be used for making small rolls.

After they have risen, rolls should be glazed with whole egg mixed with a teaspoon of milk. They may be sprinkled with caraway, poppy, or sesame seeds if desired. Bake rolls on lightly greased baking sheets in a 400 degree oven for 20 to 25 minutes, or until they are golden brown.

BRIOCHE

4 *packages dry yeast or* 2 *ounces fresh yeast*
¼ *cup sugar*
2 *teaspoons salt*
¾ *cup warm milk*
12 *egg yolks or* 6 *yolks and* 3 *whole eggs*
4 *to* 5 *cups flour*
1 *cup soft butter*
2 *egg yolks mixed with*
2 *teaspoons cream or milk*

If dry yeast is used, follow directions on package. If fresh yeast is used, cream it with sugar and salt to make a syrup. Add warm milk, egg yolks, and whole eggs if they are used. Stir well. Add 3 cups flour, then the soft butter. Knead very well, at least 10 minutes, until dough is smooth and elastic, adding more flour if necessary to make a medium-firm satiny dough.

SHAPING SMALL TWISTED ROLLS

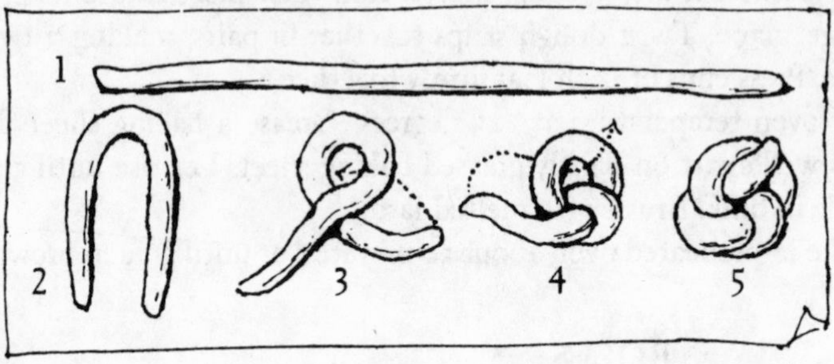

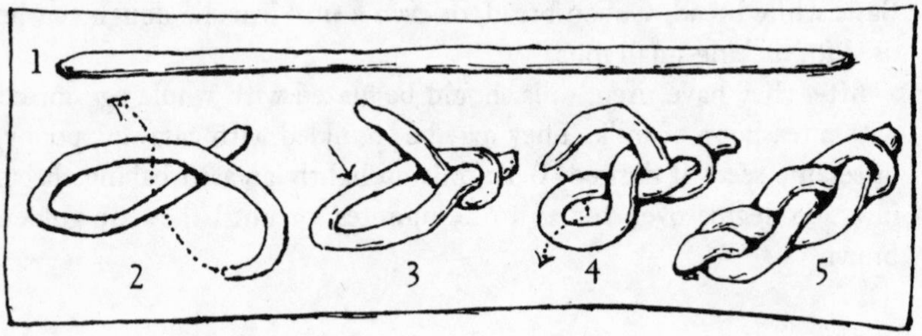

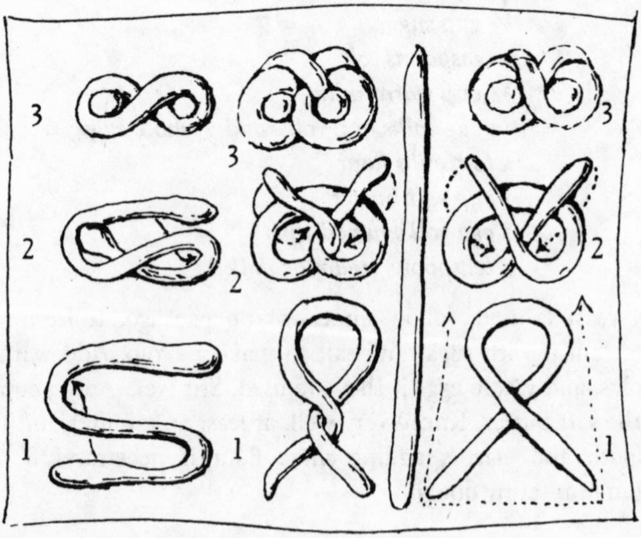

Place dough in bowl. Dust with flour. Cover bowl. Place in a draft-free place to rise until doubled in bulk, 30 to 45 minutes. Punch down thoroughly. Let rise once more, until dough has almost doubled in bulk. If dough is not to be used at once, refrigerate until it is needed.

Set oven temperature at 400 degrees. Grease small brioche tins (available at some of the shops listed on p. 49) or muffin tins.

Cut off egg-size pieces of dough. If it is important that all the brioches be exactly the same size, weigh out 2-ounce pieces of dough.

Roll dough into ovals. Using side of your hand, deeply indent about ⅓ of dough to separate it almost completely from the rest of the piece. Place dough, large end down, into greased brioche tins. Now round the smaller portion of dough on top into a knob, and press it firmly into the dough underneath. Be very sure the knob is set into rest of dough firmly or it will fall over as it rises during baking.

Let brioches rise until dough comes almost to tops of tins. With a pair of scissors, snip two or three times around knob to insure that it will retain its separate shape. Brush with egg yolk mixture. Bake in preheated oven for 20 to 25 minutes, or until brioches are a deep golden brown.

Yield: approximately 3 dozen.

CROISSANTS

After years of experimentation with croissant recipes, I have finally discovered the knack of making perfect, flaky croissants at home. Actually, the proportions given in almost any standard recipe for croissants could be followed, if only the method for making and shaping them were made clear.

2 *packages dry yeast or* 1 *ounce fresh yeast*
1 *tablespoon sugar*
2 *teaspoons salt*
4 *cups flour*
1 ½ *cups sweet butter*
1 *cup cold milk (approximately)*
2 *egg yolks mixed with*
2 *teaspoons cream*

SOME STEPS IN MAKING DOUGH FOR CROISSANTS AND DANISH PASTRY

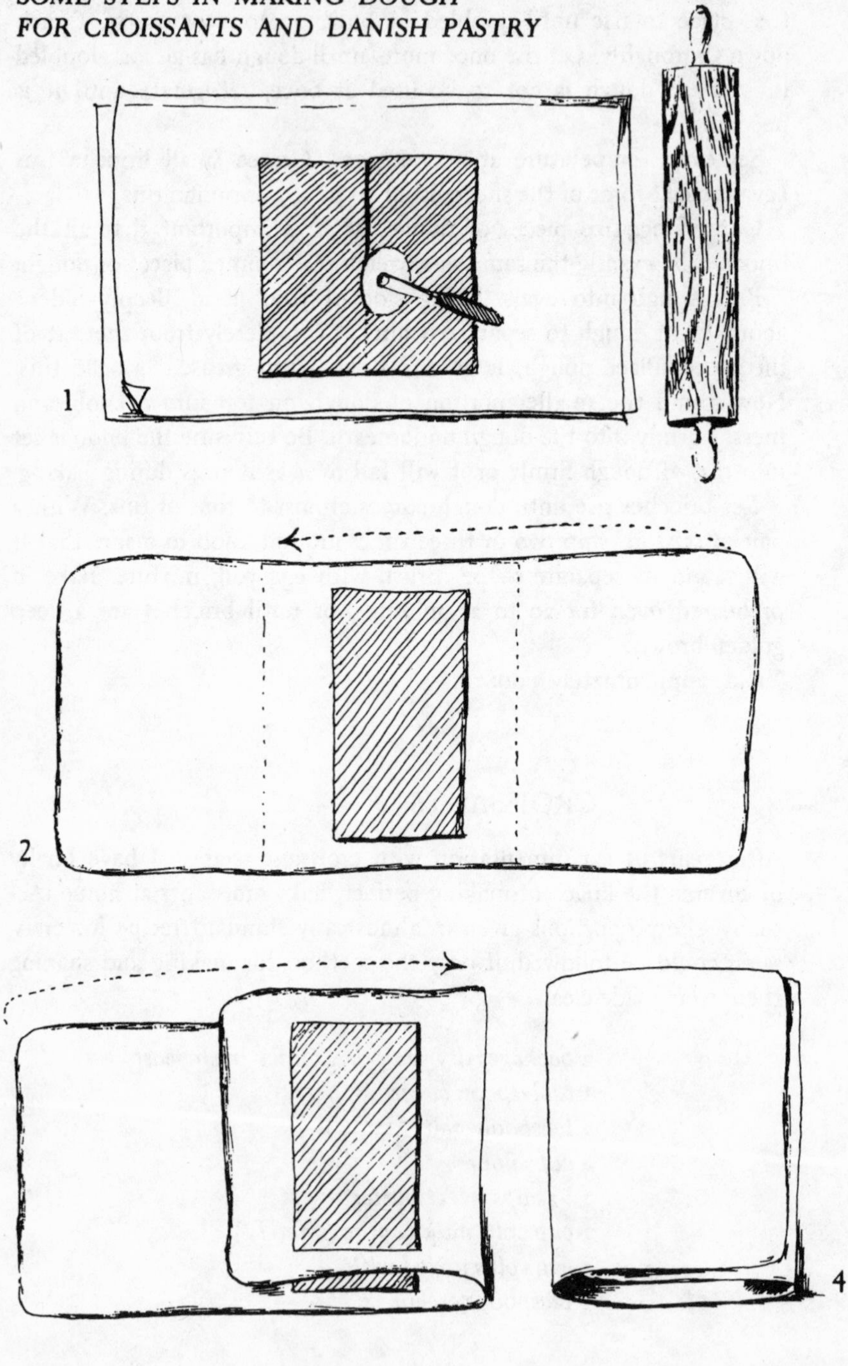

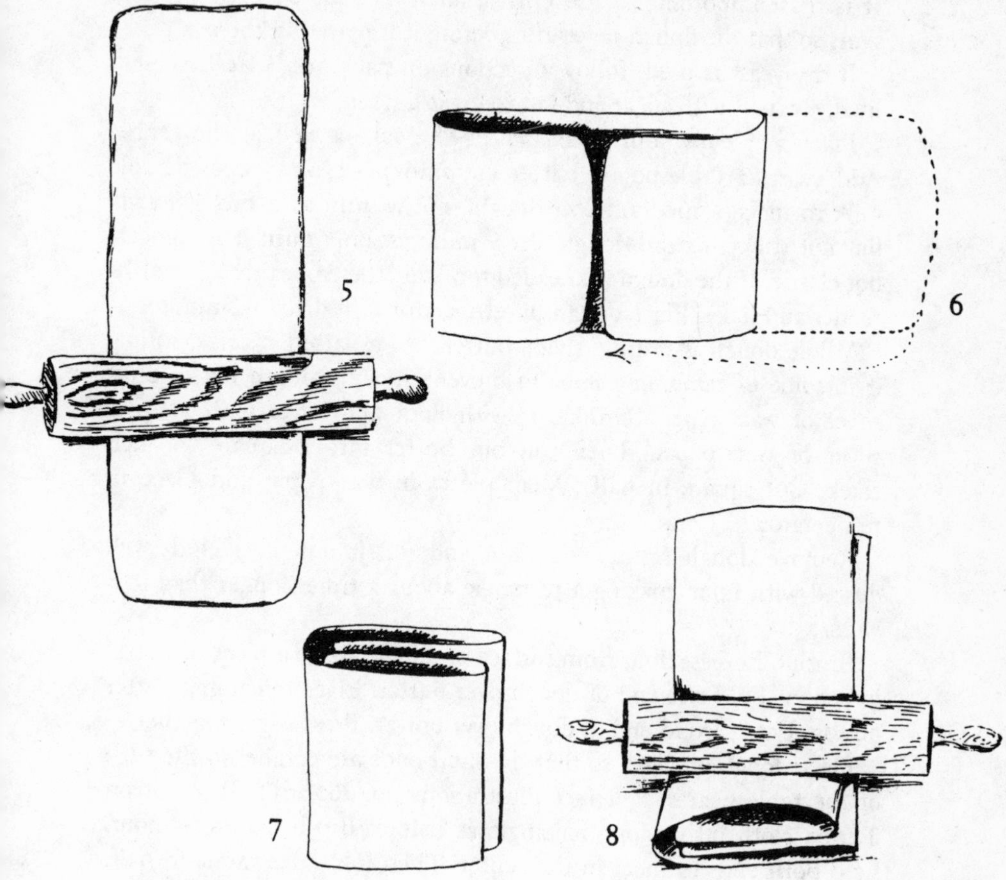

1. *Cutting rolled-out butter in half*

2. *Rolling out chilled yeast dough with one piece of butter in center*

3. *One end of dough folded over butter; second piece of butter on top*

4. *Second end of dough folded over butter, which is now entirely encased in dough*

5. *Dough after it has been rolled out*

6. *Ends of dough being folded to meet in center*

7. *Dough folded once more to make 4 layers*

8. *Position of dough before rolling out once more*

It is most important to use only a small amount of yeast in croissants so that the dough never rises before it is placed in the oven.

If dry yeast is used, follow directions on package. If fresh yeast is used, cream it with sugar and salt to make a syrup.

Place 3 ½ cups flour in a large bowl. Make a well in the center. Add yeast, 2 tablespoons butter cut into pieces, and enough cold milk to make a medium-firm dough—not as firm as a bread dough, but not sticky. Knead dough a few minutes, only until it is smooth, not elastic. If the dough is kneaded too long, the croissants will not be tender and flaky. Place dough in refrigerator to rest for 10 minutes.

While dough is resting, shape butter into a flattened brick, rolling it in some of remaining flour to prevent sticking. Place butter on a sheet of wax paper. Sprinkle it with flour and cover with another sheet of wax paper. Then roll out butter into a square ¼ inch thick. Cut square in half. Wrap pieces in wax paper and place in refrigerator.

Remove dough from refrigerator and roll it out on a cloth well dusted with flour, making a rectangle about 3 times longer than it is wide.

Brush off excess flour from surface of dough. Place a piece of butter in center. Fold one end of dough over butter. Place remaining butter on top. Fold second end of dough over butter. Press edges together.

Place dough on cloth so that the short ends are parallel to the edge of the table nearest you (see illustrations pp. 260-261). Roll out on floured cloth into a long rectangle as before. Brush off excess flour. Fold both ends to meet in the center. Then fold once more, in half, as if you were closing the pages of a book, making 4 layers.

Press all edges together. Wrap and chill for one hour. Place dough on floured cloth, again being sure that the short ends are parallel to the edge of table nearest you. Roll out dough. Fold ends to meet in the center, then fold once again as before.

Chill dough at least two or three hours, or until it is very cold.

Cut dough in half. Roll out each half separately into a sheet ⅛ inch thick. Cut into long strips 5 inches wide. Divide strips into triangles. Roll up widest side of triangles toward opposite point fairly tightly, stretching slightly as you roll to make them longer. Do not try to shape further now. First chill rolls, preferably in freezer, for ½ hour.

Then, removing only 4 or 5 at a time, make each into a thinner, longer, and more compact shape by rolling it firmly against the pastry cloth with open palm of hand. Place on greased baking sheet, curving each into a croissant. Chill again until very cold.

Set oven at 475 degrees.

Brush with egg yolks mixed with cream. Place in preheated oven for 5 minutes. Reduce heat to 400 degrees. Continue baking about 8 minutes longer, or until croissants are golden brown.

Yield: approximately 3 dozen.

Note: These freeze well after baking.

BASIC COFFEECAKE DOUGH

4 *packages dry yeast or* 2 *ounces fresh yeast*
1 *teaspoon salt*
½ *cup sugar*
1 *cup lukewarm milk*
1 *teaspoon vanilla*
½ *teaspoon grated lemon rind*
6 *egg yolks or* 3 *whole eggs*
4 *to* 5 *cups flour*
½ *cup butter*

If dry yeast is used, see directions on package. If fresh yeast is used, cream it with salt and sugar until a syrup forms. Add lukewarm milk, vanilla, and lemon rind. Beat in eggs. Add enough flour to make a medium-soft dough. Work in soft butter. Knead in bowl or on table for 10 minutes, adding more flour if necessary.

When dough has been kneaded enough, it will be shiny and elastic and have small blisters on the surface. Dust top lightly with flour. Cover bowl with a towel. Place in a draft-free place to rise. This will take 30 to 45 minutes. A smaller amount of yeast (half the amount given in the recipe) can be used to increase rising time; or, if you are in a hurry, a little extra yeast may safely be added. Dough must double in bulk before it can be used. It has risen enough if it is no longer springy when two fingers are poked into the center.

Punch dough down. Knead briefly. Shape as desired. Before baking, let rise again until almost double in bulk. Or, after punching dough down, cover bowl and place it in the refrigerator. Dough can be kept in the refrigerator up to 3 days. It must be punched down each time it rises. It will rise very often during the first 3 or 4 hours, and it must be attended to or it will sour. After it has become thoroughly chilled, it will need to be punched down no more than twice a day.

Makes 2 large coffeecakes.

EXTRA-RICH COFFEECAKE DOUGH

basic coffeecake dough (*p.* 263)
12 *egg yolks*
1 *cup soft butter*

Follow recipe for basic coffeecake dough, reducing milk to ½ cup. Substitute 12 yolks and 1 cup of butter for amounts of eggs and butter given in basic recipe.

Makes 2 large cakes.

RICH SOUR CREAM DOUGH

This, too, is a basic coffeecake dough, though a little different in texture from others. It makes a moister and less fluffy coffeecake and is especially suitable for small pastries, like schnecken, and larger cakes, like stollen, which are to be kept for a long time. Those who prefer a rich, moist, long-keeping coffeecake will particularly appreciate this recipe.

4 *packages dry yeast or* 2 *ounces fresh yeast*
½ *cup sugar*
1 *teaspoon salt*
½ *cup cold milk*
1 *cup sour cream*
2 *teaspoons lemon juice*
1 *teaspoon vanilla*
3 *egg yolks*
5 *to* 6 *cups flour*
1 ½ *cups soft butter*

If dry yeast is used, see directions on package. If fresh yeast is used, cream it with sugar and salt to make a syrup. Add milk, sour cream, lemon juice, and vanilla. Stir in egg yolks. Add enough flour to make a medium-firm dough. Beat in soft butter. Knead in bowl or on table for 10 minutes, adding more flour if necessary. When dough has been kneaded enough, it will be smooth and elastic. Cover bowl and place in refrigerator immediately for at least 4 hours before using.

Like basic coffeecake dough, this sour-cream dough will rise in the refrigerator. It should be punched down each time. After it has become thoroughly chilled, it will need to be punched down no more than twice a day. It will keep in the refrigerator up to 3 days.

It can substitute in any recipe for basic coffeecake dough.

Makes 3 cakes.

FRUIT KUCHEN

½ basic coffeecake dough (p. 263)
1 egg mixed with
1 teaspoon cream
3 cups fruit (plums, cherries, apples, or peaches, pitted or sliced as necessary)
1 teaspoon grated lemon rind
¼ cup cinnamon sugar (p. 44) or 1 cup streusel (p. 107)

Set oven temperature at 350 degrees. Grease an 11 x 16 jelly-roll pan.

Roll or pat basic coffeecake dough to fit pan. Let dough become puffy, but do not let it double. Brush with beaten egg mixture.

Arrange pitted, sliced fruit over top. Sprinkle fruit with grated lemon rind and cinnamon sugar, or with streusel.

Bake in preheated oven about 50 minutes, or until cake is golden brown. Serve warm.

CHEESE KUCHEN

¼ basic coffeecake dough (p. 263)
cheese filling (p. 103)
2 tablespoons cinnamon sugar (p. 44)

Set oven temperature at 350 degrees. Grease a 9-inch flan ring which has been placed on a greased cooky sheet. Roll or pat dough to fit into ring. Let dough become puffy, but do not let it double.

Fill with cheese filling. Sprinkle with cinnamon sugar. Bake in preheated oven about 45 minutes, or until top is golden.

POTATO CREAM KUCHEN

¼ basic coffeecake dough (p. 263)
potato cream filling (p. 106)
1 large apple, peeled, cored, and thinly sliced
2 tablespoons cinnamon sugar (p. 44)

Set oven temperature at 350 degrees. Grease a 9-inch flan ring which has been placed on a greased cooky sheet. Roll or pat dough to fit into ring. Let dough become puffy, but do not let it double.

Fill with potato cream filling. Arrange sliced apple over top. Sprinkle with cinnamon sugar. Bake in preheated oven about 45 minutes, or until cake is golden brown.

ORANGE HONEY TWIST

basic coffeecake dough (p. 263)
¼ cup melted butter
orange honey filling (p. 104)
⅔ cup finely crushed walnuts
½ cup diced candied orange peel
1 cup white sultana raisins
1 egg yolk mixed with
1 teaspoon cream
½ cup blanched, sliced almonds

Set oven temperature at 350 degrees. Grease two 9 x 5 x 3 loaf pans.

Roll dough into a large square ¼ inch thick. Brush with melted butter. Spread thinly with orange honey filling. Scatter crushed walnuts, candied orange peel, and raisins over dough. Roll up jelly-roll style.

With a rolling pin press filled dough down to a thickness of 1 inch. Divide flattened roll lengthwise to make 3 long strips. Cut in half to make 6 shorter strips. Braid cut strips together to make 2 loaves.

Fit each loaf into greased pan. Let rise until dough doubles in bulk. Brush with egg-yolk mixture. Scatter almonds over twists.

Bake in preheated oven about 45 minutes, or until they are golden brown.

APPLE ROLL

basic coffeecake dough (p. 263)
¼ cup melted butter
1 ½ cups peeled, cored, coarsely chopped apples, or apple custard filling (p. 105)
¾ cup white sultana raisins
½ cup cinnamon sugar (p. 44)
1 egg mixed with
1 tablespoon milk

Set oven at 350 degrees. Grease two 9 x 5 x 3 loaf pans.

Roll dough into a large square ¼ inch thick. Brush with melted butter. Scatter chopped apples or spread apple custard filling over dough. Sprinkle with raisins. If chopped raw apples are used, sprinkle them with half of cinnamon sugar. Roll up jelly-roll style. Divide roll into two pieces.

Fit each half into a greased pan. Let rise until dough has almost doubled in bulk. Brush with egg mixture. Sprinkle with cinnamon sugar.

Bake in preheated oven about 45 minutes, or until cakes are golden brown.

POPPY SEED ROLL

basic coffeecake dough (p. 263)
poppy seed filling (p. 102)
1 egg mixed with
1 tablespoon milk

Set oven at 350 degrees. Grease two 9 x 5 x 3 loaf pans.

Roll out dough less than ¼ inch thick. Spread poppy seed filling evenly over dough. Roll up jelly-roll style. Cut roll in half to make 2 cakes. Fit each half into a greased pan. Let rise until dough has almost doubled in bulk. Brush with egg mixture.

Bake in preheated oven about 45 minutes, or until cakes are golden brown.

STREUSEL ROLL

basic coffeecake dough (*p.* 263)
⅓ cup melted butter
⅔ cup cinnamon sugar (*p.* 44)
⅔ cup currants
1 cup finely crushed pecans
streusel topping (*p.* 107)

Set oven temperature at 350 degrees. Grease two 9 x 5 x 3 loaf pans.

Roll dough into a large square ¼ inch thick. Brush with most of melted butter and sprinkle with cinnamon sugar, currants, and crushed pecans. Roll up jelly-roll style.

Cut roll evenly into 6 slices. Fit 3 slices, cut sides flat, into each pan, squeezing them in if necessary. Press slices down into pan so that, in rising, they will grow together.

Let rise until dough has almost doubled in bulk. Brush tops lightly with remaining melted butter. Scatter streusel topping generously over each cake.

Bake in preheated oven about 45 minutes, or until streusel tops are lightly browned.

APPLE CRESCENT HORNS

rich sour cream dough (*p.* 264)
apple custard filling (*p.* 105)
streusel topping (*p.* 107)
½ cup heavy cream

Set oven temperature at 375 degrees. Grease baking sheets lightly.

Roll dough into a rectangle less than ¼ inch thick. Spread it thinly with apple custard filling. Sprinkle with ⅓ of streusel topping.

Roll up tightly, jelly-roll style, cutting off rolls as soon as they are 1 inch in diameter. Cut rolls into 3-inch lengths. Curve each one into a crescent shape.

Place on prepared baking sheet. Let rise only until dough looks puffy. Brush all over with cream. Sprinkle with remaining streusel.

Bake in preheated oven about 20 minutes, or until horns are golden brown.

Yield: approximately 6 dozen.

SCHNECKEN

½ cup soft butter
1 ½ cups well-packed light-brown sugar
1 tablespoon white corn syrup
1 ½ cups coarsely broken or whole pecans
rich sour cream dough (p. 264)
2 teaspoons cinnamon
1 cup currants or raisins
1 cup finely crushed pecans

Cream butter with ½ cup light-brown sugar. Beat in corn syrup. Grease regular size or tiny muffin tins with this mixture, using it generously. Place 2 or 3 pecan pieces into each muffin cup.

Set oven temperature at 375 degrees.

Roll dough into a long rectangle ¼ inch thick. Sprinkle with remaining sugar, cinnamon, currants or raisins, and crushed pecans.

Roll dough tightly, jelly-roll style, sealing the seam. If roll becomes much thicker than the size of muffin tins, stretch it out. If it is too thin, gently compress it.

Slice roll into pieces which will fill muffin cups halfway. Press slices into cups firmly. Let rise only until dough looks puffy.

Bake in preheated oven about 20 minutes, or until tops of schnecken are golden brown.

Turn muffin pans upside down immediately, to remove schnecken and to permit glaze to run over sides.

Yield: approximately 7 dozen small schnecken or 5 dozen larger ones.

BUTTER TWISTS

rich sour cream dough (p. 264), using only 1 tablespoon of sugar
2 to 3 cups granulated sugar

Prepare rich sour cream dough, using only 1 tablespoon of sugar. Roll chilled dough into a rectangle ⅓ inch thick. Sprinkle generously with sugar. Fold dough into thirds. Wrap in floured aluminum foil. Place in refrigerator for ½ hour.

Roll out dough twice more, each time sprinkling with sugar, folding into thirds and chilling. After dough has been rolled out, sugared, and folded 3 times, chill it for 1 hour. Divide dough in half. Roll out each half separately to make two 8 x 16 rectangles. Sprinkle with sugar. Fold rectangles in half, lengthwise, making each 4 x 16. Cut crosswise into 1-inch-wide strips. Dip strips into sugar. Twist ends in opposite directions. Chill.

Set oven temperature at 375 degrees.

Place chilled twists on ungreased baking sheets. Press down ends firmly to prevent them from unwinding.

Bake in preheated oven about 20 minutes, or until twists are golden.

Yield: approximately 6 dozen.

JELLY DOUGHNUTS

2 packages dry yeast or 1 ounce fresh yeast
2 tablespoons sugar
1 teaspoon salt
1 cup warm milk
1 egg
2 egg yolks
1 teaspoon grated lemon rind
3 to 4 cups flour
¼ cup soft butter
fat for deep frying
1 ½ cups jam
vanilla sugar (*p.* 45)

If dry yeast is used, see directions on package. If fresh yeast is used, cream it with sugar and salt to make a syrup. Add milk, egg, egg yolks, and lemon rind. Mix well. Add enough flour to make a medium-firm dough, working in soft butter at the same time. Knead well until dough is smooth and elastic. Place dough in bowl. Dust lightly with flour. Cover bowl. Place in a draft-free place until dough doubles in bulk.

After dough has risen, punch it down. Cover bowl. Let rise a second time.

Shape doughnuts by pinching off egg-size pieces of dough and forming each into a smooth, slightly flattened ball. Place on a floured towel. Let balls rise until all are doubled in size.

While doughnuts are rising, heat fat to 375 degrees.

Drop doughnuts into fat, 2 or 3 at a time. Fry until undersides are a deep golden brown. Turn and fry until second sides are also well browned, about 5 minutes in all.

Remove from fat. Drain on paper towels or brown paper.

When doughnuts are thoroughly cool, fill them by squirting jam into their centers with a long, narrow pastry tube. Dust with vanilla sugar.

Yield: approximately 3 dozen.

PANETTONE
(*An Italian Fruit Bread*)

extra-rich coffeecake dough (*p.* 264)
1 ½ *cups additional flour* (*approximately*)
½ *cup white sultana raisins*
½ *cup black sultana raisins*
⅔ *cup diced candied citron*
¼ *cup melted butter*

Follow recipe for extra-rich coffeecake dough, adding enough additional flour to make a fairly firm dough.

After dough has risen, knead in raisins and candied citron. Do not handle dough more than necessary after fruit has been added or it will turn gray.

Set oven temperature at 400 degrees. Grease a large baking sheet.

Divide dough in half. Shape each piece into a ball. Place balls well apart on greased baking sheet. Cut a cross on top of each ball.

Enclose each with a 5-inch-high collar made of greased heavy brown paper. Secure collars by tying them with string or by pinning or clipping them. If preferred, 2 deep 8-inch pans may be substituted.

Let dough rise until almost double in bulk. Brush with melted butter.

Bake in preheated oven for 10 minutes. Reduce heat to 350 degrees. Continue baking 30 to 40 minutes longer, brushing twice more with melted butter.

Bake until cakes are golden brown.

Yield: 2 loaves.

DRESDEN STOLLEN

1 cup white sultana raisins
¾ cup currants
1 ¼ cups mixed, diced candied fruit
¼ cup cognac
½ cup blanched, sliced, lightly toasted almonds
rich sour cream dough (p. 264)
½ cup melted butter
vanilla sugar (p. 45)

Mix raisins, currants, and candied fruit together in a bowl. Pour cognac over fruit. Let stand at least 1 hour. Drain excess liquid, if any, from fruit.

Knead fruit and almonds into dough. Work dough only until fruit is evenly distributed. Too much handling will turn dough gray.

Set oven temperature at 375 degrees. Lightly grease a large baking sheet.

Cut dough in half. On a floured surface, roll each piece into an oval ⅓ inch thick. Fold oval almost, but not quite, in half, so that the bottom edge of dough extends beyond the top (as in a Parker House roll). Lightly roll folded dough with a rolling pin to set fold.

Place stollens well apart on prepared baking sheet. Allow to rise until puffy but not quite doubled. Brush all over with melted butter. Bake in preheated oven about 45 minutes, until cakes are golden brown.

Brush again with melted butter while cakes are still warm; then brush with butter a final time after stollens have cooled.

Dust heavily with vanilla sugar. Wrap cooled stollens in aluminum foil. Store until needed. Just before serving, dust again with vanilla sugar. Cut into thin slices.

Makes 2 large stollens.

POLISH BABKA

2 ½ cups milk
6 cups flour (approximately)
4 packages dry yeast or 2 ounces fresh yeast
½ cup sugar
1 teaspoon salt
16 egg yolks
¾ cup soft butter
1 cup white sultana raisins
¼ cup rum
½ cup rum fondant (see Chapter 3) or vanilla sugar (p. 45)

Bring milk to a rolling boil. Add to 1 ¼ cups flour, beating it in hard until mixture is as fluffy as mashed potatoes. Cool to lukewarm.

If dry yeast is used, see directions on package. If fresh yeast is used, cream it with sugar and salt to make a syrup. Add syrup to *cooled* paste. Let rise 20 minutes, or until mixture is a light sponge. Stir it down.

Beat in egg yolks and enough flour to make a soft, sticky dough. Add soft butter.

Knead dough in bowl until it is very smooth, shiny, and elastic (see p. 20). Your hand should be clean when it is pulled abruptly from the dough. Kneading by hand will take about 40 minutes, possibly longer. Take short rests if you want. It is possible to beat this dough in the type of home mixer equipped with a kneading hook (not those with rotary beaters). When dough has been beaten enough, cover it with a towel and let rise in a draft-free place until it doubles in bulk.

Set oven temperature at 375 degrees. Grease two small kugelhopf pans. One large kugelhopf pan may be used if you desire.

Stir risen dough down. Work in raisins. Fill pan or pans halfway. Let dough rise until it almost doubles in bulk. Bake in preheated oven 30 to 45 minutes, or until cakes are a deep golden brown.

Remove cakes from pans. Sprinkle them with rum. While they are still warm, brush with rum fondant; or dust with vanilla sugar after cakes are cool.

Yield: 1 large or 2 medium-size cakes.

DANISH PASTRY

When making Danish pastry it is important to keep the dough very cold. In shaping small pastries, it is sometimes necessary to re-chill partially shaped dough until it is firm enough for the job to be completed.

When you first make Danish pastry, be careful to follow all the rules. Don't make it in the summertime unless your kitchen is air-conditioned. After you gain experience you may attempt short cuts such as rolling out and folding the dough twice in succession without re-chilling.

Another way of shortening the process is by placing the dough in the freezer between rollings. Usually 10 minutes in the freezer is sufficient. When you use this short cut, be careful not to freeze the dough solid.) The shaped pastries can also be chilled in the freezer. They can even be baked frozen if extra baking time is allowed. Any unbaked yeast pastries, however, should never be kept frozen for more than a week or so; and it is preferable to bake Danish pastry within a day or two after it has been shaped.

DANISH PASTRY

4 to 6 cups flour
2 packages dry yeast or 1 ounce fresh yeast
3 tablespoons sugar
1 teaspoon salt
3 whole eggs or 6 egg yolks
1 teaspoon grated orange rind
¼ teaspoon ground cardamom seeds (optional)
1 teaspoon vanilla
1 ¼ cups cold milk (approximately)
2 cups butter, firm, but not ice cold

Place 4 cups flour in a large bowl. Reserve remaining flour for rolling. Make a well in center of bowl.

If dry yeast is used, see directions on package. If fresh yeast is used, cream it with sugar and salt to make a syrup. Add egg yolks or whole eggs, grated orange rind, ground cardamom seeds, and vanilla.

Pour yeast mixture into well. Add one cup milk and ¼ cup butter cut into pieces. Mix with finger tips, adding more milk if necessary, to make a medium-soft dough. Knead dough in bowl for 5 minutes, or until it is smooth but not elastic. Flour it and let rest in refrigerator for 10 minutes.

While dough is resting, form remaining butter into a flattened brick. Using some of reserved flour on wax paper or a pastry cloth, roll out butter into a square about ⅓ inch thick. Use plenty of flour under and on top of butter to keep it from sticking. Loosen it frequently as you roll. Cut the square in 2 pieces. Place in refrigerator between sheets of wax paper (see illustrations pp. 260-61).

Roll out dough on well-floured cloth to make a rectangle 3 times longer than wide and about ⅓ inch thick. Brush excess flour from dough. Place a piece of butter in center. Fold one end of dough over butter. Place remaining butter on top. Fold second end over the butter. Press edges together.

Turn dough, changing its position so that the short ends are parallel with the edge of table nearest you. Roll out on well-floured cloth, using a firm, even motion to spread butter together with dough. Try to work quickly, but check frequently underneath the dough to be sure it isn't sticking. Roll out a rectangle 3 times longer than wide, about ⅓ inch thick. Brush excess flour from surface. Fold both ends of dough to meet in the center. Press edges together, then fold in half as if closing a book, which will make 4 layers of dough. Flour dough. Place on cooky sheet. Cover with aluminum foil. Refrigerate for ½ hour.

Repeat rolling and folding dough 3 more times, chilling it 20 minutes between rollings. Be sure to change position of dough each time so that the short ends of dough are parallel with the edge of table nearest you when you start rolling.

After final folding, chill dough at least 3 hours before shaping and baking. Bake as directed on p. 277.

BUTTER ROLL PASTRY

An easier, fluffier version of Danish-type pastry.

4 packages of dry yeast or 2 ounces fresh yeast
4 tablespoons sugar
1 teaspoon salt
1 cup cold milk
3 eggs
1 teaspoon vanilla
1 teaspoon grated orange rind
¼ teaspoon ground cardamom seeds (optional)
4 to 5 cups flour
1 cup butter

If dry yeast is used, see directions on package. If fresh yeast is used, cream it with sugar and salt to make a syrup. Add cold milk, eggs, vanilla, orange rind, and ground cardamom. Add enough flour to make a medium-soft dough. Knead only 5 minutes or until smooth. Place dough in bowl. Dust with flour. Cover bowl. Place in refrigerator for 20 minutes.

Roll out dough on a floured cloth to make a rectangle 3 times longer than wide. Brush off excess flour. Dot center with ⅔ cup butter. Fold ends of dough over butter so that they meet in the center. Press down edges. Dot one side of folded dough with remaining ⅓ cup butter. Fold in half, covering butter. Press all edges together. Chill for 20 minutes.

Place dough on floured cloth so that short ends are parallel with the edge of table nearest you. Roll dough into rectangle as before. Fold ends to meet in the center. Press them down. Then fold dough in half as if closing a book, again making 4 layers. Chill for 20 minutes.

Repeat rolling and folding 3 more times, chilling dough 20 minutes between rollings. Be sure short ends of dough are parallel to edge of table nearest you when you start rolling. When dough has been rolled and folded a total of 5 times, chill it for several hours more before rolling it out thin, shaping pastries, and baking them.

Bake as directed on p. 277.

BAKING DANISH OR BUTTER ROLL PASTRY

Danish pastry (p. 274) or butter roll pastry (p. 276)
filling of your choice (see Chapter 3, coffeecake fillings)
2 egg yolks mixed with 2 teaspoons cream
sliced, blanched almonds
apricot glaze (p. 92), optional
rum fondant (see Chapter 3, frostings), optional

Follow instructions in subsequent recipes for shaping either small or large Danish pastries. Chill shaped pastries until they are cold, usually about 20 minutes for small ones and up to 45 minutes for larger rings.

While pastry is chilling, set oven at 450 degrees. Lightly grease baking sheets.

Place chilled pastries well apart on baking sheets. Brush all over with egg yolk mixed with cream. Sprinkle with sliced, blanched almonds. Place in preheated oven. Bake small pastries for 10 minutes. Reduce heat to 375 degrees. Continue to bake 10 to 15 minutes, or until pastries are golden brown. Bake large cakes in a 450 degree oven for 15 minutes. Reduce heat to 375 degrees and continue baking 30 to 40 minutes, or until golden brown.

Immediately upon taking pastries from oven, brush with hot apricot glaze, then, if desired, brush very lightly with rum fondant.

Pastries which are rolled in sugar before baking need no further glaze of any kind.

Danish pastries freeze very well after baking if they are thoroughly cooled. Do not brush with rum fondant if they are to be frozen. To serve, reheat frozen pastries until they are just crisp. Glaze as desired after removing from oven.

The recipe for Danish pastry which follows will make approximately 40 small pastries, or 3 medium or 2 very large cakes.

LARGE DANISH RING

½ recipe Danish pastry (p. 274)
coffeecake filling (see Chapter 3, coffeecake fillings)

To make a filled coffee ring approximately 12 inches in diameter, roll out half of Danish pastry dough into a rectangle 6 x 25 x ¼ (pp. 280-81).

Spread dough with thin layer of any preferred coffeecake filling. Fold lengthwise into thirds, making a strip 25 x 2. Roll this strip gently with a rolling pin to flatten and lengthen it slightly.

With a knife, make 3 incisions lengthwise, spaced equally, almost the full length of the strip, leaving an inch or so uncut at the ends. Take one end in each hand. Turn and lightly roll the ends in opposite directions to form a long twist, stretching dough slightly. Continue to hold ends so they won't unwind. Shape into a ring, crossing ends and pressing them down firmly to join.

Holding joined ends down against the table with one hand, flip ring over toward you with the other hand so that ends are concealed underneath. Place on prepared baking sheet. Press down top of ring slightly to flatten it.

Bake as directed on p. 277.

LARGE DANISH TWIST

½ recipe Danish pastry (p. 274)
coffeecake filling (see Chapter 3, coffeecake fillings)

Roll out Danish pastry to make a square ⅛ inch thick. Spread dough thinly with any preferred coffeecake filling. Roll up tightly, jelly-roll style. Press down with a rolling pin to flatten the filled roll slightly.

Cut filled roll in half lengthwise, exposing the layers of filling. Entwine strips together, keeping filling turned face up. Pinch ends to seal them.

Place on prepared baking sheet. Flatten twist slightly.

Bake as directed on p. 277.

DANISH CLUSTER CAKE

Follow directions for making cinnamon buns (p. 283), using any coffeecake filling (see Chapter 3).

Cut into slices 2 inches thick. Lay slices down flat and close together in a deep, greased pan. To give cake a more interesting shape, 2 or 3 center slices may be placed upright rather than flat.

Bake as directed on p. 277.

SMALL DANISH RINGS

½ recipe Danish pastry (p. 274)
1 egg, slightly beaten
1 cup currants
3 tablespoons rum
½ cup finely crushed pecans
⅔ cup cinnamon sugar (p. 44)

Roll out Danish pastry to make a long strip ⅛ inch thick and 12 inches wide.

Brush dough with beaten egg. Sprinkle with currants which have been soaked in rum for a few minutes. Scatter crushed pecans and cinnamon sugar over dough. Roll over filling lightly with a rolling pin.

Fold dough in half lengthwise to make strip 6 inches wide. Roll lightly over folded dough. Cut crosswise into ¾-inch strips. Make an incision down the center of each strip almost to each end.

Follow twisting and shaping instructions given for large Danish ring (p. 278) and bake as directed on p. 277.

Yield: approximately 20.

CUSTARD SNAILS

½ recipe Danish pastry (p. 274)
½ recipe pastry cream (p. 95)

Roll out Danish pastry into a strip ⅛ inch thick and 18 inches long. Cut into strips 18 x ¾.

SHAPING A COFFEE RING

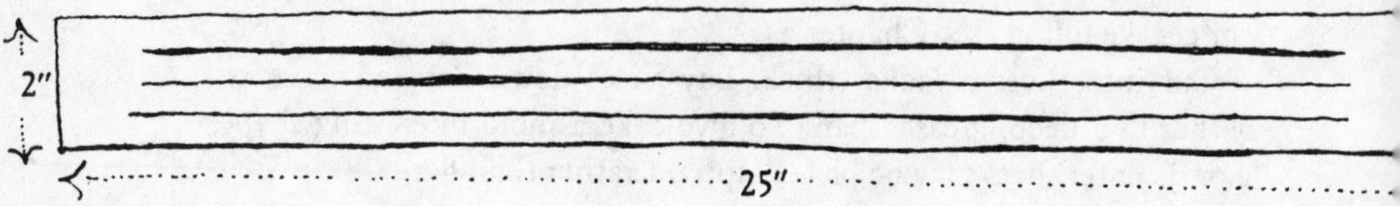

1

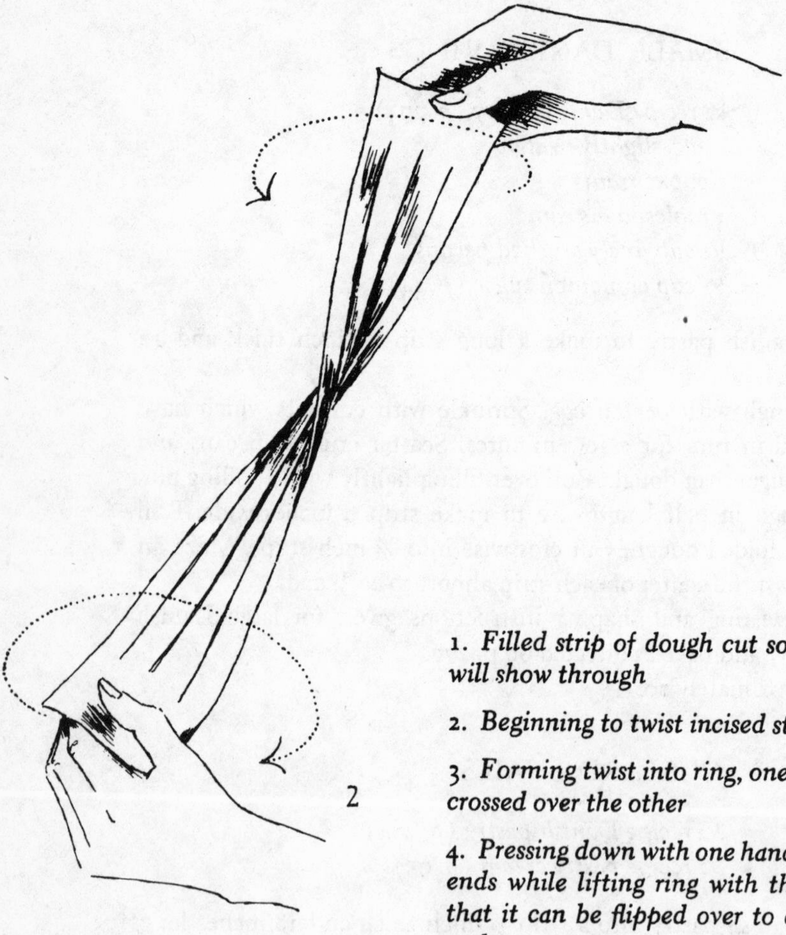

2

1. *Filled strip of dough cut so that filling will show through*

2. *Beginning to twist incised strip*

3. *Forming twist into ring, one end crossed over the other*

4. *Pressing down with one hand on crossed ends while lifting ring with the other, so that it can be flipped over to conceal the ends*

5. *Ring with ends concealed*

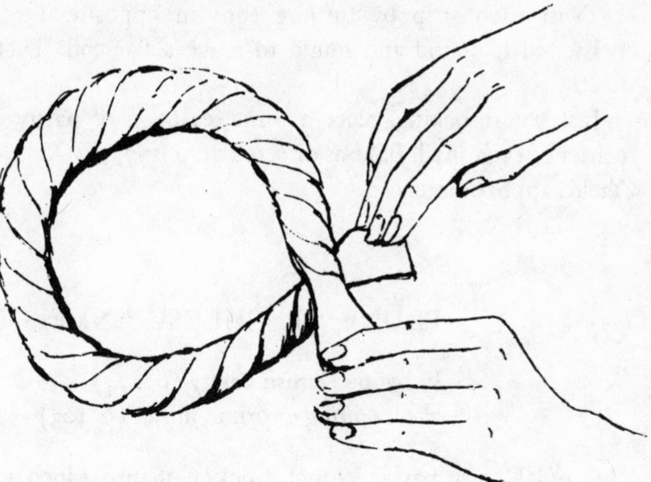

3

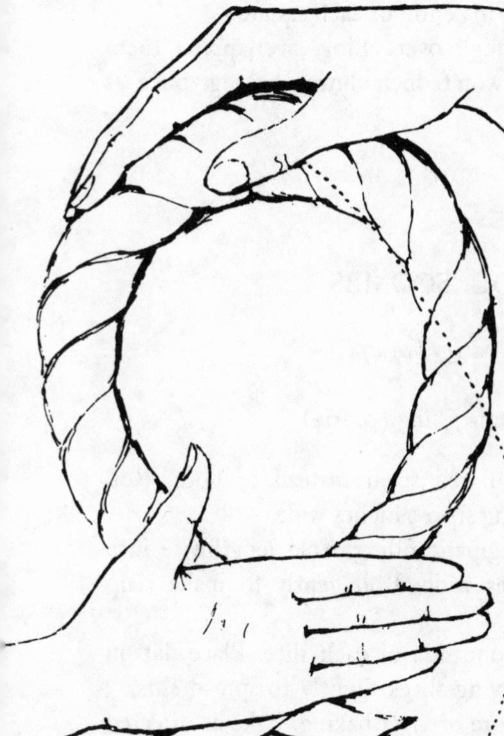

4

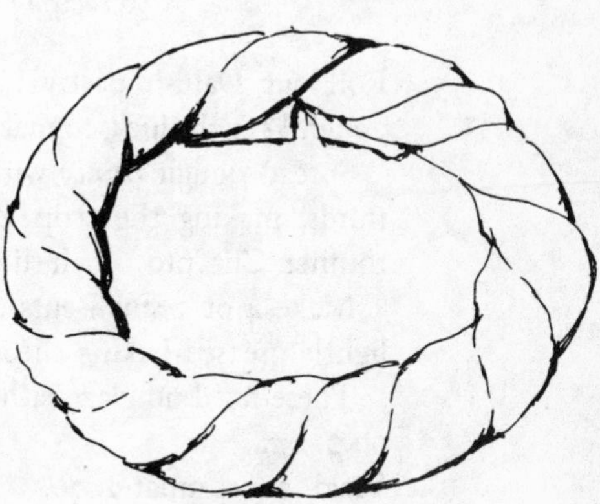

5

Twist each strip by turning ends in opposite directions. Wind twisted strip round and round to make a flat coil. Tuck end underneath.

Just before baking, place a scant teaspoon of pastry cream in the center of each snail. Bake as directed on p. 277.

Yield: approximately 20.

PRUNE OR CHEESE ENVELOPES

½ recipe Danish pastry (p. 274)
cheese filling or prune filling (p. 103)

Roll out Danish pastry ⅛ inch thick. Cut into 4-inch squares. Put a teaspoon of cheese or prune filling in center of each square.

Fold 2 opposite corners of dough over filling, overlapping them slightly. Pinch together so they won't open during baking. Bake as directed on p. 277.

Yield: approximately 20.

ALMOND COCKSCOMBS

½ recipe Danish pastry (p. 274)
granulated sugar
½ recipe frangipane filling (p. 104)

Roll out Danish pastry in granulated sugar instead of flour. Roll dough ⅛ inch thick, to make a long strip 9 inches wide.

Spread dough *thinly* with frangipane filling. Fold lengthwise into thirds, making the strip 3 inches wide. Roll gently to make strip thinner. Cut into 1-inch slices.

Make 4 or 5 small cuts along one side of each slice. Place flat on lightly greased baking sheets, curving slices slightly to spread slits.

These need no glaze either before or after baking. Bake as directed on p. 277.

Yield: approximately 20.

CUSTARD SLIPS

½ recipe Danish pastry (p. 274)
granulated sugar
1 cup apricot jam
½ recipe pastry cream (p. 95)

Roll out Danish pastry in granulated sugar instead of flour. Roll dough ⅛ inch thick to make a long strip 9 inches wide.

Spread dough thinly with apricot jam. Fold into thirds, making the strip 3 inches wide. Roll to make strip ¼ inch thick. Cut crosswise into 1-inch slices. Make a slit down the center of each slice almost to ends. Pull one end through slit. Pipe a small dab of pastry cream down center of each one.

Bake as directed on p. 277. These need no glaze either before or after baking.
Yield: approximately 20.

CINNAMON BUNS

½ recipe Danish pastry (p. 274)
1 egg, slightly beaten
¾ cup cinnamon sugar (p. 44)
1 cup currants soaked in
3 tablespoons rum

Roll out Danish pastry into a strip ⅛ inch thick and 16 inches wide. Brush with beaten egg. Sprinkle with cinnamon sugar, then with currants which have been soaked in rum for a few minutes. Press filling lightly with a rolling pin.

Roll dough tightly to make a roll approximately 2 ½ inches in diameter. Seal seam, first brushing with remaining egg.

Cut into slices ¾ inch thick. Place on lightly greased baking sheets. Press down slices slightly to flatten them.

Bake as directed on p. 277.
Yield: approximately 20.

DANISH PASTRY SHAPES

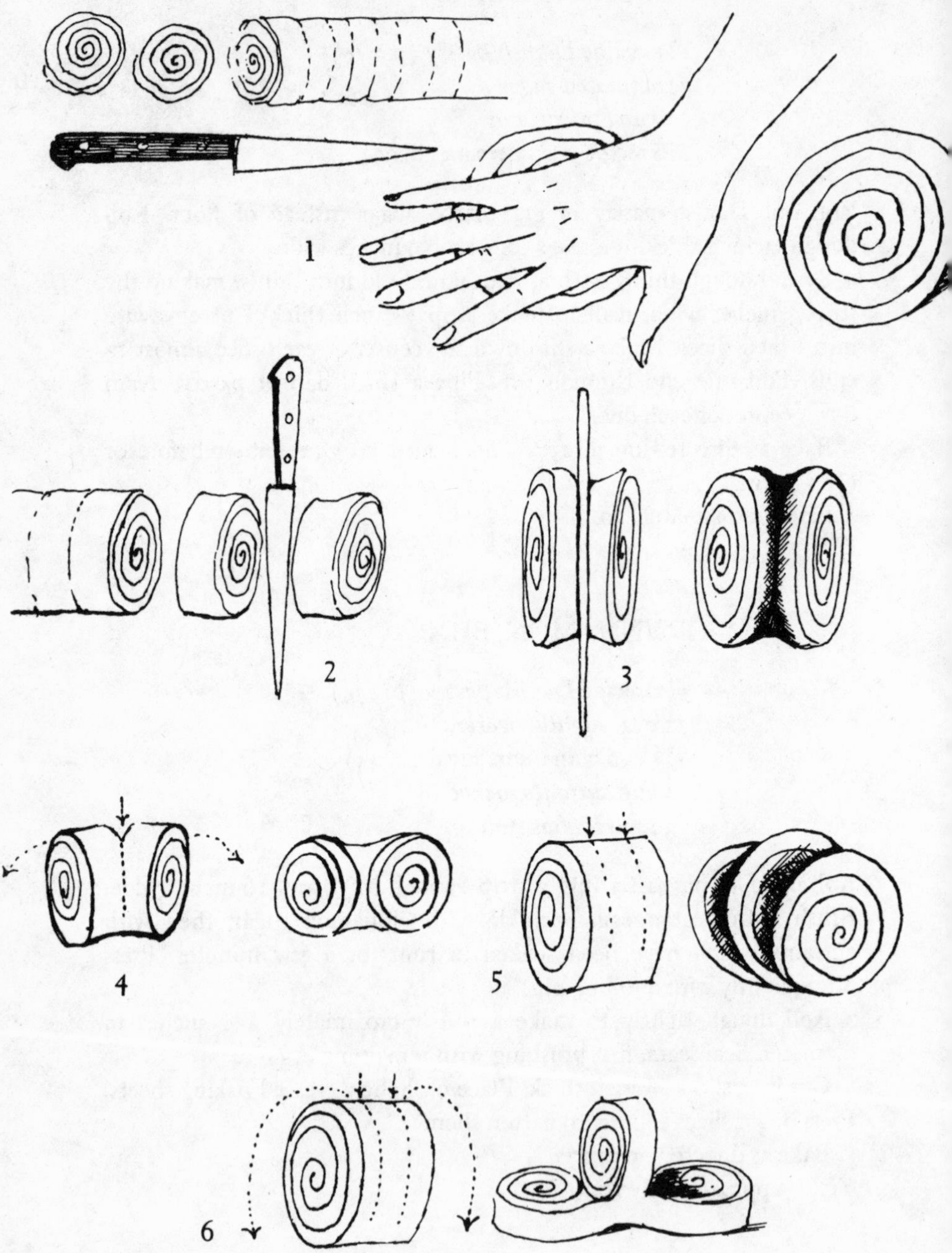

To make Spectacles, Fans, Baskets, and Butterflies from cinnamon bun rolls, follow illustrations on p. 284.

1. *Cinnamon buns*

2. *Cutting slices to make various shapes*

3. *To make butterflies: press a thin stick into center of slice.*

4. *To make spectacles: cut slice almost completely through, then open flat.*

5. *To make fans: cut slice almost completely through, twice, then lay flat and spread fanwise.*

6. *To make baskets: cut through as for fans. Lay two outside slices flat; leave center slice upright.*

Chapter 11

Pastry Appetizers and Hors d'Oeuvres

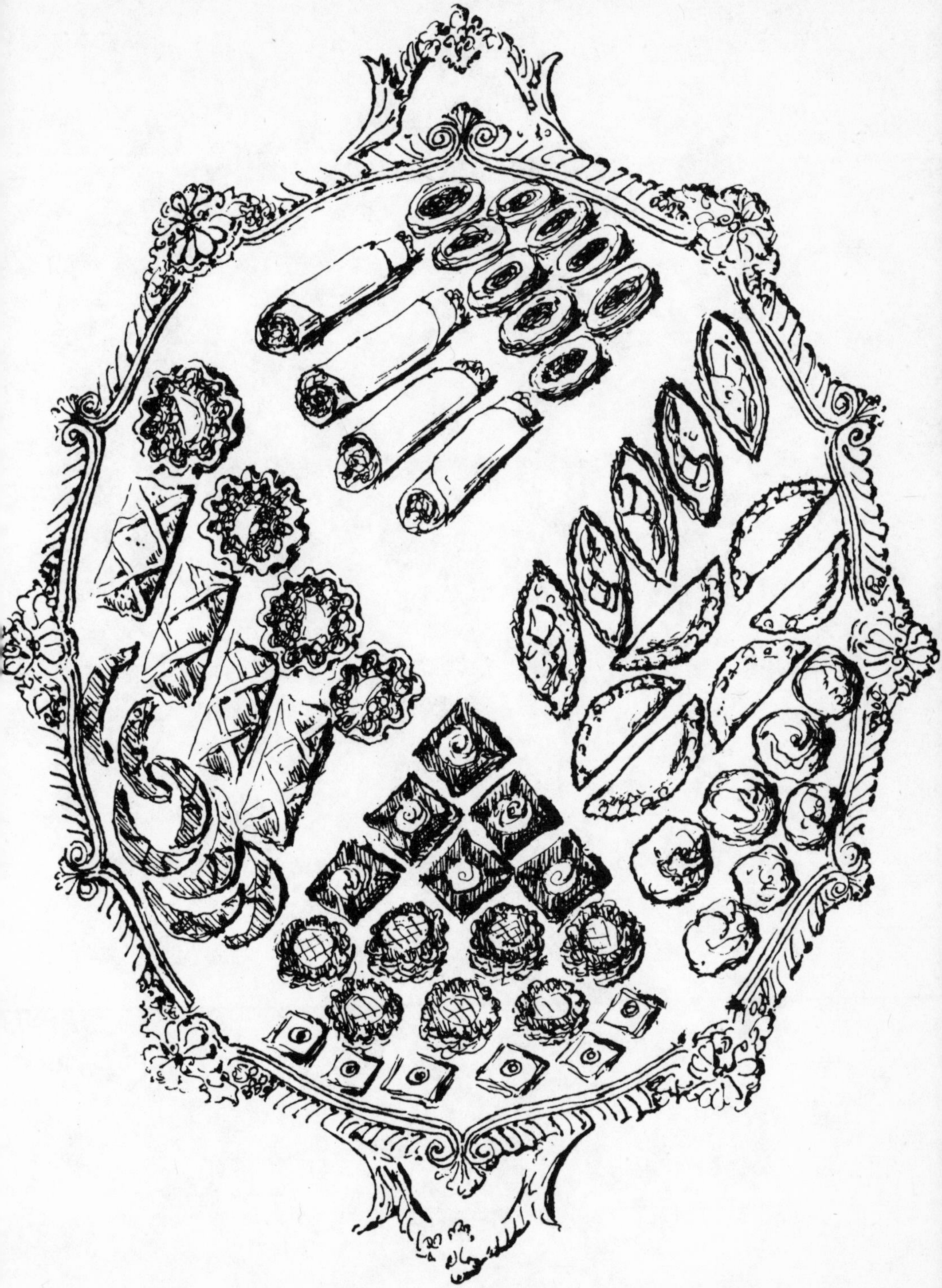

11 *Pastry Appetizers and Hors d'Oeuvres*

An entire volume could be written on using pastry to make delectable tiny appetizers and hors d'oeuvres. Here, we touch on the subject only long enough to give a generous sampling of the limitless possibilities.

The preparation of filled pastries such as cocktail puffs, barquettes, or tiny vols au vent can be made easier and more efficient by adopting a simple technique practiced by professional cooks. This involves the use of a pastry bag and tube. Using a spoon is both messy and time-consuming. Here is the simplest, quickest method of filling a great many little pastry shells:

1. Line up all the shells.
2. Place filling in a pastry bag fitted with a plain tube. Tube openings range from pinpoint size to over 1 inch. Use a tube with an opening large enough to accommodate the texture of filling. A filling containing coarse bits of nut meats or celery might need a No. 8 or even a No. 9 tube.
3. Press filling into shells. A little practice will teach you to press out the same amount each time.

An outstanding feature of almost all pastry hors d'oeuvres is that they can be made in advance and frozen for several months. Some, like turnovers and puff-paste rolls, are better if frozen unbaked and then baked when needed. A few others, like strudel, are better if frozen after they are baked, although these cooked hors d'oeuvres should not be kept in the freezer longer than three or four weeks.

When baking frozen pastry, preheat oven before removing pastry from the freezer. When oven has reached the correct temperature for specific recipe, pop pastries right in. Never thaw them first.

SHORT HORS D'OEUVRE PASTRY

2 ⅔ *cups sifted flour*
1 *cup butter, slightly softened*
½ *teaspoon sugar*
2 *teaspoons salt*
4 *hard-cooked egg yolks, mashed*
4 *raw egg yolks or 2 whole eggs*

Place flour in a bowl. Make a well in the center. Add all ingredients. With finger tips, make a paste of center ingredients, gradually incorporating the flour to form a smooth, firm ball. Squeeze dough between fingers or with heel of hand, so that flour can be completely incorporated. If dough is very soft, wrap in wax paper. Chill two or three hours, or until firm enough to roll between sheets of wax paper or hand-mold into shapes.

Note: To mix in electric mixer, see method given under rich tart pastry (p. 231).

CREAM CHEESE PASTRY

This is a quick and easy recipe that can be made in the mixer. It makes a rich, crisp pastry which can be used in many ways and can serve as a substitute for short hors d'oeuvre pastry.

The easiest way to roll cream cheese pastry is between sheets of wax paper. Remember that in rolling any pastry between sheets of paper, and especially cream cheese pastry, it is necessary to loosen the upper and lower papers several times to prevent the pastry from sticking and to allow it to spread freely.

Cream cheese pastry can be frozen, unbaked, for 3 months or more. Shape it before freezing.

1 *cup butter*
1 *cup cream cheese*

¼ cup heavy cream
2 ½ cups flour
1 teaspoon salt

Cream butter and cream cheese together. Beat in cream. Gradually add flour and salt. Wrap dough in wax paper and chill several hours, or until needed.

Bake in a 350 degree oven.

POPPY SEED STRAWS

short hors d'oeuvre pastry (p. 290)
½ cup poppy seeds

Add poppy seeds to pastry as it is being mixed. Chill pastry. Roll it out ⅓ inch thick. Cut into small bars, ½ x 2. Place on ungreased baking sheet and bake in 350 degree oven until light brown, about 10 minutes.

Yield: approximately 4 dozen.

FILBERT SLICES

short hors d'oeuvre pastry (p. 290)
1 egg mixed with
1 teaspoon milk
1 ¼ cups filberts
1 tablespoon coarse salt
½ teaspoon cinnamon

Form short hors d'oeuvre pastry into a long roll 1 inch in diameter. Chill roll until it is firm enough to be sliced. Cut slices ¼ inch thick. Brush rounds with egg-yolk mixture. Grate filberts fine. Combine with coarse salt and cinnamon. Coat rounds heavily with mixture. Bake on an ungreased baking sheet in a 350 degree oven about 15 minutes.

Yield: approximately 5 dozen.

NUT WHEELS

short hors d'oeuvre pastry (p. 290)
2 *cups filberts or walnuts*
2 *teaspoons coarse salt*
½ *teaspoon cinnamon*

Roll out chilled pastry between sheets of wax paper to make a strip ¼ inch thick.

Grind or grate nuts fine. Combine with salt and cinnamon. Sprinkle evenly over pastry. Roll over nuts lightly with a rolling pin to settle them into the pastry.

Set oven temperature at 350 degrees. Grease a baking sheet lightly.

Roll up pastry, jelly-roll style, making a long roll about 1 inch in diameter. Chill until firm. Cut into slices ¼ inch thick. Place on cooky sheet. Bake in preheated oven about 15 minutes.

Yield: approximately 5 dozen.

Note: Chopped liver, ground shrimp, or any firm filling can substitute for nuts.

SALT STICKS

short hors d'oeuvre pastry (p. 290)
1 *egg mixed with*
1 *teaspoon milk*
coarse salt
caraway seeds

Break off tablespoon-size pieces of short hors d'oeuvre pastry. Roll between hands into long thin rolls the diameter of a thickish pencil. Cut into 2-inch lengths. Brush tops with egg-yolk mixture. Roll in coarse salt and caraway seeds. Bake in 350 degree oven on an ungreased baking sheet about 10 minutes. Serve at room temperature.

Yield: approximately 7 dozen.

TURNOVERS

Turnovers can be made with any kind of pastry—puff paste (page 133), cream cheese pastry or short hors d'oeuvre pastry (p. 290). If desired, the pastry itself can be seasoned with such flavorings as chile powder, curry, caraway, celery, or poppy seeds. The filling for turnovers should never be loose. A loose filling will push its way out of the pastry as it is baking. A few simple, basic recipes for fillings are given at the end of this chapter.

To make turnovers, roll any preferred pastry ⅛ inch thick. Cut into 2-inch rounds or squares. Place a scant spoonful of filling in the center of each piece of pastry. Fold over, sealing edges of pastry firmly by pinching together. If puff paste is used, brush it with beaten egg before folding over and press pastry together ⅛ inch from edge so that the edges are disturbed as little as possible. Prick tops of all turnovers with a fork once or twice. Chill. Bake in a 350 degree oven about 25 minutes, or until golden brown. Turnovers can be brushed with an egg-yolk glaze (p. 254) before baking, if desired.
Yield: approximately 5 dozen.

TURNOVER SLICES

Another and quicker way to make individual turnovers is to roll either short hors d'oeuvre pastry or cream cheese pastry ¼ inch thick between sheets of wax paper. Remove upper sheet of paper. Trim dough to make a long rectangle 3 inches wide. Place a ¾-inch roll of well-seasoned filling down center of rectangle. Flatten filling slightly. Fold one side of pastry over filling. Press down slightly. Using paper underneath to help, roll partially enclosed filling over so that seam is at bottom and a smooth, filled pastry roll is on top. Chill at least 1 hour. Cut with a sharp knife into diagonal slices ¾ inch thick. Freeze until needed. Bake slices standing up on a lightly greased baking sheet in a 350 degree oven about 25 minutes, or until pastry is lightly browned. Serve slightly warm.
Yield: approximately 4 dozen.

BARQUETTES (TARTLETS)

Small, boat-shaped pastry shells filled with any number of savory mixtures are a classic French hors d'oeuvre. The fillings can be as simple or as elaborate as your taste and time allow. Classic cooking dictates fillings of foie gras and aspic glazes. Little tartlets are delicious when filled with any nicely seasoned mixture.

To line and bake barquettes, follow directions for lining and baking tartlet shells (p. 232), using short hors d'oeuvre pastry instead of a sweet pastry.

SOME SUGGESTIONS FOR FILLING BARQUETTES

HOT BARQUETTES

Creamed sea food or mushrooms.

Hot meat chilies or curries—with meat cut into tiny cubes.

Place a small piece of crisp bacon, a sprinkling of grated Gruyère cheese, and some parsley in bottom of 2 dozen unbaked barquette shells. Fill shells with custard made by beating 5 eggs with 2 cups light cream. Season with salt, pepper, and nutmeg. Bake barquettes on lowest rack of oven until custard is set. (When this filling is used in a 9-inch tart shell, it is called quiche Lorraine.)

Substitute sea food, sautéed cabbage filling, sautéed onions, mushrooms, or smoked salmon for the bacon and cheese in quiche barquettes.

COLD BARQUETTES

(*These fillings are also delicious in cocktail puffs.*)

Freshly cooked salmon, cooled, flaked, and mixed with mayonnaise, chopped parsley, grated onion. Garnish with a slice of hard-cooked egg or a strip of crisp green pepper.

Chopped shrimp or lobster salad.

Sour cream topped with black or red caviar.

Tuna fish salad mixed with a few bits of chopped sweet pickles.

Egg salad mixed with bits of green pepper.

Minced Nova Scotia salmon mixed with chopped green onion, dill, sour cream, horseradish, and just a touch of mayonnaise.

One of the great appeals of barquettes is their appetizing appearance. It is especially important to garnish them attractively. Chopped parsley can be used to brighten both hot and cold barquettes. Sprigs of water cress also add a refreshing touch of green.

Barquettes to be served cold can be simply but beautifully garnished with minced hard-cooked egg white or yolk, egg slices, capers, anchovies, pimiento, or olives cut into special shapes with cutters made for the purpose, chopped chives, or whole tarragon leaves.

CHEESE BITES

4 *cups shredded Gruyère or Cheddar cheese* (1 *pound*)
½ *pound butter*
½ *teaspoon salt*
dash of cayenne
2 *cups sifted flour*

Cream butter and cheese together. Add salt and cayenne. Stir in flour. Form dough into rolls 1 inch in diameter. Chill several hours, or until firm enough to slice. Rolls can be kept in the refrigerator up to a week and sliced as needed. Cut into slices ⅛ inch thick. Place on lightly greased cooky sheets. Bake in a 400 degree oven about 10 minutes. Be careful not to brown. These taste best served at room temperature.
Yield: approximately 9 dozen.

HAM OR SAUSAGE CRESCENTS

½ *puff paste recipe* (*p.* 133)
16 *small strips cooked sausage or ham*
2 *egg yolks mixed with*
2 *teaspoons cream*

Roll out puff paste to make a rectangle ⅛ inch thick. Trim off edges. Divide into long strips 2 ½ inches wide. Divide strips into triangles.

On each triangle place a small piece of cooked ham or sausage (Spanish, Italian, or any kind of cooked sausage may be used). Enclose meat, rolling triangles from wide end toward opposite point. Curve into a crescent shape. Place on ungreased baking sheet. Chill well.

Brush crescents with egg yolks mixed with cream. Bake in a 350 degree oven for 30 to 40 minutes, or until crescents are golden brown.
Yield: approximately 16.

ROQUEFORT BARS

½ puff paste recipe (*p.* 133)
⅔ cup Roquefort cheese
1 *egg yolk*
1 *teaspoon chopped parsley*
¼ teaspoon white pepper
1 *to* 2 *tablespoons heavy cream* (*approximately*)

Roll out puff paste less than ⅛ inch thick. Trim edges. Divide into strips 2 ½ inches wide. Spread half the strips thinly with Roquefort cheese filling: cream Roquefort cheese with egg yolk. Add chopped parsley, white pepper, and a spoonful or 2 of heavy cream if mixture is not soft enough to spread easily.

Cover filling with remaining strips of pastry. Place on paper-lined baking sheet. Chill. Bake in 350 degree oven for 50 to 60 minutes, or until pastry is golden brown. Cool slightly. Trim edges. Cut into 1-inch bars with a serrated knife.
Yield: approximately 2 ½ dozen.

FILLED HORS D'OEUVRE ROLL

¼ puff paste recipe (*p.* 133)
1 ½ *to* 2 *cups any well-seasoned meat or fish filling*
2 *egg yolks mixed with*
2 *teaspoons cream*

Roll out a piece of puff paste in a rectangle ⅛ inch thick. Trim to make a long strip 4 inches wide. Place a 1-inch roll of filling down center of strip. Fold 1 side of pastry over filling. Brush it with egg-yolk mixture. Fold remaining side over filling, overlapping egg-brushed side. Place on paper-lined baking sheet, seam side down. Chill.

Before baking, brush top with egg-yolk mixture. Bake in a 350 degree oven 50 to 60 minutes, or until pastry is golden brown. Before serving, reheat. Cut into 1-inch slices with a serrated knife.
Yield: approximately 16.

CHEESE PUFF PASTRY

Roll out puff pastry or puff paste trimmings into a rectangle ½ inch thick, rolling dough in plenty of finely grated Parmesan cheese instead of flour. Fold ends of dough to meet in the center. Sprinkle again with cheese. Fold in half, as if closing a book, making 4 layers. Chill 30 minutes or longer before using. From this paste you can make cheese palmiers, four-finger palmiers, etc. (See Chapter 5 for shapes and approximate yields.)

TINY VOL AU VENT

puff paste
1 egg yolk mixed with
1 teaspoon cream
any hot filling (see p. 294 for suggestions)

Roll puff paste ⅓ inch thick. Cut into 1-inch rounds. Using a slightly smaller cutter, press into centers, cutting only ¾ through. Place on paper-lined baking sheet. Brush tops with egg-yolk mixture. Bake in a 350 degree oven about 25 minutes, or until little shells are golden brown. Cut around indented top with a small knife and lift off. Using a small-size measuring spoon, scrape soft paste from inside of shells. Return to oven for a few minutes, if necessary, to dry inside of shells. Just before serving fill with hot creamed mixture such as chicken, sweetbreads, or mushrooms. Top filling with pastry caps.
Yield: approximately 5 dozen.

POTATO PUFF STICKS

1 cup mashed potatoes
½ teaspoon white pepper
1 teaspoon salt
1 ⅔ cups flour
¼ pound butter
caraway seeds

Combine mashed potatoes, pepper, salt, and enough flour (about 1 ½ cups) to make a moderately firm dough. Knead very well, at least 10 minutes, to make dough elastic. Let dough rest in refrigerator about 20 minutes. While dough is resting, coat butter with some of remaining flour and roll it between sheets of wax paper to make a rectangle ⅓ inch thick.

Remove dough from refrigerator. Roll into a rectangle 3 times longer than it is wide. Place half of butter in center. Fold 1 end of dough over butter. Place remaining butter on top. Fold opposite end of dough over butter. Press edges. Turn dough so that short ends are parallel to edge of table nearest you. (See diagrams for puff paste on pp. 134-135.) Roll out again into rectangle. Fold 2 ends of dough to meet in the center. Then fold in half, as if closing a book. Chill dough in refrigerator 30 minutes. Repeat rolling and folding 3 more times, chilling well each time. Dough is now ready to use.

Roll out ¼ inch thick on floured surface. Sprinkle dough heavily with caraway seeds. Roll lightly over seeds to set them. Cut dough into bars 1 ½ x ¾. Chill bars (or freeze them if you prefer). After chilling, bake at 450 degrees for 5 minutes. Reduce heat to 350 degrees and bake until sticks are golden.

Yield: approximately 3 dozen.

STRUDEL HORS D'OEUVRES

Small, crisp strudel slices with a nonsweet filling are a delicious snack. Here's how to make them.

strudel dough (pp. 150, 152-153)
1 *cup melted butter or other fat*
3 *cups nonsweet strudel filling (see filling recipes at end of chapter)*
2 *to* 3 *cups sautéed bread crumbs*

After strudel dough has been stretched thin and dried for a short time, brush all over with melted butter, olive oil, chicken fat, or any fat which is related to the filling used. Cover dough with a generous sprinkling of sautéed bread crumbs. Place a long narrow strip of filling, ¾ inch wide, across one end of dough. Begin to roll up strudel, following instructions for rolling large strudel. When roll reaches

1 ¼ inches in diameter, cut it away from remaining sheet of dough. Place in a greased, shallow pan, forming a horseshoe shape, if necessary, to make it fit. Place another thin roll of filling on remaining dough. Repeat entire process as often as necessary to use up sheet of dough. One large sheet of stretched dough generally will make 2 or 3 long thin strudels.

Before baking, slice strudel into 1-inch pieces in order to facilitate serving, but cut only halfway through each slice.

Brush with melted butter or other fat. Bake in a 375 degree oven 35 to 40 minutes, basting with fat occasionally until golden brown. Serve warm.

Yield: approximately 5 dozen pieces.

SPONGE PINWHEEL SLICES

This nonsweet sponge roll is the basis for a number of unusual, savory appetizers.

One especially good filling consists of half a pound of cream cheese creamed with 1 small can of peeled green chilies, finely chopped. If green chili, which is mildly hot, doesn't appeal to your taste, substitute pimiento.

Any creamed or spiced cheese mixture makes an excellent filling. So does thinly sliced boiled ham spread with mustard and finely chopped pickles. Liver paté as a filling is also delicious, as is a paste made of ground, leftover chicken or meat, seasoned and beaten to spreading consistency with an egg yolk or a little cream. Other ideas may be found among the hors d'oeuvre fillings at the end of this chapter.

4 *eggs*
½ *teaspoon salt*
1 *teaspoon sugar*
¼ *cup sifted flour*
¼ *cup sifted cornstarch*
¼ *cup grated Parmesan or Gruyère cheese*
1 *teaspoon finely chopped parsley, well dried before chopping*

Set oven temperature at 400 degrees. Grease an 11 x 16 jelly-roll pan. Line the bottom with wax paper and grease again.

Separate eggs. Beat egg whites with salt until they hold soft peaks. Add sugar and continue beating until whites are very stiff, about 3 minutes longer.

Stir yolks with fork to break them up. Mix approximately ¾ cup stiffly beaten whites into yolks, folding quickly together. Pour yolk mixture over remaining whites. Sprinkle flour, cornstarch, grated cheese, and chopped parsley on top. Fold all together, working rapidly. Fold until no large pieces of white show. Pour into prepared pan. Bake about 10 minutes, or until puffed and light brown.

Slightly cool this sponge in pan. Loosen, then turn out on rack. When completely cool, cut in half, making 2 pieces 5½ x 16. Spread each thinly with filling. Roll up, jelly-roll style, making two long, thin rolls. Wrap in waxpaper and chill in refrigerator at least 1 hour.

Before serving, cut into ¼-inch slices with a serrated knife. Place each slice flat on a greased baking sheet. Place in a 325 degree oven about 10 minutes, or until edges are slightly crisp. Serve warm. Filled sponge roll slices may be frozen for 2 or 3 weeks.

Yield: approximately 10 dozen.

Note: 1 teaspoon chopped fresh dill, 1 teaspoon curry powder, or 1 teaspoon chili powder can be added to this basic recipe to make variations.

COCKTAIL PUFFS

Cocktail puffs should be smaller than walnuts. They freeze well after they are baked.

Make tiny cream puffs (pp. 79-80). Split each one and fill as desired, or press filling into puffs with a pastry bag filled with tube No. 5 or No. 230. Do not allow filled puffs to stand more than an hour or two. Place in refrigerator until needed.

As these are crisp, bland little shells, they lend themselves to a great many cold fillings. See suggestions for filling barquettes on p. 294.

GOUGÈRE

Filling is unnecessary. These are delicious as they are. They can be frozen and reheated. Gougère may also be baked as a large ring and shaped with a pastry bag, as for Paris brest (p. 160).

pâte à chou (p. 79)
¾ cup grated Gruyère or mixed Gruyère and Parmesan cheese

Beat cheese into pâte à chou. With a pastry bag or spoon form small, high mounds on a lightly greased cooky sheet. Bake in a 375 degree oven about 35 minutes, or until puffs are golden brown and there are no beads of moisture showing. Serve warm.

SPICY SEED PUFFLETS

1 *teaspoon cracked coriander seed or curry powder*
1 *teaspoon cracked black pepper*
pâte à chou (p. 79)
½ teaspoon celery seed
coarse salt
caraway seeds

Crush coriander seed and black pepper with a mortar and pestle or use blender, but be careful not to grind them too fine. Mix into pâte à chou, adding celery seed at the same time. Shape with a pastry bag or spoon into small, high puffs on a lightly greased cooky sheet. Sprinkle with coarse salt and caraway seeds. Bake in a 375 degree oven about 50 minutes, or until puffs are brown and completely dry. These may be kept like crackers and, like crackers, can be served at room temperature.

RUSSIAN ROLLS

On a floured cloth, roll out firm brioche dough (p. 257) ¼ inch thick. Cut into 1 ½-inch rounds. Place a spoonful of cabbage filling (p. 307), meat filling (p. 303), or cooked sausage in center of each round. Gather edges of dough together and pinch firmly, enclosing filling in center. Mold rolls by hand into a round or slightly oval shape. Place on lightly greased baking sheet, pinched side down. Let rise until almost double in bulk. Brush with egg yolk mixed with 1 teaspoon cream. Sprinkle with poppy or caraway seeds if desired. Bake in a 375 degree oven 20 to 30 minutes, or until rolls are golden brown. These are best served slightly warm.

MEDITERRANEAN PIE

brioche dough (p. 257)
1 medium onion, chopped
1 green pepper, chopped
2 cloves garlic, chopped
½ cup olive oil
anchovies
black olives, pitted and halved

Lightly grease an 11 x 16 jelly-roll pan. Set oven at 375 degrees.

Sauté onions, green pepper, and garlic in half the olive oil until soft. Let cool.

Roll brioche dough ¼ inch thick. Press firmly into greased jelly-roll pan. Let rise until dough becomes puffy but not double in bulk. Brush lightly with olive oil. Spread dough with sautéed vegetables. Make a lattice top with anchovy strips. (If anchovies are packed in salt rather than oil, rinse them first in water, then dry them on paper towels.) In the center of each square place a pitted olive half. Bake in a 375 degree oven 50 to 60 minutes. To serve, cut into small squares. Serve warm.

Yield: approximately 4 dozen squares.

PIZZA PENNIES

½ cup cornmeal
¼ Cuban bread dough (p. 255)
60 to 75 thin slices onion, or ⅔ cup chopped garlic
¼ cup olive oil (approximately)
60 to 75 thin slices sausage (peperoni, fresh cooked Italian sausage), or 25 anchovies cut into thirds
oregano to taste
freshly ground pepper

Sprinkle baking sheets with cornmeal.

After bread dough has risen once, roll it out ⅛ inch thick. Using a cooky cutter, cut rounds 1 ½ inches in diameter. Place on baking sheets.

Place a thin slice of onion on top or sprinkle with chopped garlic. Dab or brush each round lightly with olive oil. Garnish top with a slice of sausage or a piece of anchovy. Sprinkle lightly with oregano and freshly ground pepper.

Place in a cold oven. Set temperature at 425 degrees. Bake about fifteen minutes, or until pizza pennies are puffed and golden. Serve warm.

Yield: approximately 6 dozen.

FILLINGS FOR HORS D'OEUVRES

BASIC MEAT FILLING

For turnovers, sponge pinwheel slices, filled hors d'oeuvre roll, Russian rolls, and similar pastries.

2 *well-packed cups any cooked meat, poultry, or giblets, coarsely ground*
1 *large onion, finely chopped*
½ *cup fat*
½ *cup chopped green onions*
2 *eggs (approximately)*
½ *cup chopped parsley*
salt and pepper to taste

Sauté chopped onion in fat (butter, olive oil, pork, bacon, or chicken fat) until soft and yellow. Add chopped green onions. Stir a few minutes, then add ground meat. Mix well. Remove from heat. Beat in eggs. If mixture is very dry, it may be necessary to add an additional egg. The consistency should be like that of mashed potatoes.

Stir in chopped parsley. Season with salt and pepper to taste. Cool before using.

Yield: approximately 2 ½ cups.

VARIATIONS ON BASIC MEAT FILLING

Add *one* of the following combinations:

1 tablespoon curry powder, ½ cup chopped black olives, and ¼ cup finely chopped sweet pickles or chutney

2 tablespoons Hungarian paprika, ¼ cup sour cream and 1 teaspoon tomato paste

1 tablespoon chili powder, ½ cup mashed, cooked pinto beans, 2 tablespoons grated cheese and 1 teaspoon tomato paste

2 cups finely chopped mushrooms, sautéed slowly in butter until they are brown

Use sweetbreads as the meat, chopped medium fine—not ground. Add ½ cup thick cream sauce made with half white wine and half cream. Season with a pinch of nutmeg and chopped parsley.

BASIC SEA FOOD FILLING

1 ½ cups dry white wine
1 teaspoon salt
6 peppercorns
1 bay leaf
¼ teaspoon thyme
1 stalk celery with leaves
1 large sprig parsley
2 pounds bay scallops or shelled, cleaned shrimp
1 cup heavy cream
2 tablespoons butter
2 tablespoons flour
2 egg yolks
1 tablespoon chopped parsley
½ cup chopped pimiento (optional)

Pour wine into a saucepan. Add salt, peppercorns, bay leaf, thyme, celery, and parsley. Bring slowly to a boil. Cook for 5 minutes. Add shellfish. Simmer until sea food is just firm, about 5 minutes. Remove from heat. Cool slightly. Remove fish from liquid. Chop medium fine with a knife. Strain remaining liquid.

Place pan containing liquid on stove. Cook over high heat 5 to 10 minutes, or until liquid is reduced to less than 1 cup.

Place cream in another saucepan. (Use a deep saucepan to prevent cream from boiling over.) Cook over high heat to reduce cream to ½ cup. Cream will thicken considerably.

Melt butter in a heavy pan. Stir in flour. Cook over low heat for 5 minutes, stirring constantly. Add reduced fish stock and reduced cream. Stir briskly with wire whisk to prevent lumps from forming.

Stir 3 tablespoons of hot sauce into egg yolks. Pour yolks back into remaining sauce, continue to beat with whisk. Continue to cook over low heat about 3 minutes, or until yolks further thicken the sauce.

Remove from heat. Add chopped parsley and pimiento. Season with salt and pepper to taste. Stir this heavy cream sauce into chopped cooked sea food. Cool before using.

Yield: approximately 2 ½ cups.

VARIATIONS ON BASIC SEA FOOD FILLING

Use 2 pounds fish fillets instead of shellfish. Mash cooked fish to a fine paste, adding cream sauce as a binder. Especially good for turnovers.

Use 6 pounds well-cleaned mussels or clams. Simmer only until shells open. Remove sea food from shells and chop.

Use leftover, cooked sea food (lobster, crabmeat, shrimp). Combine white wine and spices, adding any juices of cooked fish. Reduce wine as in basic recipe. Proceed to make sauce.

Add 1 teaspoon curry powder.

To make filling for tiny vols au vent, chop sea food less fine, and use only 1 tablespoon butter and 1 tablespoon flour to make a slightly thinner cream sauce.

CHICKEN LIVER FILLING

This chicken liver filling can be used to fill *any* of the various hors d'oeuvre pastries. It is especially delicious.

1 *pound unrendered chicken fat*
4 *large onions*
1 ½ *pounds chicken livers*
salt and pepper

Cut chicken fat into small pieces. Place it in a saucepan over very low heat. Cook until the yellow color has disappeared and the pieces of fat look gray. Add 1 cup finely chopped onion. Continue to cook fat over low heat until onions and cracklings are golden brown. Cool before straining through cheesecloth. Save cracklings. This part of the recipe can be done days ahead.

Slice remaining onions coarsely. Place in a saucepan. Barely cover onions with cold water. Bring quickly to a boil. Drain onions.

Heat ½ cup chicken fat in a large skillet. Add onions. Sauté slowly until they are very soft and yellow. Push onions to side of skillet. Add halved chicken livers. Raise heat and quickly sauté livers, adding more chicken fat if necessary, until they are just cooked. Test by cutting one liver with a knife. When it is cooked enough, there will be no pink color in the center. Season livers and onions with salt and pepper.

Grind livers, onions, and reserved cracklings through finest blade of meat grinder. To the resulting paste, add the juices and fat left in skillet. Season with salt and pepper. Add a little more chicken fat. Cool before using. If filling is to be kept more than a day, pour hot chicken fat over top and place in refrigerator. This filling can be kept about five days if top is well coated with fat, or it can be frozen for several weeks. This is also a delicious pâté-like spread.

Remaining rendered chicken fat will keep indefinitely in the refrigerator and makes an excellent cooking fat.
Yield: approximately 2 ½ cups.

QUICK AND EASY LIVER FILLING

1 ½ pounds good liverwurst
½ cup chicken fat or butter
1 medium-size onion, finely chopped
¼ cup heavy cream
¼ cup cognac

Remove casing from liverwurst. Place in a bowl.

Sauté finely chopped onion in chicken fat or butter until yellow and very soft. Add to liverwurst.

Cream mixture together, adding cream and cognac gradually. Use as a substitute for chicken liver filling.
Yield: approximately 2 cups.

SPINACH FILLING

This makes a delicious filling for almost any of the filled pastry hors d'oeuvres.

¾ cup olive oil
2 large onions, chopped
3 pounds spinach, trimmed, washed, towel-dried

1 clove garlic, chopped
1 bunch green scallions
¾ cup chopped parsley
¾ cup chopped dill
salt and pepper
½ cup pine nuts (pignola)

Heat olive oil in a large skillet or pan. Add chopped onions and sauté until soft. Raise heat to high. Add spinach and sauté quickly, stirring and turning vegetables. Just before spinach has completely wilted, add chopped garlic, scallions, parsley, and dill. Continue cooking over high heat until the only liquid left in the pan is olive oil. Cool. Chop spinach fine with a knife. Season with salt and fresh black pepper. Add pine nuts.

In using spinach filling for puff paste hors d'oeuvre roll, first place a layer of boiled ham on rectangle of puff paste.

Yield: approximately 1 ½ cups.

CABBAGE FILLING

Delicious as a stuffing for strudel, this cabbage filling is also delectable in Russian rolls and in almost any filled pastry hors d'oeuvre except possibly vols au vent and cocktail puffs.

⅔ cup butter or ½ pound fresh, fat pork
6 cups finely chopped cabbage
1 large onion, minced
4 dried Polish mushrooms, soaked in water 1 hour or until soft (optional)
salt and pepper to taste

If fat pork is used, cut it into small pieces. Place it in a heavy saucepan and cook slowly until bits of pork turn light brown. Transfer fat and cracklings to a skillet or pot large enough to hold cabbage. If butter is used, melt it in a large pan.

Add cabbage and minced onion to fat. Chop softened mushrooms and add these also. Stir vegetables until they are coated with fat. Reduce heat to low, cover, and simmer for 10 minutes, or until vegetables begin to steam in their own juices. Remove cover. Continue to cook slowly, stirring occasionally, until cabbage is soft and lightly

browned. If necessary, add a little more fat so vegetables do not burn. Season with salt and pepper. Cool before using.
Yield: approximately 2 ½ cups.

HAM FILLING

Primarily for filling strudel, this is also good in Russian rolls and tiny vols au vent.

1 cup onions, chopped finely
ham fat or butter for sautéing
2 cups cooked ham, chopped coarsely
1 cup sour cream
4 egg yolks
¼ cup chopped parsley
pepper

Sauté onions in ham fat or butter until they are soft and yellow. Add ham. Cook briefly. Remove from heat. Mix sour cream with egg yolks, adding parsley. Pour over ham and mix well. Season with pepper only, as ham is generally salty enough. Cool before using.
Yield: approximately 2 ¼ cups.

ONION FILLING

Follow recipe for cabbage filling, substituting 6 cups thinly sliced onions for cabbage. Omit mushrooms. Add 1 cup chopped green onions. Use as a substitute for cabbage filling.

CHEESE FILLING
(*For Strudels*)

3 tablespoons butter
3 tablespoons flour
1 cup light cream, heated
½ pound grated cheese, such as Gruyère, Greek feta, or large-curd pot cheese
1 tablespoon parsley, chopped
1 tablespoon fresh dill, chopped (optional)
salt and pepper

Melt butter in a saucepan. Add flour. Cook, stirring over low heat about 5 minutes, or until mixture looks bubbly. Remove from heat. Stir in hot cream. If mixture should lump, stir quickly with a wire whisk and it will become smooth again. Cook over low heat 2 or 3 more minutes, or until sauce is thick. Remove from heat.

Stir in cheese, chopped parsley, and dill. Season with salt and pepper. Cool before using.

Yield: approximately 2 cups.

Index

continued